INTIMATIONS OF
POSTMODERNITY

Zygmunt Bauman

London and New York

First published 1992
by Routledge
2 Park Square, Milton Park, Abingdon, Oxon, OX14 4RN

Simultaneously published in the USA and Canada
by Routledge
270 Madison Ave, New York NY 10016

Reprinted 1992, 1993, 1994, 1997 and 2000

Transferred to Digital Printing 2006

Routledge is an imprint of the Taylor & Francis Group

© 1992 Introduction, selection and other editorial matter,
Zygmunt Baumanu; Appendix, Richard Kilminster and Ian Varcoe

Typeset in Bembo by Selectmove Ltd, London

British Library Cataloguing in Publication Data
A catalogue record for this book is available from the British Library

Library of Congress Cataloguing in Publication Data
A catalogue record for this book is available from the Library of Congress

ISBN 0–415–06749–9 (hbk)   ISBN 0–415–06750–2 (pbk)

Publisher's Note
The publisher has gone to great lengths to ensure the quality of this
reprint but points out that some imperfections in the original
may be apparent

CONTENTS

INTRODUCTION
The re-enchantment of the world,
or, how can one narrate postmodernity?

Postmodernity means many different things to many different people. It may mean a building that arrogantly flaunts the 'orders' prescribing what fits what and what should be kept strictly out to preserve the functional logic of steel, glass and concrete. It means a work of imagination that defies the difference between painting and sculpture, styles and genres, gallery and the street, art and everything else. It means a life that looks suspiciously like a TV serial, and a docudrama that ignores your worry about setting apart fantasy from what 'really happened'. It means licence to do whatever one may fancy and advice not to take anything you or the others do too seriously. It means the speed with which things change and the pace with which moods succeed each other so that they have no time to ossify into things. It means attention drawn in all directions at once so that it cannot stop on anything for long and nothing gets a really close look. It means a shopping mall overflowing with goods whose major use is the joy of purchasing them; and existence that feels like a life-long confinement to the shopping mall. It means the exhilarating freedom to pursue anything and the mind-boggling uncertainty as to what is worth pursuing and in the name of what one should pursue it.

Postmodernity is all these things and many others. But it is also – perhaps more than anything else – a *state of mind*. More precisely – a state of those minds who have the habit (or is it a compulsion?) to reflect upon themselves, to search their own contents and report what they found: the state of mind of philosophers, social thinkers, artists – all those people on whom we rely when we are in a pensive mood or just pause for a moment to find out whence we are moving or being moved.

This is a state of mind marked above all by its all-deriding, all-eroding, all-dissolving *destructiveness*. It seems sometimes that postmodern mind is a critique caught at the moment of its ultimate triumph: a critique that finds it ever more difficult to go on being critical just because it has destroyed everything it used to be critical about; with it, off went the very urgency of being critical. There is nothing left to be opposed to. The world and the life in the world have become themselves nothing but an unstoppable and obsessive self-criticism – or so it seems. Just as modernist art, bent on censoring modern reality, ended up in taking apart the very subject-matter of its critique (painting ended up in a clean canvas, writing in an empty page, music in silence;[1] in the desperate attempt to purify the work of the artist, Walter de Maria dug a deep hole near Kassel, Yves Klein invited the art connoisseurs to a private view of blank gallery walls, Robert Barry transmitted his art ideas telepathically to bypass the polluting blight of word and paint, and Rauschenberg put up for sale erased drawings of his artistic friends),[2] so the critical theory confronts an object that seems to offer no more resistance; an object that has softened, melted and liquidized to the point that the sharp edge of critique goes through with nothing to stop it. Past tragedies mock themselves in a no-smile-raising grotesque. How ridiculous it seems to try to change the direction of history when no powers give an inkling that they wish to give history direction. How empty seems the effort to show that what passes for truth is false when nothing has the courage and the stamina to declare itself as truth for everybody and for all time. How farcical it seems to fight for genuine art when one can no more drop anything incidentally without the dropped object being proclaimed art. How quixotic to debunk the distortion in the representation of reality once no reality claims to be more real than its representation. How idle it seems to exhort people to go there rather than somewhere else in a world in which everything goes.

The postmodern state of mind is the radical (though certainly unexpected and in all probability undesired) victory of modern (that is, inherently critical, restless, unsatisfied, insatiable) culture over the modern society it aimed to improve through throwing it wide open to its own potential. Many little victorious battles added up to a victorious war. One after another, hurdles have been taken apart, ramparts crushed and locks broken in the incessant, stubborn work of emancipation. At each moment a particular constraint, an especially painful prohibition was under attack. In the end, a *universal dismantling of power-supported structures* has been the result. No new and improved order has emerged, however, from beneath the debris of the old and unwanted one. Postmodernity (and in this it differs from modernist culture of which it is the rightful issue and legatee) does not seek to substitute one truth for another, one standard of beauty for another, one life ideal for another. Instead, it splits the truth, the standards and the ideal into already deconstructed and about to be deconstructed. It denies in advance the right of all and any revelation to slip into the place vacated by the deconstructed/discredited rules. It braces itself for a life without truths, standards and ideals. It is often blamed for not being positive enough, for not being positive at all, for not wishing to be positive and for pooh-poohing positivity as such, for sniffing a knife of unfreedom under any cloak of saintly righteousness or just placid self-confidence. The postmodern mind seems to condemn everything, propose nothing. Demolition is the only job the postmodern mind seems to be good at. Destruction is the only construction it recognizes. Demolition of coercive constraints and mental blocks is for it the ultimate purpose and the end of emancipatory effort; truth and goodness, says Rorty, will take care of themselves once we have taken proper care of freedom.

When it happens to be in a self-reflective, philosophical cast, the postmodern mind would point out, against its critics, that despite appearances to the contrary it is not a 'destructive destruction', but a *constructive* one, in which it has been engaged all along. Its job has been a sort of a site-clearing operation. While renouncing what merely passes for the truth, dismantling its past, present and future putative, ossified versions, it uncovers the truth in its pristine form which modern pretensions had maimed and distorted beyond recognition. More than that: the demolition uncovers *the truth of the truth*, truth as residing in the being itself and not in the violent acts performed upon it; truth that has been belied under the domination of legislative reason. The real truth is already there before its laborious construction has started; it is re-posited in the ground on which the elaborate artifices have been erected: ostensibly to display it, in fact to hide and stifle it.

Of this demolition of false pretences the postmodern mind claims to be performing, the 'second Copernican revolution' of Heidegger is often seen as the archetype and trend-setter. As Paul Ricoeur explains, since *Sein und Zeit* appeared in 1927, understanding began to be recognized as the 'mode of being before defining the mode of knowing. It consists essentially in the capacity of *Dasein* to project its most proper possibilities inside the fundamental situation of being in the world'. Heidegger's seminal insight has been taken up and put to manifold uses by his followers – for instance by Gadamer, who took it upon himself to re-examine Dilthey's worried question through Heideggerian spectacles. That question has been subjected to the test in three areas:

> that of the arts, in which our hold of aesthetic reality precedes the distanced judgment of taste; that of history, where the consciousness of being exposed to the labours of history precedes the objectifications of documentary historiography; that of language, where the universally linguistic character of human experience precedes all linguistic, semiotic and semantic methodology.[3]

All in all, postmodernity can be seen as restoring to the world what modernity, presumptuously, had taken away; as a *re-enchantment* of the world that modernity tried hard to *dis-enchant*. It is the modern artifice that has been dismantled; the modern conceit of meaning-legislating reason that has been exposed, condemned and put to shame. It is that artifice and that reason, the reason of the artifice, that stands accused in the court of postmodernity.

The war against mystery and magic was for modernity the war of liberation leading to the declaration of reason's independence. It was the declaration of hostilities that made the unprocessed, pristine world into the enemy. As is the case with all genocide, the world of nature (as distinct from the house of culture modernity set out to build) had to be beheaded and thus deprived of autonomous will and power of resistance. At stake in the war was the right to initiative and the authorship of action, the right to pronounce on meanings, to construe narratives. To win the stakes, to win all of them and to win them for good, the world had to be *de-spiritualized*, de-animated: denied the capacity of the *subject*.

The dis-enchantment of the world was the ideology of its subordination; simultaneously a declaration of intent to make the world docile to those who would have won the right to will, and a legitimation of practices guided solely by that will as the uncontested standard of propriety. In this ideology and in the practice it reflected and legitimized, spirit was all on one side and matter all on the other. The world was an *object* of *willed action*: a raw material in the work guided and given form by human designs. Meanings and designs became one. Left to itself, the world had no meaning. It was solely the human design that injected it with sense and purpose. So the earth became a repository of ores and other 'natural resources', wood turned into timber and water – depending on circumstances – into an energy source, waterway or the solvent of waste. The link that may be spotted between earth, forest and water was difficult to perceive between ores, timber and waste disposal; in their new incarnations they were parcelled out between distinct and distant functions and purposes and all their once pristine links were now subject solely to the logic of the latter. And as nature became progressively 'de-animated', humans grew increasingly 'naturalized' so that their subjectivity, the primeval 'givenness' of their existence could be denied and they themselves could be made hospitable for instrumental meanings; they came to be like timber and waterways rather than like forests and lakes. Their dis-enchantment, like that of the world as a whole, stemmed from the encounter between the designing posture and the strategy of instrumental rationality. The achievement of that encounter was the world split between wilful subject and will-less object; between the privileged actor whose will counted and the rest of the world whose will did not count – having been denied or disregarded. It is against such a disenchanted world that the postmodern re-enchantment is aimed.

MODERNITY, OR DESPERATELY SEEKING STRUCTURE

The kind of society that, retrospectively, came to be called modern, emerged out of the discovery that human order is vulnerable, contingent and devoid of reliable foundations. That discovery was shocking. The response to the shock was a dream and an effort to make order solid, obligatory and reliably founded. This response problematized contingency as an enemy and order as a task. It devalued and demonized the 'raw' human condition. It prompted an incessant drive to eliminate the haphazard and annihilate the spontaneous. As a matter of tact, it was the sought-after order that in advance construed everything for which it had no room or time as contingent and hence lacking foundation. The dream of order and the practice of ordering constitute the world – their object – as chaos. And, of course, as a challenge – as a compulsive reason to act.

Discovery of contingency was not a feat of reason. One does not see the given-to-hand, much less does one think of it, until it goes bust and lets one down. One does not conceive of regularity unless one is buffeted by the unexpected, one does not notice monotonousness until the fashion in which things behaved yesterday stops being a reliable guide to their conduct tomorrow. Contingency was discovered *together* with the realization that if one wants things and events to be regular, repeatable and predictable, one needs to do something about it; they won't be such on their own. Awareness of the world's contingency and the idea of order as the goal and the outcome of the *practice of ordering* were born together, as twins; perhaps even Siamese twins.

The dissipation of socially supervised routine (theorized as the preordained order of being) could have been an exhilarating experience. But it also kindled a heretofore unknown fear. The weakening of routine was the blessing of freedom for the strong and bold; it was the curse of insecurity for the weak and diffident. The marriage between freedom and insecurity was prearranged and consummated on the wedding night; all subsequent attempts at separation proved vain, and the wedlock remained in force ever since.

The Renaissance celebrated the collapse of the preordained (and thus visible only in its collapse) order as liberation. The withdrawal of God meant a triumphant entry of Man. In Pico della Mirandola's rendering, the Divine Creator said to Adam: 'thou shouldst be thy own free moulder and overcomer; thou canst degenerate to animal, and through thyself be reborn to godlike existence. . . . Thou alone hast power to develop and grow according to free will.'⁴ This sort of freedom, if contemplated at all, was previously thought of as a Divine attribute. Now it was human; but as it was human by Divine order (the *only* briefing given by God to man), it was also man's duty. Freedom was a chance pregnant with obligation. It was now up to man to 'be reborn to godlike existence'. This was a life-long task, brandishing no hope of respite. Nothing was to be satisfactory if short of the ultimate, and the ultimate was no less than *perfection*, described by Leon Battista Alberti as a harmony of all the parts fitted together in such a way that nothing could be added, diminished or altered, but for the worse. Human freedom of creation and self-creation meant that no imperfection, ugliness or suffering could now claim the right to exist, let alone claim legitimacy. It was the contingency of the imperfect that spurred the anxiety about reaching perfection. And perfection could be reached only through action: it was the outcome of laborious 'fitting together'. Once a matter of providence and revelation, life had turned into the object of *techne*. The urge to re-make the world was planted in the primary experience of liberation. It was forced into buoyant growth by the fear of the chaos that would overwhelm the world were the search for perfection to be abandoned or even slackened in a moment of inattention.

A pure, unclouded celebration was therefore short; just a brief interlude between the Divine and the man-made orders, between *being what one was* and *making oneself what one should be*. From Erasmus, Mirandola, Rabelais or Montaigne to Descartes or Hobbes there was but the distance of a generation. And the celebration was confined to those lucky few who could concentrate on 'moulding themselves' thanks to the concentration of ample resources, not yet questioned as a right, and therefore enjoyable without the attendant worry about foundations. (The celebrations were not go on for long, however, and could not be universal, as the foundations were bound to prove shaky or altogether absent, the resources to dry up, and thus the effort to secure their unhampered flow to clash with the right to enjoy one's contingency.)

It was in that brief interlude, and among those who could savour the sweet fruits of the sudden collapse of power-assisted certainties, that diversity was not merely accepted as the human fate, but lovingly embraced and hailed as the sign and condition of true humanity. Openness, readiness to refrain from condemnation of the other and to argue with, rather than to fight the antagonist, cognitive and cathexic modesty, settling for the credible instead of chasing the absolute – were all conspicuous marks of the humanist culture (later, from the heights of modern ambitions, to be redubbed as the 'Pyrrhonian crisis', a moment of weakness before the resurgence of strength) that for all practical intents and purposes was to be shortly shelved in dust-gathering libraries for the centuries to come. Harsh realities of politics in the aftermath of religious wars and the final collapse of the feudal order made the diversity of lives and relativity of truths much less attractive, and certainly not at all laudable. Enlightened and not-so-enlightened rulers set out to build anew, wilfully and by design, the order of things which the anointed monarchs of the past had stupidly allowed to crumble. When seen from the watchtowers of new ambitious powers, diversity looked more like chaos, scepticism like ineptitude, tolerance like subversion. Certainty, orderliness, homogeneity became the orders of the day.

What followed was a long (roughly three centuries long) age of *Cosmopolis* (to borrow the apt term recently coined by Stephen Toulmin).[5] In the Cosmopolis, the vision of visionaries joined hands with the practice of practitioners: the intellectual model of an orderly universe blended with the ordering bustle of the politicians. The vision was of a hierarchical harmony reflected, as in a mirror, in the uncontested and uncontestable pronouncements of reason. The practice was about making the pronouncements, adorned with the badges of reason, uncontested and uncontestable. As St Augustine's *City of Man* reflected the glory of the *City of God*, so the modern, obsessively legislating, defining, structuring, segregating, classifying, recording and universalizing state reflected the splendour of universal and absolute standards of truth. Whoever questioned St Augustine's wedlock between the mundane and the divine could only speak in the name of evil and devil; whoever questioned the modern wedlock between absolute truth and absolute power could only speak in the name of unreason and chaos. Dissent had been discredited and delegitimized even before it was spoken – by the very absoluteness of the dominant syndrome, the universalism of its proclaimed ambitions and the completeness of its domination. The new certainty had defined scepticism as ignorance or ill will, and difference as fossilized backwardness, or as a rudiment of bygone ignominy living on borrowed time.[6] In an apt expression of Harry Redner, 'just as in the language of faith God cannot be denied or even seriously questioned, so too in the languages of Progress it is Progress itself that has that status'.[7]

The different – the idiosyncratic and the insouciant – have been thereby dishonourably discharged from the army of order and progress (as Comte put it, of orderly progress and progressive order). The degradation was unequivocal, complete and irrevocable. There was really no good reason to tolerate the Other who, by definition, rebelled against the truth. As Spinoza justly pointed out – if I know the truth and you are ignorant, to make you change your thoughts and ways is my moral duty; refraining from doing so would be cruel and selfish. Modernity was not merely the Western Man's thrust for power; it was also his *mission*, proof of moral righteousness and cause of pride. From the point of view of reason-founded human order, tolerance is incongruous and immoral.

The new, modern order took off as a desperate search for structure in a world suddenly denuded of structure. Utopias that served as beacons for the long march to the rule of reason visualized a world without margins, leftovers, the unaccounted for – without dissidents and rebels; a world in which, as in the world just left behind, everyone will have a job to do and everyone will be keen to do the job he has to: the *I will* and *I must* will merge. The visualized world differed from the lost one by putting assignment where blind fate once ruled. The jobs to be done were now gleaned from an overall plan, drafted by the spokesmen of reason; in the world to come, design preceded order. People were not born into their places: they had to be trained, drilled or goaded into finding the place that fitted them and which they fitted. No wonder utopias chose architecture and urban planning as both the vehicle and the master-metaphor of the perfect world that would know of no misfits and hence of no disorder; however much they differed in detail, they all lovingly detailed the carefully segregated and strictly functional urban quarters, the straight, unpolluted geometry of streets and public squares, the hierarchy of spaces and buildings which, in their prescribed volumes and austerity of adornment, mirrored the stately sovereignty of the social order. In the city of reason, there were to be no winding roads, no cul-de-sacs and no unattended sites left to chance – and thus no vagabonds, vagrants or nomads.

In this reason-drafted city with no mean streets, dark spots and no-go areas order *was to be made*; there was to be *no other order*. Hence the urge, the desperation: there would be as much order in the world as we manage to put into it. The practice stemming from a conviction that order can be only man-made, that it is bound to remain an artificial imposition on the unruly natural state of things and humans, that for this reason it will forever remain vulnerable and in need of constant supervision and policing, is the main (and, indeed, unique) distinguishing mark of modernity. From now on, there would be no moment of respite, no relaxing of vigilance. The ordering impulse would be fed ever again by the fear of chaos never to be allayed. The lid of order would never seem tight and heavy enough. Escape from the wilderness, once embarked on, will never end.

In a recent study,[8] Stephen L. Collins put the spotlight on the 'Hobbesian problem' as the epitome of this modern spirit:

Hobbes understood that a world in flux was natural and that order must be created to restrain what was natural. . . . Society is no longer a transcendentally articulated reflection of something predefined, external, and beyond itself which orders existence hierarchically. It is now a nominal entity ordered by the sovereign state which is its own articulated representative. . . . [Forty years after Elizabeth's death] order was coming to be understood not as natural, but as artificial, created by man, and manifestly political and social. . . . Order must be designed to restrain what appeared ubiquitous (that is, flux). . . . Order became a matter of power, and power a matter of will, force and calculation. . . . Fundamental to the entire reconceptualization of the idea of society was the belief that the commonwealth, as was order, was a human creation.

To create order means neither to cultivate nor to extirpate the differences. It means *licensing* them. And it means a *licensing authority*. Obversely, it means also de-legalizing unlicensed differences. Order can be only an all-inclusive category. It must also remain forever a belligerent camp, surrounded by enemies and waging wars on all its frontiers. The unlicensed difference is the main enemy: it is also an enemy to be eventually conquered – a temporary enemy, a testimony to inadequacy of zeal and/or resource of the fighting order (for early modern thinkers – one may repeat after Peter de Bolla – 'the heterogenous experiences of the real indicate a number of differences which must be brought to similarity, which must be homogenized into a unitary subject through comparison and combination').[9] The subversive power of *unlicensed* difference resides precisely in its *spontaneity*, that is in its indeterminacy *vis-à-vis* the decreed order, that is in its unpredictability, that is in its uncontrollability. In the shape of the unlicensed difference, modernity fought the real enemy: the grey area of ambivalence, indeterminacy and undecidability.

One can hardly imagine a social group more strictly differentiated, segregated and hierarchic than the population of the Panopticon – Jeremy Bentham's grand metaphor of an orderly, reason-led society. Yet *all* residents of the Panopticon – the Overseer, the supervisors and lowliest of the inmates alike – are *happy*. They are happy because they live in a carefully controlled environment, and thus know exactly what to do. Not for them the sorrows of frustration and the pain of failure. The gap between the will and duty has been bridged.[10] Bridging of this gap was, indeed, the *focus imaginarius* of the modern struggle for rationally designed order. It was left for Bentham's genius to perceive that by no other arrangement is the purpose better served and secured than by prison. Or, rather, that the main task of the day overtakes and dwarfs the 'merely functional' distinctions between prisons, houses of detention, houses of correction, workhouses, poorhouses, hospitals, lunatic asylums, schools, military barracks, dormitories and factories. Modernity was a long march to prison. It never arrived there (though in some places, like Stalin's Russia, Hitler's Germany or Mao's China, it came quite close), albeit not for the lack of trying.

POSTMODERNITY, OR HIDING FROM FEAR

We have been brought up in the shadow of the sinister warning of Dostoyevsky: if there is no God, everything is permissible. If we happen to be professional social scientists, we have been also trained to share the no less sinister premonition of Durkheim: if the normative grip of society slackens, the moral order will collapse. For whatever reason, we tend to believe that men and women can only be goaded or cajoled, by superior force or superior rhetoric, into peaceful coexistence. So we are naturally inclined to view the prospect of levelling up of hierarchies with horror: only universal mayhem can follow the disappearance of universality-claiming truths. (This is, probably, the main reason why many a philosopher and politician, and that part of each of us where a philosopher or a politician resides, militates against facing contingency as inescapable fate; let alone embracing it as a welcome destiny.) I propose that it is precisely in that horror and this resentment that the most dangerous potential of the postmodern condition lay in ambush.

The threats related to *postmodernity* are highly familiar: they are, one may say, thoroughly *modern* in nature. Now, as before, they stem from that *horror vacui* that modernity made into the principle of social organization and personality formation. Modernity was a continuous and uncompromising effort to fill or to cover up the void; the modern mentality held a stern belief that the job can be done – if not today then tomorrow. The sin of postmodernity is to abandon the effort and to deny the belief; this double act appears to be indeed a sin, once one remembers that abandoning effort and denying belief does not, by itself, neutralize the awesome propelling force of the *fear of void*; and postmodernity has done next to nothing to support its defiance of past pretence with a new practical antidote for old poison.

And thus men and women have been left alone with their fears; they are told by philosophers that the void is here to stay, and by politicians that coping with it is their own duty and worry. Postmodernity has not allayed the fears which modernity injected into humanity once it left it to its own resources; postmodernity only *privatized* these fears. This may be good news: after all, in its collectivized form the struggle against the void all too often ended up in the missions of classes, nations or races – a far cry from the philosophers' dream of eternal peace brought about by the universality of human reason. The privatization of fears may not bring peace of mind, but it just may take away some of the reasons for the wars of classes, nations or races. And yet, the news is not unambiguously good. With fears privatized, the temptation to run for cover remains as potent as ever. But there is no hope left that human reason, and its earthly agents, will make the race a guided tour, certain to end up in a secure and agreeable shelter.

The privatization of fears means privatization of escape routes and escape vehicles. It means a DIY escape. The only thing collectivity is expected to offer is a set of self-assembly kits for the DIY work. As it stands, the social world appears to the individual as a pool of choices; a market, to be exact. How meaningful the work on the assembly and its result will be depends on the chooser–cum–assembly worker: at least this is what he or she has been made to believe. But then he or she would not have the means to find out just how sensible and/or gratifying that meaning is, once they put it together. For this they need confirmation that can only come in the form of supra-individual approval. The latter need is in no way novel or specifically postmodern. What is indeed peculiarly postmodern is the absence of 'official approving agencies', able to force through, with the help of sanction-supported norms, their approval or disapproval (hence the new feeling of an eerie 'softness' of the habitat; the pleasurable yet disturbing 'everything goes' feeling). Like the approval-seeking proposals, so the approving agencies themselves must be more often than not construed in the DIY way – exactly like the choices one would wish (and hope) them to approve.

It is for this reason that postmodernity, having privatized modern fears and the worry of coping with them, had to become an age of *imagined communities*.[11] For the philosophers and the ordinary folk alike, community is now expected to bring the succour previously sought in the pronouncements of universal reason and their earthly translations: the legislative acts of the national state. But such a community, like its predecessor, universal reason, does not grow in the wilderness: it is a greenhouse plant, that needs sowing, feeding, trimming and protection from weeds and parasites. Even then it leads but a precarious existence and can wither away overnight once the supply of loving care runs out. It is precisely because of its vulnerability that community provides the focus of postmodern concerns, that it attracts so much intellectual and practical attention, that it figures so prominently in the philosophical models and popular ideologies of postmodernity.

Communities are *imagined*: belief in their presence is their only brick and mortar, and imputation of importance their only source of authority. An imagined community acquires the right to approve or disapprove in the *consequence* of the decision of the approval-seeking individual to invest it with the arbitrating power and to agree to be bound by the arbitration (though, of course, the reverse order must be *believed* to be the case to make the whole thing work). By itself, an imagined community would have no resources to enforce its arbitration in the case of the grant of authority being withdrawn; it would not even have the institutionalized agency capable of reaching the decision in the case under arbitration. And yet the imagined community may be, on occasion, by far more powerful than the Tönnies-type 'communities by inertia' (communities that lingered effortlessly, as if merely by dint of physical proximity and absence of movement) ever were. What it lacks in stability and institutionalized continuity, it more than compensates for with the overwhelming affective commitment of its self-appointed 'members'. In the absence of institutional support, the commitment tends to be fickle and short-lived. At the moments of condensation, however, it may reach literally breath-taking intensity. And it does; often enough to arouse anxiety.

To exist is to be enacted; I am seen, therefore I exist – this might have been the imagined community's own version of the *cogito*. Having no other (and above all no objectified, supra-individual) anchors except the affections of their 'members', imagined communities exist solely through their manifestations: through occasional spectacular outbursts of togetherness (demonstrations, marches, festivals, riots) – sudden materializations of the idea, all the more effective and convincing for blatantly violating the routine of quotidianity. In the postmodern habitat of diffuse offers and free choices, public attention is the scarcest of all commodities (one can say that the political economy of postmodernity is concerned mostly with the production and distribution of public attention). The right of an imagined community to arbitrate is established (though for a time only; and always merely until further notice) in proportion to the amount and intensity of public attention forced to focus on its presence; 'reality', and hence also the power and authority of an imagined community, is the function of that attention. Seeking an authority powerful enough to relieve them of their fears, individuals have no other means of reaching their aim except by trying to make the communities they imagine more authoritative than the communities imagined by others – and this by heaving them into the centre of public attention. This can be achieved by spectacular display – so spectacular and so obtrusive as to prevent the public from turning their eyes the other way. Since no imagined community is alone in its struggle for public attention, a fierce competition results that forces upwards the stakes of the game. What was sufficiently spectacular yesterday loses its force of attraction today, unless it lifts to new heights its shocking power. Constantly bombarded, the absorptive powers of the public are unable to cling to any of the competing allurements for longer than a fleeting moment. To catch the attention, displays must be ever more bizarre, condensed and (yes!) disturbing; perhaps ever more brutal, gory and threatening.

In the world of imagined communities, the struggle for survival is a struggle for access to the human imagination. Whatever events therefore succeed in gaining such access (street battles before and after football matches, hijacking of planes, targeted or haphazard acts of terrorism, desecration of graves, daubing offensive graffiti on cult buildings, poisoning or contaminating supermarket food, occupying public squares, taking hostages, stripping in public, mass marches or city riots) do so first and foremost in their semiotic, symbolic quality. Whatever the damage actually visited upon the intended or accidental victims of display, it is the *symbolic* significance that counts – the capturing of public imagination. As a rule, the magnitude of the latter effect is but feebly related to the scale of the 'material' devastation that the spectacles could accomplish.

This last observation contains, perhaps, a glimmer of hope. But the fact remains that the postmodern privatization of fears has prompted and will prompt a furious search for communal shelters all the more vehement and potentially lethal for the brittle, imagined existence of communities; that this search will generate increasingly daring (and possibly violent, since nothing attracts attention so well as thoughtless, motiveless violence) displays of communal togetherness; and that displays will remain perforce competitive, and hence infused with inter-communal hostility. How much chance for tolerance?

For all intents and purposes, rampant tribalism is the currently practiced way of 'embracing contingency'[12] (to use Agnes Heller's memorable expression) already privatized with the advent of postmodernity. We are bound to live *with* contingency (aware of contingency, face to face with contingency) for the foreseeable future. If we want this future to be also a long one, tolerance must be secured in the only form in which it may put a brake on tribal hostilities: in the form of *solidarity*.[13] One may go a step further and propose that tolerance as such is possible *only* in the form of solidarity: that is, what is needed is not just refraining from converting ambitions (an abstention that may well result in a breakdown in communication, in the declaration of indifference and the practice of separation), but a practical recognition of the *relevance* and *validity* of the other's difference, expressed in a willing engagement in the dialogue.

Tolerance requires the acceptance of the subjectivity (i.e. know-ledge-producing capacity and motivated nature of action) of the other who is to be 'tolerated'; but such acceptance is only a necessary, not the sufficient condition of tolerance. By itself, it does nothing to save the 'tolerated' from humiliation. What if it takes the following form: 'you are wrong, and I am right; I agree that not everybody can be like me, not for the time being at any rate, not at once; the fact that I bear with your otherness does not exonerate your error, it only proves my generosity'? Such tolerance would be no more than just another of the many superiority postures; at the best it would come dangerously close to snubbing; given propitious circumstances, it may also prove an overture to a crusade. Tolerance reaches its full potential only when it offers more than the acceptance of diversity and coexistence; when it calls for the emphatic admission of the *equivalence* of knowledge-producing discourses; when it calls for a *dialogue*, vigilantly protected against monologistic temptations;[14]

when it acknowledges not just the *otherness* of the other, but the legitimacy of the other's interests and the other's right to have such interests respected and, if possible, gratified.

THE ETHICAL PARADOX OF POSTMODERNITY

I suggest that ethical choice and moral responsibility assume under the postmodern condition a totally new and long forgotten significance; an importance of which modernity tried hard, and with a considerable success, to divest them, moving as it did toward replacement of ethical discourse with the discourse of objective, translocal and impersonal truth. Modernity was, among other things, a gigantic exercise in abolishing individual responsibility other than that measured by the criteria of instrumental rationality and practical achievement. The authorship of moral rules and the responsibility for their promotion was shifted to a supra-individual level.[15] With societies (institutionalized as nation states) losing interest in the promotion of cultural uniformity and renouncing their role as spokesmen of universal reason, agents face ethical confusion and lack of clarity of moral choices as a permanent condition rather than a temporary (and in principle rectifiable) irritant. They also face them as their own problems and their own responsibility. Last but not least, they face them as harrowing challenges that can never be resolved to one's full, unclouded satisfaction; as tasks with no guaranteed 'true' and 'proper' solutions, unlikely ever to be rid of uncertainty and ambivalence.

The ethical paradox of the postmodern condition is that it restores to agents the fullness of moral choice and responsibility while simultaneously depriving them of the comfort of the universal guidance that modern self-confidence once promised. Ethical tasks of individuals grow while the socially produced resources to fulfil them shrink. Moral responsibility comes together with the loneliness of moral choice.

In a cacophony of moral voices, none of which is likely to silence the others, the individuals are thrown back on their own subjectivity as the only ultimate ethical authority. At the same time, however, they are told repeatedly about the irreparable relativism of any moral code. No code claims foundations stronger than the conviction of its followers and their determination to abide by its rules. Once embraced, the rules tell what one must do; but nothing tells one, at least convincingly, why these rules (or any other rules for that matter) should be embraced in the first place. The deposition of universal reason did not reinstate a universal God. Instead, morality has been *privatized*; like everything else that shared this fate, ethics has become a matter of individual discretion, risk-taking, chronic uncertainty and never-placated qualms.

Under the circumstances, there are no obvious social agencies that may guide the choice between indifference and solidarity – the two sharply opposed versions of postmodern tolerance. The choice will eventually have to be practical and do without the support of philosophical assurances. It will have to be built from the bottom up, out of the ethical convictions and moral conduct of the multitude of individual agents. Which form the postmodern tolerance will take is in no way guaranteed in advance. Each of the two forms has its own powerful reinforcements, and there is no knowing which one might eventually prevail.

This is because behind the postmodern ethical paradox hides a genuine practical dilemma: acting on one's moral convictions is naturally pregnant with a desire to win for such convictions an ever more universal acceptance; but every attempt to do just that smacks of the already discredited bid for domination. A truly consistent rejection of the heteronomy entailed in the monologic stance would lead, paradoxically, to lofty and derisive indifference. One would need, after all, to refrain from prompting the other to act according to the rules one accepts as morally sound, and from preventing the other following rules one views as odious or abominable; such self-restraint, however, cannot be easily detached from its corollary: the disdainful view of the other as an essentially inferior being, one that need not or cannot lift himself or be lifted to the level of life viewed as properly human. One may say that the zealous avoidance of the monologic stance leads to consequences strikingly similar to those one wished to stave off. If I consider corporal punishment degrading and bodily mutilations inhuman, letting the others to practice them in the name of their right to choose (or because I cannot believe any more in the universality of moral rules) amounts to the reassertion of my own superiority: 'they may wallow in barbarities I would never put up with . . . that serves them right, those savages'. The renunciation of the monologic stance does not seem, therefore, an unmixed blessing. The more radical it is, the more it resembles moral relativism in its behavioural incarnation of callous indifference.

There seems to be no easy exit from the quandary. Humanity paid too high a price for the monologic addiction of modernity not to shudder at the prospect of another bout of ordering-by-design and one more session of social engineering. It will not be easy to find the golden mean between colonizing temptations and the selfishness of tribal self-closure; none of the alternatives seems to be an attractive proposition – yet none of their mixtures promises to be foolproof and, above all, stands a chance of persevering. If the civilizing formula of modernity called for surrendering at least a part of the agent's freedom in exchange for the promise of security drawn from (assumed) moral and (prospective) social certainty, postmodernity proclaims all restrictions on freedom illegal, at the same time doing away with social certainty and legalizing ethical uncertainty. Existential insecurity – ontological contingency of being – is the result.

ABOUT THIS BOOK

It is not easy to narrate postmodernity. If the purpose or the effect of narration is to bring order into a semantically loaded yet confused space, to conjure up logical consistency where chaos would otherwise rule – any narrative aiming to serve well its *raison d'être* stands a risk of implying more coherence than the postmodern condition could possibly uphold. Once we remember that incoherence is the most distinctive among the attributes of postmodernity (arguably its defining feature), we need to reconcile ourselves to the prospect that all narratives will be to a varying extent flawed. The closer they come to picturing the postmodern condition as a balanced system, the graver their faults will risk being. It is for the fear of such an (all too easy to commit) error that the essays collected in this volume bear no other ambition but to report a number of sightings, or glimpses, of the postmodern scene – each conscious of being partial and perceived from just one of the many possible observation points. Most of them have been conceived and written at various stages of the postmodern debate; each one resulted from a separate entry into the postmodern world, at a somewhat different point of its own development and the development of its perception, and with the benefit of hindsight of a different knowledge. Brought together, the essays offer a picture produced by the rotation of a 'hermeneutic circle': the successive re-cycling of a number of basic insights.

The first group of essays is united by a common intention: to situate the work of sociology in a new world, strikingly dissimilar from that in which its orthodox goals and strategies had gestated. Can sociology enter this new world? If so, at the expense of what accommodation? Can the traditional status of sociology as a *privileged* discourse, as a supplier of rational models of social reality and managerially useful knowledge of its processes, be rescued and retained? In particular, how are the orthodox goals of sociology likely to fare under conditions of endemic pluralism of authority? In a nutshell, the essays of this group ask what (if anything) has the advent of postmodernity changed in the relation of sociology to the state and prospects of freedom and justice.

The second group of essays add up to a case study of sorts. They focus on one, clinically sharp (because pushed to a radical extreme relieved by no 'extenuating circumstances') attempt to act on the ambitions of the modern, Enlightenment-born mind, and to put its precepts into practice. They focus therefore on the least ambiguous and most resounding defeat of the modern project (and, by the same token, on the most spectacular triumph of postmodern values which came to replace it); they deal, in other words, with the prohibitively costly communism-building venture – but try to establish what general lessons about the inner potential and inner dangers of the modern and the postmodern conditions can be learned from its failure.

The collapse of communism was the final nail in the coffin of the modern ambitions which drew the horizon of European (or Europe-influenced) history of the last two centuries. That collapse ushered us into an as-yet-unexplored world: a world without a collective utopia, without a conscious alternative to itself. Its survival and self-propagation needs to be understood from inside – a formidable task, likely to be repeatedly undertaken and unlikely to be fulfilled in anything approaching a lastingly satisfactory manner. The last essay of the volume is a daring attempt to come to grips with this task; like many other attempts that have already appeared and undoubtedly will go on appearing, this one is what it must be at this stage of the exploration: tentative and inconclusive, more a record of a mind's struggle with the unfamiliar, than a comprehensive theoretical model of a reality-in-the-process-of-becoming, a reality thus far stubbornly defying all efforts of rational ordering.[16]

NOTES

1 Modernist art, in a desperate attempt to cut links with the world it deplores, systematically destroys anything that this world could accept, absorb and turn to its own use: it 'destroys the figure, cancels it, arrives at the abstract, the white canvas, the slashed canvas, the charred canvas. In architecture and the visual arts, it will be the curtain wall, the building as steel, pure parallelepiped, minimal art; in literature, the destruction of the flow of discourse, the Burroughs-like collage, silence, the white page; in music, the passage from atonality to noise to absolute silence (in this sense, the early Cage is modern). But the moment comes when the avant-garde (the modern) can go no further. . .' (Matei Calinescu, *Five Faces of Modernity: Modernism, Avant-Garde, Decadence, Kitsch, Postmodern*, Durham: Duke University, 1987, pp. 176–7).

2 Cf. Suzi Gablik, *Has Modernism Failed?* (London: Thames & Hudson, 1984).

3 In: *Au jardin des malentendus*, textes édités par Jacques Leenhardt et Robert Picht (Actes Sud, 1990), pp. 173–4.

4 Otto Rank, who quotes Mirandola, supplies a psychological commentary to the notion of human genius born of the Renaissance experience. He interprets the concept as 'the apotheosis of man as a creative personality; the religious ideology (looking to the glory of God) being transferred to man himself'. Man 'takes over the role of the divine hero' (*Art and Artist: Creative Urge and Personality Development*, trans. by Charles Francis Atkinson, New York: Alfred A. Knopf, 1932, p. 24).

5 Comp. Stephen Toulmin, *Cosmopolis: The Hidden Agenda of Modernity* (New York: Free Press, 1990).

6 In a highly perceptive study of the use of time in the practice of modern power (*Time and the Other: How Anthropology Makes its Object*, New York: Columbia University Press, 1983), Johannes Fabian points out that 'geopolitics has its ideological foundations in chronopolitics' (p. 144). The modern perspective 'denied coevality' to any form of life different from its own; it construed the Other of itself as 'living in another time'. The allochronic distancing device (Fabian's felicitous term) seems to be a variant of a more general expedient: construing the Other (defining the Other) in a way that a priori decides its inferior and, indeed, transient and (until disappearance) illegitimate status. In an age of the forward march of reason-guided progress, describing the Other as outdated, backward, obsolete, primitive, and altogether 'pre-', was equivalent to such a decision.

7 Harry Redner, *In the Beginning was the Deed: Reflections on the Passage of Faust* (Berkeley: University of California Press, 1982), p. 30. Redner summarizes the process that followed:

> The story is well known how we Europeans launched ourselves

on an unparalleled drive for power, which we called Progress. . . . All other societies and cultures were crushed or
exterminated or forced to engage with us in our race of Progress;
eventually perhaps, some of them will even outdistance us. All
the natural and human resources were put at our disposal to be
transformed in accordance with our sovereign will. This willed
thrust of power was justified in the name of an unlimited future
of Man.

(p. 13)

The theoretical/practical posture that defines the modern era has been
succinctly described by Redner as a

way of systematically dominating, controlling, and disposing of
things, which in the first place was directed against Nature but
which [humans] now find is also turning on themselves and
depriving them of their human nature. . . .They can make
themselves irrelevant, if not redundant, to their own schemes
and so dispose of themselves.

(p. 5)

8 Comp. Stephen L. Collins, *From Divine Cosmos to Sovereign State: An
   Intellectual History of Consciousness and the Idea of Order in Renaissance
   England* (Oxford: Oxford University Press, 1989 p. 28–9).
9 'For the earlier theorist', says de Bolla, 'difference represents the
   division of society and, therefore, the division of the self; here the
   reflective surface. . .is external, public, within the social, cultural
   and political' (Peter de Bolla, *The Discourse of the Sublime: Readings
   in History, Aesthetics and the Subject*, Oxford: Basil Blackwell, 1989,
   p. 285). The autonomous individual may be conceived of only
   as an excess, a surplus, an uncontrolled effluent of the discourse
   of control; he is, one may say, an 'unfinished business' of the
   ordering scheme, burdened with the reconciliation or smoothing up
   of differences – the tasks that would have been rather settled at the
   public level.
10 I have analysed the psycho-social consequences of panoptical structure
   more fully in the first chapter of *Freedom* (Milton Keynes: Open
   University Press, 1988).
11 I owe the idea of *imagined community* to Benedict Anderson (comp. his
   Imagined Communities: Reflections on the Origin and Spread of Nationalism,
   London: Verso, 1983) – though I accept the responsibility for the uses to
   which I put it. Compare as well Michel Maffesoli, *Les Temps de tribus: Le
   déclin de l'individualisme dans les sociétés de masse* (Paris: Klincksieck, 1988)
   for a similar idea of *neo-tribes*.
12 Agnes Heller, 'From hermeneutics in social science toward a hermeneutics of social science', *Theory and Society* 18 (1989).
13 Richard Rorty (*Contingency, Irony and Solidarity*, Cambridge: Cambridge University Press, 1989, p. 198) gives the following descriptive
   definition of the (logical) conditions of solidarity: ours is

the first epoch in human history in which large numbers of

people have become able to separate the question 'Do you believe and desire what we believe and desire?' from the question 'Are you suffering?'. In my jargon, this is the ability to distinguish the question whether you and I have the same vocabulary from the question of whether you are in pain.

One may entertain some doubts as to just how large is the 'large number of people' Rorty is referring to; but there is little doubt as to the centrality of Rorty's distinction for the fate of postmodern solidarity.

14 On the conditions/cognitive assumptions warranting the strategic difference between the 'monologic' and 'dialogic' discourses, Mikhail Bakhtin had the following to say: 'in a monologic discourse, there is only one consciousness, one subject; in a dialogic one – two consciousnesses, two subjects' (cf. M.M. Bakhtin, *Estetika slovesnovo trorchestra, (Aesthetics of Verbal Creativity)*, Moscow: Iskusstvo, 1986, p. 306). In the monologic frame, 'the intellect contemplates an object and makes statements about it. In this case, there is only one subject, both cognitive (contemplating) and speaking (locutionary). It confronts a numb object' (ibid., p. 383).

15 I have developed this theme more fully in my 'Effacing the face', in *Theory, Culture and Society* 7.

16 Some essays collected in this book have been published in the current or previous versions of *Political Quarterly, Praxis International, Sociological Review, Theory, Culture and Society, Thesis Eleven* and *TLS*.

1

LEGISLATORS AND INTERPRETERS

Culture as the ideology of intellectuals

Antonio Gramsci (1957) reserved the marker, 'organic', for those intellectuals who articulated the world view, interests, intentions and historically determined potential of a particular class; who elaborated the values which needed to be promoted for such a potential to be fully developed; and who legitimized the historical role of a given class, its claim to power and to the management of social process in terms of those values.

Ideologies were the product of such articulation, elaboration and legitimation. Their production, discursive defence and dissemination were the work of organic intellectuals: the activity that simultaneously defined the specifically intellectual praxis and the function played by the intellectuals in the reproduction of the social system.

As 'organic', intellectuals remained invisible as the authors of ideological narratives. The pictures of society or history they painted seldom contained their own representation. As a rule, the organic intellectuals hid behind the broad shoulders of their ostensible heroes. In class-related ideologies, the role of historical actors was normally assigned to classes defined by activities different from those that distinguished their intellectual authors.

A closer scrutiny, however, would pierce the camouflage. It would reveal the uncanny resemblance the stage actors of ideological scenarios bore to the intellectual scriptwriters. Whoever happened to be named as the sitter in a given portrait-painting session, the product was invariably a thinly disguised likeness of the painter. In organic ideologies, the intellectuals painted their self-portraits, though only rarely did they admit this to be the case.

Like other authors of narratives, organic intellectuals could hardly eradicate or dissolve their presence in the products of their work; this much has been readily admitted of virtually all kinds of authorship, though paradoxically the pretensions of objectivity in the field of ideological narratives tend to be defended with more zeal than elsewhere. Yet in organic ideologies the intellectual authorship leaves a particularly heavy imprint – and this in two respects above all.

First, the intellectuals' own mode of praxis serves as the natural base line against which the features of the ostensible sitter of the portrait are plotted. The sitter's own characteristics tend to be trimmed, underplayed or domesticated, while the painter's experience is projected onto the finished work. Thus the portraits invariably represent heroes accredited with acute interest in knowledge, disinterested pursuit of truth, moral proselytism and other traits inextricably associated with the self-interpretation of the intellectual mode of life.

Second, the ostensible heroes of organic ideologies are assigned the role of 'historical agents' in so far as they are believed to promote a kind of society in which the continuation of the intellectual mode of life is guaranteed to be untrammelled and is assigned a considerable, if not the central, importance in the work of the social system. In other words, the 'good society' of which the heroes are believed to be agents, is a projection of the intellectual mode upon the society as a whole; alternatively, it is a model trusted to provide optimal conditions for the proliferation of such a mode.

There is, however, one ideology in which the intellectual authors of the narrative appear virtually undisguised; in which they constitute, so to speak, part of the plot. To use Gramsci's terms again, in this ideology the intellectuals appear as the 'organic intellectuals of themselves'. This unique ideology is one of culture: that narrative representing the world as man-made, guided by man-made values and norms and reproduced through the ongoing process of learning and teaching.

The notorious diversity of definitions of culture given currency in sociological, anthropological and non-academic literature – even of discursive contexts in which the concept of culture is situated and given meaning – should not conceal the common basis from which all such definitions and approaches derive. However the phenomenon of culture is defined, the possibility of the definition, of the very articulation of culture as a phenomenon of the world, is rooted in a particular vision of the world that articulates the

2

potential, elaborates the values and legitimizes the role of the intellectuals.

The vision in question is directed by three tacitly, yet axiomatically accepted premises.

First, human beings are essentially incomplete and not self-sufficient. Their humanization is a process taking place after birth, in the company of other human beings. The distinction between the inherited insufficiency and acquired completeness is conceptualized as the opposition between 'biological' and 'social' aspects of the 'homo duplex', or between 'nature' and 'nurture'.

Second, humanization is essentially a learning process, split into the acquisition of knowledge and the taming, or repressing, of animal (and almost invariably antisocial) predispositions. The distinction between knowledge to be put in place of the natural predispositions, and the predispositions it is to replace, is often conceptualized as the opposition between 'reason' and 'passions', or between 'social norms' and 'instincts' or 'drives'.

Third, learning is just one side of the relation of which the other side is teaching. The completion of the humanization process, therefore, requires teachers and a system of – formal or informal – education. The educators hold the key to the continuous reproduction of cohabitation as a human society.

Thanks to the profuse historical studies (originated by Lucien Febvre, Febvre *et al.* 1930) we can locate the birth of this thoroughly modern vision of the world fairly precisely. It took place in the later part of the seventeenth and the first half of the eighteenth centuries and coincided with the birth and the institutionalization of the modern intellectuals.

The ideology of culture represents the world as consisting of human beings who are what they are taught. It therefore brings into relief the induced diversity of human ways of life; it makes possible the articulation of a plurality of 'ways to be human'. This feature of the ideology of culture lends plausibility to a supposition that the birth of the 'cultural vision' of the world was linked primarily to the newly acquired modern sensitivity to cultural differences. The story often found in the sociological and anthropological texts is that of Europe suddenly opening its eyes to the diversity of cultural modes of life previously unnoticed or considered uninteresting. This story, however, misses the point crucial for the birth of cultural ideology: the perception of diversity *as* culturally induced, of differences *as* cultural differences, of variety *as* man-made and brought about by the teaching/learning process. It was a particular *articulation* of diversity, and not newly aroused sensitivity to differences, that was the constitutive act of the ideology of culture.

Europeans were avid travellers; pilgrims to the Holy Land, late medieval sailors could not help noticing strange ways of life alongside unfamiliar shapes of shelters or unusual physiques of people they met on their way. They recorded what they saw in a similar 'alongside' manner; all perceived differences appeared as if on the same plane, variety of skin colors being a part of the order of things in the same way as the variety of customs and revered idols. Fashionable travelogue literature revelled in reporting genuine and fantastic findings as so many curiosities in the same fashion the early-modern *Kunstkamera* collected them – mixing double-headed calves with strange man-made implements of unknown destination. The founder of modern taxonomy, Linnaeus, considered the differences between straight and curly hair equally symptomatic for the differentiation of human species as the variety of the forms of government.

The contemplative mood in which European travellers viewed the richness of human forms they found in the foreign lands was an attitude trained at home. The premodern society was split into self-enclosed ranks; each rank carried a life deemed uniquely suited to it and to no one else, and advised to 'stick to its own kind' or admonished for peeping beyond the confines of its own station. Ranks were part of the 'great chain of being', a testimony to the preordained order of things; they lived together, equally ancient and immutable, guarded against contaminating each other; emulation across the boundaries was frowned upon and considered morally morbid – a tinkering with the divine order. Not that the idea of self-improvement was totally unheard of; individual members of the ranks were indeed encouraged to strive for perfection. But the ideals of perfection were as numerous as the ranks themselves; and as impenetrable, separate, and – in theory – immune to change. 'Self-perfection' meant becoming more like the model assigned to the rank and avoiding confusion with other models.

Such a coexistence of forms of life, with none considering itself as a universal model for imitation and none bent on submerging or eradicating the others – provided no room for the 'nature–culture' or 'nature–nurture' distinction. Only once it had broken, could the 'culture vision' as a peculiar modern intellectual ideology emerge.

The cultural ideology became possible when the ostensibly peaceful coexistence between forms of life turned untenable; either through the malfunctioning of its reproductive mechanism, or because of its unsuitability for the novel form of social domination, or for both reasons. The reality cultural ideology reflected at its birth was one of the abruptly changing relations between rank-ascribed forms of life: with some forms of life becoming *problems* for some others, problems calling for being acted upon. Forms of life (or their selected aspects) came to be seen as 'culturally produced' after they had turned into objects of *practice*, became things one 'had to do something about' in order to contain, change or replace them. It was the intention to terminate their existence, and the underlying practice of enforced uniformization, that cast the diversity of the forms of life as an artificial, contingent, 'merely man-made' phenomenon. A 'historical origin' of forms of life was postulated once their 'historical end' had been envisaged as a practical and desirable possibility.

It was the extent of ambitions to interfere with forms of life, and of resources available to support such ambitions, that determined the newly discovered boundary between 'nature' and 'culture' and its subsequent shifts. In the previously uniformly preordained world, an enclave had been cut out that invited human designs (and had been theorized, therefore, as humanly designed). Its growth, at the expense of shrinking 'nature', followed closely the expansion of proselytizing ambitions, systemic needs that made such ambitions necessary, and the mobilization of social power that rendered them realistic.

The appearance of proselytizing practices and ambitions in early-modern Europe was linked to a number of far-reaching structural dislocations; among the latter, the breakdown of the traditional mechanisms of social control and societal reproduction and the gestation of the modern state must be offered pride of place.

Surveillance-based, disciplinary power was the major tool of social control throughout the history of premodern Europe (a fact glossed over in the otherwise seminal analysis of Foucault 1980). This particular tool was not, however, employed by the state, confined as it were to the 'sovereign' power of the prince, focused almost solely on securing the princely and the aristocratic share in economic surplus. Instead, disciplinary power was deployed within communities and corporations small enough to make surveillance reciprocal, ubiquitous and comprehensive. Social order at the level of daily life was reproduced through the pernickety and oppressive surveillance exercised matter of factly, thanks to the permanent physical proximity of its, simultaneously, subjects and objects.

It was the breakdown of self-enclosed communities and the ensuing appearance of the 'masterless men' – vagabonds, vagrants, shifting population nowhere at home, belonging to no specific community or corporation, at no locality subject to continuous and all-embracing surveillance – that rendered the issue of social control, and of the reproduction of social order, problematic. The heretofore invisible, 'natural' flow of things had been brought abruptly into relief as a 'mechanism' – something to be designed, administered and monitored, something not functioning, or not functioning properly, unless attended to and operated skilfully. The timeless, yet never before problematized, control through surveillance, reproduction of order through disciplining bodily drill, had turned into an object of systematic inquiry, specialized skills and a function of experts. The diffuse activity of community had been transformed into an asymmetrical relationship between the subjects and the objects of the supervision. As such, it called for a support in a supracommunal authority. It needed resources no community could provide. It required deployment by the state; it rendered the state a systemic prerequisite of the reproduction of social order, the mainstay of the perpetuity of social domination. By the same token, the crisis of traditional vehicles of social control ushered in the modern state.

The latter meant first and foremost the centralization of social powers previously localized. This, however, was not simply a matter of transferring power from one setting to another; the very character of power changed considerably in the process. The destruction of *les pouvoirs intermédiaires*, which the entrenchment of the modern absolutist state was about, was tantamount to the annihilation of the only institutional setting in which control could be exercised in a 'traditional' way (i.e. unreflectively) without the purpose of the exercise having been clearly articulated and the exercise itself transformed into a specialized function. The advent of the absolutist state was hence tantamount to the transformation of control into a consciously administered, purposeful activity conducted by specially trained experts. The state had now to take care of creating conditions in which surveillance and bodily drill could be effectively operated.

6

If the community-based social control resulted in perpetuating and reinforcing local differentiations of the forms of life, the state-based control could only promote supracommunal uniformity. Universality as an ideal and a measure of social improvement was born of this need of the modern state; and of its practical ability to act on such a need.

Bent on uniformity, the unprecedented practice of the early-modern state was bound to clash with the still well-entrenched reproductive mechanisms that constituted the substance of communal autonomy. Concentration of power could never be complete without that autonomy being shattered – weakened or preferably uprooted. An indispensable part of the absolutist state bid for comprehensive power was therefore the notorious culture crusade that took off in the seventeenth century and continued well into the nineteenth. The crusade redefined the relations between diverse forms of life; mere superiority turned into hegemony.

Ranks were 'lower' or 'higher' well before the advent of modernity. So were their ways of life. Yet they were seen as separate entities, to be prevented rather than encouraged to come into direct contact with each other – each being viable in its own right and dependent but on itself for its own reproduction. 'Superiority' of one rank over another (and of corresponding ways of life) was hence a category of comparison, and not a concept standing for a specific task the 'superior' rank bore in relation to other ways of life. Such a task, on the other hand, is the essence of the thoroughly modern idea of 'hegemony': the role of the 'superior' way of life and its carriers as the moral mentor, missionary and pattern to be followed by all the others.

The universalistic ambitions of the modern state led inevitably to further weakening of the localized mechanisms of reproduction of previously autonomous ways of life; such mechanisms appeared to central power as so many obstacles on the way to the kind of society it projected, given its tendency to uniform administrative principles. Differences between ways of life were correspondingly redefined as relations of active mutual engagement. Popular, locally administered ways of life were now constituted, from the perspective of universalistic ambitions, as retrograde and backward-looking, a residue of a different social order to be left behind; as imperfect, immature stages in an overall line of development toward a 'true' and universal way of life, exemplified by the hegemonic elite; as grounded in superstition or error, passion-ridden, infested with animal drives, and otherwise resisting the ennobling influence of the truly human – shortly to be dubbed 'enlightened' – order. Such a redefinition placed the elite, for the first time, in a position of a collective *teacher* on top of its traditional role as the collective *ruler*. Diversity of ways of life has become now a temporary phenomenon, a transient phase to be left behind in the effort aimed towards a universal humanity.

The new character of relations between forms of life inside the society, now claimed by the absolutist state, served as a pattern for consideration of the relations between ways of life in general. The same active, proselytizing stance – once extended beyond the confines of its own society – constituted alien forms of life as ossified relics of the past, or otherwise artificially arrested stages of human development. Such aspects of human life as the emerging absolute power was bent on reshaping, or bound to reshape, had been selected as the bearers of a special status: men were about to reform them, hence they had to be conceived of as man-made in the first place. Those aspects were now seen as distinguished by their plasticity, temporariness, transitoriness – and, above all, amenability to purposeful regulation. The relative inferiority of the strange forms of life was interpreted, therefore, as the outcome of wrong regulation, and the local equivalents of the judging powers were charged with responsibility for the evil. On the whole, the inferiority of other forms of life, and the range of those of their aspects to which the judgment of inferiority was applied, were a function of the judging power's ambitions – their scope and administrative skills to back them.

The aspects of human life now picked up for conscious regulation came to be known as 'culture'. Historians agree that for almost a century, up to the last quarter of the eighteenth century, 'culture' (its French form of 'civilisation', German of 'Bildung', English of 'refinement') was used in the public discourse as a name of an activity, of something some people were doing, or exhorted to do, to others – much as a farmer cultivated his plants to ennoble the seeds and enrich the crop. The immediate interest that led to the coining of the idea of 'culture' as such aspects of human life as can be consciously regulated and given deliberately selected shape (unlike the other aspects that human powers were still unable or unwilling to reach) was one in the practice of changing the ways of life viewed as a symptom, and a source, of the morbid resilience of local autonomy pitted against the universalistic ambitions of the modern state. Culture, civilizing, refining were so many names given to the crusade proclaimed against the 'vulgar', 'beastly', 'superstitious' habits and customs and the forces allegedly presiding over their perpetuation.

The givers of names were the first modern intellectuals – the members of *la république des lettres*, of *les sociétés de pensée*, men free of all institutional dependencies and loyalties, united solely by their voluntary participation in a discussion of issues that, thanks to the public nature of the discussion, came to be defined as 'public'. It was the action of that new brand of educated elite (brilliantly analysed by François Furet (1978), in reference to the rich ideas contained in the literary legacy of Alexis de Tocqueville, and to heretofore little-known studies of Augustin Cochin (1978)) that provided an experience from which the new vision of the social world, as constituted by the learning/teaching activity, was to be extrapolated. I have described the process at length in Bauman (1987).

In response to the demand potentially present in the expanding ambitions of the absolutist state, *la république des lettres* offered the ideal design of the polity toward which the lawgivers should strive, the method of its attainment (the process of enlightenment through the diffusion of right ideas), and their own skills as the guarantee that the method would be applied effectively. The overall effect of the triple offer was the constitution of knowledge as power; the establishment of a privileged, foolproof access to right knowledge as the legitimation of the right to tell the others, deprived of such an access, what to do, how to behave, what ends to pursue and by what means.

The cognitive perspective grounded in the practice of *la république des lettres* rearranged the vision of the diversity of forms of life, now seen as first and foremost a *cultural* diversity. Other forms of life were now seen as products of a wrong kind of teaching, of malice or error, of ignorance at best. Behind the teaching, teachers were surmised in the image of the conscious educators of the day. *Les philosophes* named the clergy, old wives and folk proverbs as the teachers responsible for the lamentable state of popular habits. In the new vision of the social world, nature did not tolerate void – for every way of life there had to be a teacher responsible for its shape. The choice was not any more between a guided and regimented education and the autonomous self-constitution of forms of life – but between good and bad education. Not only was knowledge power; all power was knowledge. All efficient power had to rely on good knowledge for its efficiency.

The power/knowledge syndrome was, from the very start, a double-edged phenomenon, and hence prone to internal contradiction. On the one hand, it contained what later came to be called the 'rational government' – a global administration of the society as a whole aimed at creating and maintaining conditions eliciting 'good' behaviour and eliminating or preventing the 'bad'.

On the other, it entailed a direct manipulation of cognitive maps, values and motives of the individual members of the society in order to prompt what later came to be called 'rational behavior'. In the cultural ideology of the Enlightenment, rational society and rational individuals were presumed harmoniously to reinforce each other, though their articulation as separate phenomena, subject to relatively autonomous sets of determinants, took some time (and a certain amount of frustration) to set up.

The idea of rational government constituted a true novelty. It was concerned not merely with a substitution of a better policy for an inferior one, good laws for bad. It entailed a wholly new concept of government, its scope and responsibilities. The government was now seen as the force that – knowingly or by default – shapes the external framework of human life; the idea that society is 'man-made' represented the unprecedented ambition of the modern state to actually *make* the society; and an unheard-of mobilization of resources that rendered such making a viable proposition. The concept of state laws was also new; the idea of their postulated 'rationality' represented a new intention to use legislation for moulding social reality according to the precepts of reason. All in all, rational government meant the newly perceived malleability of social life, its need to be shaped, its amenability to being remade according to designs embodied in the action of external agencies – power being tantamount to the effectiveness of such action.

The idea of the rational individual was also novel in a revolutionary way. The gist of the idea was not a mere substitution of something for something else; reasonable and reliable thinking for error or superstition – but a wholly new concept of the human being whose conduct is shaped by his/her knowledge, and whose knowledge is shaped by knowledge givers, those who are, truly or ostensibly, 'in the know'. Again, the true novelty consists in the vision of the individual, his thoughts and his behaviour, as flexible and malleable entities, as objects of practice, of purposeful redirection. The vision of the individual who determines his conduct by writing the motives he selects into his cognitive map of the world was something that could have been achieved only from the perspective of the new active stance toward the aspect of the world defined as 'culture', that is, as man-made (as men were bent on remaking it). The latter could pursue their intention through supplying the individuals with the determinants of their conduct, and thus indirectly determining that conduct for them.

Metaphorically, the kind of authority in which such a vision of the world established men of knowledge could be described as 'legislative'. The authority involved the right to command the rules the social world was to obey; and it was legitimized in terms of a better judgment, a superior knowledge guaranteed by the proper method of its production. With both society and its members found wanting (i.e. shapeable yet heretofore shaped in the wrong way), the new legislative authority of men of knowledge established its own necessity and entitlements.

It is only too easy to misinterpret, after the years, the 'cultural-ization' of the world as necessarily involving this 'cultural relativism' with which the idea of culture seems today inextricably linked. The intellectual ideology of culture was launched as a militant, uncompromising and self-confident manifesto of universally bind-ing principles of social organization and individual conduct. It expressed not only the exuberant administrative vigor of the time, but also a resounding certainty as to the direction of anticipated social change. Indeed, forms of life conceived as obstacles to change and thus condemned to destruction had been relativized; the form of life that was called to replace them was seen, however, as universal, inscribed in the essence and the destination of the human species as a whole.

The original, legislative, version of cultural ideology thrived under conditions of certainty. It was advanced as a solution to a protracted 'Pyrrhonian crisis' of western philosophy; as a decisive rejection of half-hearted, proto-pragmatist compromises like those suggested by Mercenne or Gassendi (cf. Popkin 1979), and a refusal to accept the attitude of modesty (and, in general, admit the temporarily and spatially 'local' nature of the European form of life) best exemplified by the sceptic reflections of Montaigne. Intellectual legislators entertained no doubts as to representing history and reason; and the authority of both history and reason stemmed from the fact that – unlike the parochial errors they were bound to leave behind – they were grounded in universal traits of the human species and thus suffered no competitors.

It is tempting to connect this remarkable upsurge of certainty, coming in the wake of the early-modern crisis of self-confidence, with the formidable advances of the absolute state in neutralizing and subordinating 'traditional' seats of power; with the spectacular penetration by purposefully acting administrators into the areas of social and individual life previously left to their own 'natural' flow; with the powerful strides of state power away from the 'gamekeeping' and toward the 'gardening' practice of authority; with – last but not least – the rapid growth of West European economic and military superiority over the rest of the world. Limits to new, modern powers were prominent only by their ability to be broken; the capacity of such powers to impose one chosen pattern over everything and everybody did seem a matter of time, will and technique. As long as the practical capacity of ecumenical ascendancy was believed to be boundless, there was no clear reason why the absolute character of knowledge that underpinned such practice should have been questioned.

Certainly, this intellectual reflection of the apparent infinity of power was to become the major characteristic of this peculiar West European mental climate known as 'modernity'. I take here the concept of 'modernity' to stand for a perception of the world, rather than (as it has been misleadingly intimated) the world itself; a perception locally grounded in a way that implied its universality and concealed its particularism. It had been the decisive feature of modernity so understood that it relativized its (past and contemporary) adversaries and thereby constituted relativity itself as an adversary; as a spoke in the wheel of progress, a demon to be exorcized, a sickness to be cured.

The spirit of modernity inspired ever renewed, though never conclusive, attempts to pinpoint the universally binding, apodictically correct resolutions to the questions of truth, judgment and taste. It is all too easy to pronounce with the benefit of hindsight the failure, or even misdirectedness, of such trials. What, however, constituted the formative features of cultural ideology in its 'legislative', optimistic and audacious, modern phase, was not so much the success of the enterprise, as the possibility of its continuation, and of the absorption of successive drawbacks with no irreparable harm to the ongoing discourse. The remarkable resilience of purpose so typical of the modern mentality was grounded in the unshakable belief that the efforts have history and invincible reason on their side and that the ultimate success was not just attainable in principle, but a foregone conclusion. The conviction had in turn all the backing of social, economic and political realities. Paradoxically, though modernity militated against the pragmatist compromise, it was in the end the *pragmatic* argument from the ever more evident superiority of the western mode of life and thought that kept lending credibility to the hopes of finding the clinching proof for the species-wide validity of western science, morality and aesthetics; or for the form in which they had been conceptually sublimated.

The other side of philosophical certainty was cultural self-confidence. It was the latter that gave the unreflective and unyielding resolution to that Europe's missionary zeal, for which the colonial episode of modernity was so notorious. The full history of the relentless suppression of locality- and class-related forms of life at home remains still to be written, though many long-forgotten alternative narratives have been unearthed in recent years. Extirpation of local and class autonomy was waged doggedly and unswervingly under the banner of objectively superior cultural values, at war with not-fully-human, erroneous, retarded or superstitious forms of life and thought. Again, it was the apparent irreversibility of early-modern power struggles, the ostensible finality of the established structure of societal and world-wide domination that offered a truly supracultural, quasi-natural sanction to the unflinching dedication of cultural crusaders. No room was left for second thoughts, hesitation, scruples.

The conviction of the objective superiority of the social order formed in the north-western tip of the European peninsula was not partisan in terms of European politics. It united the intellectuals regardless of their political allegiance, or declared class loyalty. Cultural ideology was shared, as was its underlying premise that the human world has been always man-made, that the time has arrived to make it in a conscious, reasonable manner, and that the way contemporary society has been organized opens the way to do it. To put it bluntly, the intellectuals' self-identification with what they articulated as 'western values' could (and did) remain unfaltering as long as the expectation that the western sociopolitical system would be hospitable to knowledge-based (i.e. 'rational') sociopolitical blueprints, could be seen as plausible. This expectation suffered many blows, and finally yielded to the accumulated pressure of adversary evidence; its slow and painful demise was only partly concealed by occasional, always short-lived, resurrections.

The deepest cause of the gradual dissolution of modern self-confidence can be, arguably, traced back to the slow but steady disengagement between the intellectuals, as collective guardians of societal values, and the modern state. Much in the same way as Marx took the last desperate attempt of yesterday's free producers to arrest the industrial steamroller for the prodromal symptom of the future anticapitalist militancy of the industrial proletariat, *les philosophes* of the sanguine and expectant Enlightenment era took the young modern state's longing for guidance and legitimation for the promise of an imminent kingdom of reason. Both mistakes proved to be pregnant with frustration. Post-Marxian socialists and post- Enlightenment intellectuals alike are still reeling in the face of the world reluctant to conform to the model in terms of which they originally defined their role and function. Rather than admit their error, they would explain away the gap pointing to the world betraying its promise, taking a wrong turn or otherwise failing to live up to its potential.

The openness of the early-modern state to intellectual guidance was genuine enough. The territory that state was to invade was, for all practical intents and purposes, a virgin land, unexplored and uncharted. In a situation of acute uncertainty one had to rely on the loyalty of the crew. Turning the crew away from their old allegiances and realigning them around the new ones called for mobilization: dissemination of ideas simultaneously discrediting the old creed and showing the new one worthy; and for a new kind of expertise, required by the gigantic task of massive conversion. With the intellectuals ready to satisfy both needs, the state seemed to depend on them for its survival. Because of that dependency, it also seemed a pliable and grateful object of intellectual legislation.

Dependency proved, however, short-lived. Political technology developed by the modern state was soon to render the legitimizing services of the intellectuals increasingly redundant; or reduce them to a subordinate role, thus revealing the reversal of the original dependency.

The twin technique of panoptical power and seduction (with the balance between them gradually shifting in the direction of the latter) were increasingly put in charge of the reproduction of social order. With their efficiency and effectiveness growing, the role of legitimation shrank. In a fully developed modern state, effectiveness of state power, and indeed its performance in the systemic reproduction, may be maintained and perfected regardless of the scope and intensity of social commitment to the 'ruling values' – or to any values for that matter. The 'legal rationality', which Weber (1948) counted among historical forms of legitimation, in fact sounded the death knell to the legitimation era; as if to emphasize the fact by selecting 'value rationality' as its opposition, it proclaimed the modern freedom of the state from ideology; to wit, from the ideology writers. The latter would try to console themselves through presenting the demotion of legitimation as 'legitimation crisis'; hoping against hope that the state can go on doing without legitimation only at its peril.

To describe the consequences of new political technology as the dispossession of the intellectuals' needs, however, two important qualifications must be made.

First, the fading of the 'legislative' role has not been connected with material deprivations. If anything, the opposite has been the case. The 'general intellectuals' of yore have spawned numerous, still ramifying and growing in size, educated professions who command large incomes and – by all standards – privileged social standing. The failure of the bid for power has been compensated, so to speak, in a different currency – that of material gain. However dismissive (and, on occasion, hostile) of the 'legislative' ambitions of the intellectuals, the modern state presided over an unprecedented growth of 'experts' – this thoroughly modern phenomenon, transforming on a massive scale esoteric, minority knowledge into bureaucratic power. The experts did become an indispensable part of the system's reproductive mechanism, however strongly their role differed from one sketched, and worked toward, by *les philosophes*. Technologies of panoptic control and of seduction proved particularly fertile as a breeding ground for the ever new, and ever more numerous, ranks of experts and fields of expertise. Among the expert-intensive techniques, one spots immediately those central to panoptic control, like surveillance, 'correction', welfare supervision, 'medicalization', or 'psychiatrization', as well as the servicing of the general legal/penal system; or the many professions called into service and prominence due to the growing importance of needs-creation and entertainment as a paramount network of social control. Many more areas particularly hospitable to experts can be seen, however, as ultimately related to the modern techniques of power, though in a somewhat less obvious way. To name just one

15

example: modern weapons, ostensibly destined for an external enemy in some ill-defined future, while at present serving as a most powerful lever lifting the state out of the reach of effective political control (and thus reinforcing its independence from the legitimizing discourse).

Second, while rendering the 'legislative' function of the intellectuals irrelevant, the modern state disposed of any reason why the intellectual discourse should be subject to political control or otherwise externally limited or regulated. Having reached the nadir of their political relevance, modern intellectuals enjoy freedom of thought and expression they could not dream of at the time that words mattered politically. This is an autonomy of no practical consequence outside the self-enclosed world of intellectual discourse; and yet this is an autonomy all the same, a most precious and cherished consolation for the eviction from the house of power. The House of Solomon is now placed in a prosperous suburb, far away from ministerial buildings and military headquarters, where it can enjoy in peace, undisturbed, the elegant life of mind complete with a not inconsiderable material comfort. Intellectual freedom is not something to be treated lightly. It offers a unique chance to make the pursuit of matters of intellectual concern into a total, self-contained and self-sufficient form of life; and it offers the practitioners of such a form of life the gratifying feeling of being in full and exclusive control of the life-process and its products: truth, judgment, taste. Given the memory of the intimate link between political engagement and intellectual unfreedom, the autonomy of intellectual discourse turns into a highly attractive value in its own right; an attainment to be taken pride in, used to the full, staunchly defended – defended against the governments which from time to time make half-hearted attempts to cut what they see as useless expenditure; and against the rebels from its own ranks who jeopardize the comforts of freedom, drawing the dusty skeleton of political commitment out of the old family cupboard.

Political dispossession of the intellectuals has not been, therefore, a disaster pure and simple. It has brought in its wake unexpected bonuses, some of them undoubtedly attractive, and all endowed with the quality of rendering themselves desirable and indispensable through protracted use and habituation. For this reason, it does not necessarily breed discontent. On the other hand, however, it certainly does not add life to the old legislative ambitions. To remain eligible for the bonuses, contemporary intellectuals must stick unswervingly to the Weberian injunction of keeping the poetry of values away from the prose of bureaucratically useful expertise.

Among the areas of social life that lost their significance for the reproduction of social order and hence have been freed from direct supervision by the state, was one that the intellectuals considered as their domain of right; they hoped to be the direct and only beneficiaries of the withdrawal of political control and the new disinterestedness of the state. This special area was, of course, one of culture – now reduced to things of no concern to political powers. Here, as elsewhere, the overstretched, global ambitions entailed by the original concepts have been realistically tapered so that they will never trespass on the grounds reserved for the administrative interference of the state. In its new, more modest boundaries, however, culture seemed a natural domain of the intellectual, direct and unshared, rule. It is in this domain, therefore, that the legislative ambitions of the intellectuals have suffered the final and decisive blow.

As the interest of the state in culture faded (i.e. the relevance of culture to the reproduction of political power diminished), culture was coming within the orbit of another power the intellectuals could not measure up to – the market. Literature, visual arts, music – indeed, the whole sphere of humanities – was gradually freed from the burden of carrying the ideological message, and ever more solidly set inside market-led consumption as entertainment. More and more the culture of consumer society was subordinated to the function of producing and reproducing skilful and eager consumers, rather than obedient and willing subjects of the state; in its new role, it had to conform to needs and rules as defined, in practice if not in theory, by the consumer market.

Publishers, art galleries, record companies, managers of the mass communication media wrested the hoped-for cultural domination from philosophers, literary theorists, musicologists, aestheticians. Offended and outraged, the latter responded with accusations typical of the language used over the ages by the rightful game-keepers against poachers (i.e. imposter gamekeepers). The new rulers of the cultural domain were accused of demeaning the quality of 'cultural objects' by being brash, undiscerning, crude and on the whole not up to the task that required a degree of sophistication they did not possess, and of care they were not capable of. Most interestingly, the new managers were accused of the very action the accusers considered the major cultural mission of their own at the time when they seemed to be holding the political assignment of cultural leadership: of extirpating the autonomous seats of culture, the 'natural', 'spontaneous', cultural processes, and the very diversity of cultures that such natural processes may support. The new managers were accused of imposing one, 'middle-brow', homogenized standard upon the original richness of diversified cultural traditions; of substituting factory-produced 'popular' culture for community-sustained 'folk' culture. Cultural uniformity lost its attractiveness once it had become clear that someone else – forces beyond the intellectuals' control – was to set its standards and preside over its implementation.

It is arguable whether market domination of culture does indeed promote cultural uniformity, middle-, low-, or any other brow. There is plenty of evidence that the opposite is the case. The market seems to thrive on cultural diversity; there is hardly a cultural idiosyncrasy the market cannot take in its stride and make into another tributary of its power. Neither is it evident that cultural uniformity is 'in the interest' of market forces; again, the opposite seems to be the case. It is plausible that in the new domination of market forces culture has recovered a mechanism of the reproduction of diversity once located in autonomous communities and later ostensibly lost for a time in the era of politically sponsored cultural crusades and enlightened proselytism.

Whatever is the case, and whatever are the reasons for such a remarkable turnaround, the intellectuals of our times tend to deploy the 'cultural vision' of the world in a way that is almost totally opposite to the context in which this vision had been first shaped. The overwhelming tendency today is to see culture as the ground of perpetual, irreducible (and, in most cases, desirable and worth conscious preservation) diversity of human kind. As before, culture is understood as the process of 'humanization'; but it is emphasized now that there is an infinite variety of ways in which humans may be, and are, humanized; and it is strongly denied that one way is intrinsically better than another, or that one can prove its superiority over another, or that one should be substituted for another. Variety and coexistence have become 'cultural values' – ones the intellectuals are most zealously committed to defending.

There are numerous symptoms of this tendency, which exerts a truly formidable influence on the direction taken by contemporary social theory. Among the symptoms, the passage from the 'negative' to the 'positive' concept of ideology is arguably the most significant, being an emphatic rejection of the earlier claim to the 'legislative' role of philosophers, and of the supracommunal, extraterritorial intellectuals in general, in questions of truth, judgement and taste; if the 'legislative' role is retained by the new vision, it is confined to the intracommunal territory, to legislation from 'the inside' of a tradition, always acutely aware of the limits of its application and the relativism of its validity claims. In the intercommunal space, no room is left for the 'legislative' ambition. Either the very possibility of extraterritorial grounds of reason is denied, or the impotence of reason in the face of power-supported traditions is recognized; in both cases, the effort to invalidate alternative traditions, forms of life, positive ideologies, cultures, etc. as erroneous, biased, or otherwise inferior, has been all but abandoned.

The same tendency of the intellectual perception of the world, and of the way the position of the intellectuals is defined within the world so perceived, may result, and does result, in a variety of strategies. This variety often prevents the observers of the contemporary intellectual scene from spotting the shared outlook from which all strategies, however diverse, derive and from which they draw their meaning.

Leaving aside academic philosophy as a technical discipline, which conceivably can go on indefinitely reproducing its own institutionalized discourse, by and large unaffected by the changing world in the absence of all interface with social praxis – one can attempt to synthesize a few basic types to which all strategies can be in the end reduced.

One strategy is perhaps best encapsulated by the melancholic admission of Wittgenstein: philosophy leaves everything as it is. Practical impotence of value, truth or judgment discourses is not just overlooked and not merely tacitly accepted or reflected upon as an unpleasant possibility, as an eventuality one would rather avoid or at any rate one would rather not look in the face (there would be nothing particularly novel about such an attitude) but brought into the very centre of reflection; more than that, made into a new source of philosophical courage and determination. From Adorno (or, perhaps, Nietzsche?) to Rorty philosophers demand the continuation of legislative function for the sake of the importance intrinsically carried by concern with reason, ethical norms, aesthetic standards; that importance does not diminish, so they say – on the contrary, it attains particularly huge proportions for the fact that there is no one to legislate for, and that the legislative debate is in all probability bound to remain a self-contained, private affair of the legislators. This strategy abandons the intention of proselytizing; it puts paid to the hope entertained by the enlighteners that truth, if only discovered, will out and vanquish ignorance and error. In no way, however, does the resignation detract from the resolution to go on with the task given reality by the centuries of western intellectual tradition.

There is, of course, an inner differentiation among the followers of this strategy, as there is a not insignificant difference between Adorno and Rorty. On one extreme, there is a genuine feeling of defeat, despair and desperation; the fact that the hopes of *les philosophes* have been dashed is regretted and bewailed, and the culprits are sought; capitalist rule, bourgeois philistinism, or ruthless market forces are alternatively selected and condemned as villains of the sad piece. Step by step, social reality itself comes to be seen as doomed and is duly condemned. As if following August Bebel's commandment 'Beware the praise of your enemies', practical success of philosophical critique is detracted in advance as a sign of blunder or lack of fortitude, which is to be avoided at all costs. Even in their surrender (particularly in their surrender?) philosophers remain incessantly and painfully conscious of the practical connection of the cultural ideal. Its impotence is as much a constituting factor of their discourse as its assumed all-conquering potency was of the discourse of their Enlightenment ancestors. Impotence itself becomes now potency; the cultural ideal stays pure and truly worthy as long as it is not contaminated by intrinsically impure reality; it stays pure and worthy because it steers clear of practical success. And yet, in a curious twist of mind, this pure, ethereal, cultural ideal is believed to be reality's best chance.

On the other extreme (best exemplified by numerous 'protreptic' statements by Rorty, cf. Bernstein 1985), torments and agony Adorno style are replaced with a simple 'so what?' Indeed, the hope of converting the world to better standards of truth, judgment or taste was at best naive; indeed, it would be naive in the extreme to hold it still today. Yet the worst naivety was to suppose that the validity of the 'civilizing' enterprise of cultural discourse was at any time dependent on realism or irrealism of that hope; on the feasibility of proselytizing success. Now that we know that the massive conversion of the world to our standards is not on, we can better concentrate on the task at hand. And the task at hand is to keep the unique values of western civilization alive, if only as the content and the pragmatics of philosophical discourse; to continue a cultural tradition out of conviction of its intrinsic worth, all the more zealously for the realization that it is indeed a 'local' tradition and in all probability would at best remain so. Insiders as we are, we need not wax humble or cynical as we admit the 'locality' of tradition we guard: it is not just a local tradition, it is *our* local tradition, and we would go on praising its virtues even if the rest of the world refuses to join in the accolade.

Again, like in the case discussed before, culture as a basically converting, proselytizing action remains very much a subliminal ground of the strategy. In the face of the improbability of practical conversion, the emphasis shifts however to the gospel itself: yet the very insistence on its superiority over other evangelical traditions draws its sense and its importance solely from the original missionary context of cultural discourse.

What makes the two extreme points plotted on the same continuum of attitudes is their refusal to abandon the legislative mode of intellectual discourse. Legislation now lacks a vehicle of enforcement; old vehicles have been either scrapped or captured by powers impervious to intellectual counsel, if not downright hostile to it; that circumstance is however denied the force of an argument in favour of renouncing the legislative mission. One could say that the legislative mode of the new strategy differs from its older version first and foremost by the way it is grounded and legitimized (or, rather, by the way in which the precept of legitimation is declared redundant).

Another strategy is, in a sense, more radical: it entails a formidable redefinition of the intellectual role and social position, to a point where the metaphor of the 'legislator' ceases to be an adequate description of the latter. Another metaphor is called for instead – that of the 'interpreter'.

Empirically evident relativity of knowledge, dependence of truth judgment, and taste on overt or tacit assumptions embedded in communally based traditions was a vexing problem for the legislatively oriented cultural discourse; a difficulty to be resolved theoretically *and* removed practically. For the 'interpretive' strategy, relativity is not just a transitory state, but an apodictically given existential condition of knowledge. Something not to be frowned upon and objected to, but to be drawn conclusions from and adjusted to. The 'interpretive' strategy gestates an ontology that legitimizes it in terms of the intellectual mode: an ontology within which language only is accredited with the attribute of reality. The world within this ontology is an intersubjective world of communication, where 'work', as in Schutz (Schutz and Luckmann 1974), consists in making irreversible changes in the conversationalists' respective cognitive maps, stocks of knowledge or distributions of relevances. Within such a world, knowledge has no extralinguistical standards of correctness and can be grasped only inside the communicatively supported, shared stock of knowledge of the members. Pluralism is an irremovable feature of such a world. The most salient practical problem in such a world – one with which the ordinary competence of otherwise knowledgeable members cannot cope without assistance – is communication between systems of knowledge enclosed within their respective stocks of knowledge and communal systems of relevance. Here interpretation, in other situations accomplished by members matter-of-factly and on the whole adequately, calls for special skills not normally available in daily life.

Interpretation between systems of knowledge is recognized, therefore, as the task of experts armed with specialist knowledge, but also endowed, for one reason or another, with a unique capacity to lift themselves above the communication networks within which respective systems are located without losing touch with that 'inside' of systems where knowledge is had unproblematically and enjoys an 'evident' sense. Interpretation must make the interpreted knowledge sensible to those who are not 'inside'; but having no extraterritorial references to appeal to, it has to resort to the 'inside' itself as its only resource.

Social-scientific and philosophical approaches to culture converged upon such a breathtakingly paradoxical strategy in the course of several decades and from different sides. One can point out many tributaries to the current. Simmel's concept of the intellectual as essentially a stranger; Mannheim's (cf. Bauman 1978) association between true knowledge and homelessness, the state of being *'freischwebend'*; Kroeber's, Kluckhohn's, Sapir's or Benedict's (cf. Bauman 1973) ideas of 'ethos', 'style', 'pattern', which make for the uniqueness of each culture and offer the only acceptable criteria for its understanding, establishing simultaneously their ontological equality; Frank Cushing's personal exploration of the possibility of making Zuni understandable to the non-Zuni only by becoming *plus Zuni que les Zunis*; Clifford Geertz's precept of 'thick description' – an intellectual immersion in ever deeper layers of localized meanings too routine for the locals to be articulated. The themes of 'outsidedness' turned over and promoted primarily by cultural anthropology, converged in the present array of hermeneutic strategies taking the essentially philosophical sources (Heidegger, late Wittgenstein, Gadamer) as their discursive home.

The redefinition of the study of culture as an essentially hermeneutic enterprise does not only recognize the relativity of all knowledge and perpetuity of cultural pluralism. On the way, it also revises the idea of culture. The most striking of all revisions is the novel 'impersonality' of culture, elimination from the model of culture of the 'author' – be it the legislator or the educator. The vision of culture as, essentially, an activity performed by a part of the population and aimed at another part, is replaced with a vision of a spontaneous process devoid of administrative or managerial centres, free of an overall design and perpetuated by diffusely deployed powers. Language stands out as a most seminal epitome of such spontaneity and impersonality of culture. Alongside language, 'traditions', 'universes of meaning', or meaning, or 'forms of life' replace the educators and the educated as major categories of cultural discourse.

A case can be made that the total disappearance of the issues of politics and domination from the vision implied by the 'interpretive' strategy has more than an accidental connection with the currently experienced dislocations in the social function of intellectuals, and particularly in their relation to the effective powers that be; from the perspective of the present-day intellectuals, culture does not appear as something to be 'made' or 'remade' as an object for practice; it is indeed a reality in its own right and beyond control, an object for study, something to be mastered only cognitively, as a meaning, and not practically, as a task.

When related processually, rather than juxtaposed laterally, 'legislative' and 'interpretive' strategies can be recast as, respectively, 'modern' and 'postmodern'. Indeed, the recently fashionable opposition between 'postmodernity' and 'modernity' makes most sense as an attempt to grasp the historical tendency of the last centuries, and the most crucial discontinuities of recent history, from the perspective of the changing social position and function of the intellectuals (it is because of this specific vantage point from which it has been made that this opposition is not simply restating the propositions entailed in other, ostensibly similar, oppositions). The postmodernity/modernity opposition focuses on the waning of certainty and objectivity grounded in the unquestioned hierarchy of values, and ultimately in the unquestionable structure of domination; and on the passage to a situation characterized by a coexistence or armistice between values and a lack of the overall structure of domination, which makes the questions of objective standards impracticable and hence theoretically futile. In this opposition, 'modernity' is seen in a new way, redefined retrospectively by the novel experience encapsulated in the idea of 'postmodernity'. Modernity is reconstructed ex-post-facto as an era possessing the selfsame features the present time feels most poignantly as missing, namely the universal criteria of truth, judgement and taste seemingly controlled and operated by the intellectuals. Like all reconstructions, this one tells more about the reconstructors than about the reconstructed epoch, and in this respect it is highly illuminating.

The prevalence of interpretive strategy, sometimes problematized as the advent of postmodernity, signifies a most radical departure in the cultural discourse since the introduction of the concept of culture and the establishment of the culture-oriented vision of society. Indeed, the radicality of shift has induced some analysts, notably George Steiner, to speak of a 'postculture', on the assumption that the cultural situation is inextricably associated with a clear notion of superiority and inferiority in the realm of values, and that the current situation of the west, when such notion is questioned or ridiculed, cannot be described as 'cultural' and ushers us into heretofore uncharted waters.

It is the central suggestion of this chapter that the contemporary reorientation of cultural discourse can be best understood as a reflection on the changing experience of intellectuals, as they seek to re-establish their social function on a new ground in a world ill-fit for their traditional role.

REFERENCES

Bauman, Zygmunt (1973) *Culture as Praxis*, London, Routledge & Kegan Paul.

Bauman, Zygmunt (1978) *Hermeneutics and Social Science, Approaches to Understanding*, London, Hutchinson.

Bauman, Zygmunt (1987) *Legislators and Interpreters: On Modernity, Postmodernity, and the Intellectuals*, Oxford, Polity Press.

Bernstein, Richard (1985) *Philosophical Profiles; Essays in Pragmatic Mode*, Oxford, Polity Press.

Cochin, Augustin (1978) *Les sociétés de pensée et la démocratie moderne*, Paris, Gallimard.

Febvre, Lucien *et al.* (1930) *Civilisation, le mot et l'idée*, Paris, La Renaissance de Livre.

Foucault, Michel (1980) *Power/Knowledge*, Brighton, Harvester Press.

Furet, François (1978) *Penser la Révolution Française*, Paris, Gallimard.

Gramsci, Antonio (1957) *The Modern Prince and Other Writings*, London, Lawrence & Wishart.

Habermas, Jürgen (1974) *Theory and Practice*, London, Heinemann.

Popkin, Richard H. (1979) *The History of Scepticism from Erasmus to Spinoza*, Berkeley, University of California Press.

Schutz, Alfred and Luckmann, Thomas (1974) *The Structures of the Life World*, London, Heinemann.

Simmel, Georg (1968) *The Conflict in Modern Culture and Other Essays*, New York, Teachers College Press.

Weber, Max (1948) *From Max Weber*, ed. H.H. Gerth and C. Wright Mills, London, Routledge & Kegan Paul.

2

SOCIOLOGICAL RESPONSES TO POSTMODERNITY

Most current concepts of postmodernity refer solely to intellectual phenomena. In some cases, they focus narrowly on arts. In some others, they spill over to include a wider spectrum of cultural forms and precepts. In a few cases they reach deeper, into the fundamental preconceptions of contemporary consciousness. Rarely, if at all, they step beyond the boundary of the spiritual, into the changing social figuration which the artistic, cultural and cognitive developments, bracketed as postmodern, may reflect.

Such a self-limitation of the postmodernity discourse, and its legitimacy, is of crucial importance for the future of sociology. Indeed, if postmodernity means what the current concepts imply: a reform of culture, of world-perception, of the intellectual stance – then sociology faces the task of an essentially strategical adjustment. It must make itself resonant with new, postmodern culture, and break its links with the ontological and epistemological premises of modernity. It must transform itself into a *postmodern sociology*. In particular, it must follow other elements of postmodern culture by accepting (in theory as much as in practice) the self-containment and the self-grounding of the production and reproduction of meanings. It must abandon its traditional identity of a discourse characterized by an attempt to decode such meanings as products, reflections, aspects or rationalizations of social figurations and their dynamics. If, on the other hand, the self-containment of contemporary culture, and the associated implosion of vision, signal processes which reach beyond the realm of culture proper (if they accompany transformations in, say, principles of systematic organization or power arrangements) – then it is not the traditional strategy of sociology which calls for revision, but a new focus of inquiry is needed, and a new set of categories geared to the changed social reality. In this case – without resigning its formative questions – sociology must develop into a *sociology of postmodernity*. In particular, it must accept the distinctiveness of the postmodern figuration, instead of treating it as a diseased or degraded form of modern society.

CONTEMPORARY ART AS THE PARADIGM OF POSTMODERNITY

The most salient feature of contemporary art is its defiance of order. To portray this quality, Deleuze and Guattari deployed the metaphor of rhizome: that peculiar rootstock which resists the regulating pressure of tropisms, and thus seems to possess no sense of privileged direction, expanding instead sideways, upwards and backwards with the same frequency and without detectable regularity which would enable a prediction of the next move. New stems arise in spots impossible to locate in advance.

Contemporary art, it is said, knows of no synchronic order. In a sharp opposition to the modern period of art history (or, indeed, to any other period), there are today no clearly recognizable dominant schools or styles which tend to subordinate the whole field of artistic activity, and force any unorthodox artistic act to justify itself in reference to it. Moreover, in the absence of an obligatory canon the very meaning of 'heresy' (as much as the 'orthodoxy' itself) turns elusive and virtually escapes operative definition. The field of art is populated instead by creators of most diverse and aesthetically incompatible styles. Contemporary art knows of no diachronic order either. No more can one conceive of the history of art as a succession of ruling schools and styles. Moreover, the imagery of evolution has lost its grip on the reality of art's stasis (i.e. movement without change; change without direction). Later periods of artistic activity reveal little relation to the preceding stages, they do not seem to 'result' from them (in the sense of developing further their achievements, or resolving their unsolved problems, or offering alternative responses to the questions they asked or inadvertently brought forth). New phenomena in art appear to surface at random and apparently bear no relation to everything which went on before. It appears that the changes no longer constitute development.

And yet certain predilections seem to be common to contemporary art.[1] One of them is the artistic form of pastiche – the conscious or unconscious invoking, alluding to, emulating past or distant moods, styles, techniques, devices. Concepts like borrowing, eclecticism, even plagiarism, have lost their once starkly derogatory meaning. To be more precise, they lost all meaning: contemporary art has transformed the history and ethnography of art into a pool of extemporal and extraterritorial, permanently usable resources, which can be picked at will and at random. Another is the use of collage – an artistic form which does the same to the single work of art as the pastiche has done to art history. Collage denies the traditional principle of stylistical (and often compositional) unity, and practises instead the equivalence and non-contriety of artistic genres, styles or techniques. That plurality which the pastiche substitutes for the temporal order of art styles, collage incorporates into the style itself, thereby invalidating the notion of style (at least in its received sense). One more peculiarity of contemporary art is its self-referentiality – ostentatious rejection of the programme of mimesis. The challenge to the intention and the practice of 'reality-representation' goes in the case of contemporary art much further than in the 'high modernity' era. Indeed, in the light of the present practice, that era looks utterly 'representationalist'. What modernist art defied was the naive, superficial perception which could no longer distinguish between pristine experience and the conventional figurational images. Modernism struggled to penetrate the 'deeper' reality, to represent what has been made invisible for the convention-bound eye. To attain such 'better', correct, true representation, they sought the guidance of science: that recognized authority on what reality is really like. Thus the impressionists took inspiration (and legitimation for their practices) from optics, cubists from the relativity theory, surrealists from psychoanalysis.[2] Contemporary artists, on the contrary, would overtly abandon all pretension, and denigrate all intention, of representation. They would aspire to represent nothing but their own practice: the canvas, its flatness, the media and their inherent qualities. The very notion of representation will be difficult to define in terms meaningful inside contemporary art (that is, if it is considered in relation to non-artistic reality) – as it is no more clear what reality is 'objectively', whether it is predicated with objective existence, and can thus provide ontological grounding for the measurement of representational accuracy.

Marcel Duchamp's insolent act of entering a urinal for an art salon was seen at the time as the genuine beginning of a radically new era in art – breaking free from the straightjacket imposed by aesthetic theory. In retrospect, Duchamp's iconoclastic venture looks more like an ultimate triumph of modernism: that artistic game the rules of which required most brazen acts of impudence to be legitimized by a theory – a logical and internally consistent theory, however wayward and irreverent to its predecessors. Duchamp did supply his urinal with a shocking, yet congruent definition of art (something chosen by the artist), theory of artwork (cutting off an object from its mundane context), method of artistic creation (infusing the object with a new meaning).[3] Most present-day artists would bother with none of these. With the benefit of hindsight, we can see that Duchamp's defiant gesture was aimed at art critics and academic theorists. It was an attempt to wrest the power of definition, distinction and evaluation of art from the hands of those who drew their authority from the expertise in aesthetic discourse rather than the artistic practice (and do so in a fight conducted according to the rules they themselves ostensibly promoted). For present-day artists, such people constitute only a minor threat. Forces and factors which discriminate between art (i.e. something fit for display and selling it in art galleries) and non-art, between good (i.e. successful in the above terms) and bad art, are only in a small part affected by their activities. This is why contemporary art displays its striking immunity to theorizing, programming, argument, principle validation. But in the absence of theory (or, rather, with the growing irrelevance and dwindling authority of theory), 'both the rhetoric of destruction and that of novelty have lost any trace of heroic appeal.[4] 'The possibility that a given school can present itself with the claim to universal validity'[5] has been thereby effectively dashed.

The combined effect of all these departures from the axioms and canons of modern art is the overall impression of disorientation and chaos. It is this impression which, more than anything else, is conveyed by the characterization of contemporary art as postmodern ('postmodernity' being a semantically negative notion, defined entirely by absences – by the disappearance of something which was there before – the evanescence of synchronic and diachronic order, as well as of directionality of change, count among its most decisive defining features).

And yet one can make sense out of this apparent chaos – on condition one accepts the irreducibility and permanence of the plurality of human worlds, something which modern philosophy refused to admit, and modernist art refused to resign itself to.

Dick Higgins wrote ten years ago of the passage from cognitive questions asked by the twentieth-century artists till about 1958 – How can I interpret this world of which I am a part? And what am I in it? – to the postcognitive questions: Which world is this? What is to be done in it? Which of my selves is to do it?[6] 'Postcognitive questions' capture well the ontological, rather than epistemological, preoccupations of postmodern artists (according to Brian McHale, ontology constitutes the dominant of postmodern writing). For the art called postmodern, the central question is how to locate, identify, set apart a particular world, knowing well that this world is merely one of the many possible and coexisting, and that the exploration of this world, however profound, is unlikely to bring us any closer to universally binding truth, or findings able to rightfully claim either general, or exclusive validity.

If this is the case, then the notorious lack of interest in accuracy of representation, even the emphatic rejection of the very idea of the derivative, reflective status of art regarding reality, can be seen as an updated version of mimesis, resonant with the postmodern perception of the world as incurably pluralistic. Far from abandoning the role of the *speculum mundi*, postmodern art 'does hold the mirror up to reality; but that reality, now more than ever before, is plural'.[7] The postmodern artist's insistence that the 'project of truth' is ontologically flawed and hence impossible to achieve and unworthy of pursuing, conveys the truth about contemporary reality. Through its own plurality and abrogation of hierarchies, postmodern art *represents* the existential modality of the extra-artistic world.

I suggest that we can go beyond McHale and observe that the mimetic function of postmodern art is not exhausted by its inner plurality and its 'rhizomic' growth. Postmodern art imitates reality also in its exposition of the essentially under-determined character of action, as well as the feeble grounding of reality as something which results from ongoing motivated action, from the exercise of freedom and choice. More than ever before, the work of art is now blatantly and emphatically *construed*. It has no authority to invoke in order to legitimize and validate itself, except the decision of its author. It has no ecumenically dominant, or ecumenically ambitious code to refer to, in order to reveal its meaning; instead, it has to construct and deploy its own explanatory potential. In the absence of all wider referential frameworks, a postmodern work of art is moreover open to a multiplicity of interpretations which are bound to stop short of reaching 'authoritative' status, and thus to remain inconclusive. The selfsame polyvalence which in the times of modernity was resented as an irritant, as evidence of the imperfection of extant theory and a challenge, turns now into the defining and permanent feature of art. In this, as in its previously discussed traits, postmodern art points to something other than itself and conveys information about a non-artistic reality. Even its ostentatious and exuberant autonomy contains information about the world of which it is a part.

POSTMODERN CULTURE

The world of which postmodern art is most immediately a part is, of course, the world of culture. Culture, which has postmodern art as its constituent, shares with it the attributes of pluralism, absence of universally binding authority, levelling up of hierarchies, interpretive polyvalence. It is, as Baudrillard has argued,[8] a culture of excess. It is characterized by the overabundance of meanings, coupled with (or made all the more salient by) the scarcity of adjudicating authorities. Like postmodern art, it is in constant change, yet devoid of a distinctive line of development. Its elements appear both under-determined and inconsequential. It is, one may say, a culture of over-production and waste. With it, that tragedy of culture which Georg Simmel (only now beginning to be understood, and acknowledged, as the sole 'postmodern' thinker among the founding fathers of sociology) anticipated almost a century ago, has reached its completion; the body of objectively available cultural products is well in excess of the assimilating capacity of any member of society. To the individual, culture appears as a pool of constantly moving, unconnected fragments. The old expression 'cultural scene' implied a scenario, a plot, a dénouement, inter-twining of roles, a director. None of these can be sensibly implied under the conditions of postmodern culture (which, for that reason, Baudrillard dubbed *obscene*).

Most students of contemporary culture agree on the unique role of the media as the principal vehicle of culture production and distribution. It has been assumed (since Marshall McLuhan's memorable phrase 'media are the message' was first uttered) that whatever the explicit message of the media (i.e. that aspect of the message which can be verbalized as a series of falsifiable assertions about the ostensible topic of discourse) – the most powerful influence on the shape of contemporary culture is exerted by the way and the form in which the message is conveyed. Thus the most consequential impact of the centrality of media in cultural reproduction appears to consist in the general tendency to construct the world as an assembly of images which are neither causally determined nor leave a lasting trace once they vanish, of happenings, of mutually unconnected and self-enclosed episodes, events grounded solely in the elusive and protean motivation of the actors; and the massive invalidation of memory (except the peculiar, programmatically chaotic and random, form of rota-memory deployed in Trivial Pursuits) – the very faculty on which the construction of changeable reality as development must rest.

Focusing on television, as – arguably – the most representative and influential of contemporary cultural media, Martin Esslin observed: 'whatever else it might present to its viewers, television as such displays the basic characteristics of the dramatic mode of communication – and thought, for drama is also a method of thinking, of experiencing the world and reasoning about it.' The 'dramatic mode of communication' Esslin had in mind is distinguished by a number of traits, all strikingly reminiscent of the characteristics we have noted before in contemporary art. To begin with, 'real events happen only once and are irreversible and unrepeatable; drama looks like a real event but can be repeated at will'.9 Thus the news is sandwiched between two pieces of dramatized (and overtly fictional) stories, with which they share presentation of events as eminently repeatable; as happenings which may be seen (re-enacted?) over and over again, in fast and slow motion, from this angle or that. Existing only as images shown and seen, or better still video-recorded and then re-enacted at the time and in the circumstances of one's choice – the events are non-inevitable, inconclusive, revocable, until further notice (one can say that Judas's request 'can we start again, please?' in *Jesus Christ, Superstar*, could be made only in the Age of the Television). The world split into a multitude of mini-dramas has no clear-cut cohesiveness or direction. This world itself is soft – one in which time can be easily reversed, so that the episodes which fill it can be re-arranged in any order of succession (and are subject to no order but that of haphazard succession). As all consequences such episodes may have are eminently temporary and redeemable, such a world must and can do without standards, moral standards included. Morality, as it were, is a functional prerequisite of a world with an in-built finality and irreversibility of choices. Postmodern culture does not know of such a world.

Some recent studies imply that contemporary media do more than present the 'real world' as drama. They make the world into drama, as they shape its actual course after the pattern of drama-like events. It has been suggested that with the co-operation of television, the 'real world' has already become to a large extent a staged spectacle. In most strategic sites of the 'real world' events happen because of their potential fitness to be televised (politicians and terrorists alike play for television, hoping to elevate private actions into public events, biography into history). In the words of Benjamin Barder, 'it is difficult to imagine the Kennedy generation, the '60s, Watergate, the Woodstock generation, or even the Moral Majority, in the absence of national television'.[10] Daniel Dayan and Elihu Katz suggest that the provision of television's own, original events slowly takes precedence over the mere reproduction of events, or the mere offer of access to events which would have taken place anyway in the absence of the viewer. Such media events 'are not descriptive of the state of affairs, but symbolically instrumental in bringing that state of affairs about'.[11] The overall effect is the growing lack of clarity as to the meaning and the boundaries of 'real history'. Baudrillard asserts[12] that it is no longer the case that the television supplants reality with images, distorts it or lies about it; it is not even the case that the television stands between the viewer and his/her life, moulds the fashion in which life is lived or interprets its meaning (or, rather, substitutes its repetition for hermeneutics). For Baudrillard, society itself is now made to the measure of television: history is nothing but spectacle. History is a debauchery of signs; an endless play of simulation, drama and grotesque political minuet, an immoral promiscuity of all forms. One can no longer speak of the distortion of reality: there is nothing left to measure the image against. This is soft, disjointed, insubstantial reality, of which Sartre's Roquentin said that 'everything is born without reason, prolongs itself out of weakness, and dies by chance'.

In the halcyon days of modern self-confidence and optimism, Matthew Arnold wrote: 'Culture indefatigably tries, not to make what each raw person may like, the rule by which he fashions himself; but to draw ever nearer to a sense of what is indeed beautiful, graceful, and becoming, and to get the raw person to like that'.[13] Arnold knew – and knew beyond reasonable doubt – what is 'indeed' beautiful and becoming; equally well he knew which person is 'raw', and why. In his world, culture was an image of order and perfection standing ahead and above the world of practice, and thereby reducing it to 'mere reality'. Culture was, above all, a confident effort to lift reality to the level of such an image.

In contrast, one can read George Steiner's essay entitled 'In a post-culture'[14] as an insight into the world from which Arnold's confidence is all but gone. Not to know what we know today, Steiner says, was Arnold's, or Voltaire's privilege: it was their ignorance which gave them confidence. We know what they did not: that humanities do not humanize. From the heights of what legitimately passed at the time for the peak of civilization, it seemed obvious that there was a pre-ordained 'congruence between the cultivation of the individual mind and a melioration of the commanding qualities of life'. This does not seem obvious at all to us. Worse still, we would find it very difficult to make a case for something being a 'melioration', as we do not believe in the axiom of progress, have lost the technique of forward dreaming, ceased to be animated by the ontological utopia, and – with all that – lost the ability to tell the better from the worse. Our time is marked by the end of the hierarchic value structure and the rejection of all the 'binary cuts which represented the domination of the cultural over the natural code', like the cuts between the west and the rest, learned and untutored, upper and lower strata. The superiority of western culture (cultures?) seems neither self-evident nor assured as a prospect. We have lost the confident centre, without which, in Steiner's view, there is no culture. Culture, Steiner insists, must be self-consciously elitist and have the nerve to evaluate. With these two faculties in dispute or under attack, the future of our civilization is 'almost unforeseeable'. One can say that Steiner agrees with Arnold that the choice is between culture or anarchy; unlike Arnold however, he believes that the choice has been already made – and not in the way Arnold expected, and Steiner would see as indispensable for the survival of the cultural mode as such.

One can interpret Steiner's view in the following way: the concept of postmodern culture is a contradiction in terms, an oxymoron. Culture is about hierarchy, discernment and evaluation; postmodernity, on the contrary, is about flattening of hierarchies, absence of discretion, and equivalence. Postmodernity, in other words, is a post-cultural condition. One needs not necessarily agree with Steiner in his tying the phenomenon of culture down to its radical Enlightenment-born meaning, to accept that the postmodern setting does invalidate many an essential constituent of the cultural discourse. Central precepts of that discourse, like dominant culture, or cultural hegemony, seem to have lost much of their meaning, or (as far as their missionary, crusading stance is concerned) run out of energy. The contemporary world is, rather, a site where cultures (this plural form is itself a postmodern symptom!) coexist alongside each other, resisting ordering along axiological or temporal axes. Rather than appearing as a transitory stage in the as-yet-unfinished process of civilizing, their coexistence seems to be a permanent feature of the world, with no authority in sight aspiring to an ecumenical, universal role. Like postmodern art – postmodern culture seems doomed to remain disorderly, to wit plural, rhizomically growing, devoid of direction.

THE POSTMODERN WORLD-VIEW

It is this new cultural experience, briefly sketched in the preceding section, which has been distilled in the postmodern view of the world as a self-constituting and self-propelling process, determined by nothing but its own momentum, subject to no overall plan – of the 'movement toward the Second Coming', 'universalization of human condition', 'rationalization of human action' or 'civilization of human interaction' type. Postmodernity is marked by a view of the human world as irreducibly and irrevocably pluralistic, split into a multitude of sovereign units and sites of authority, with no horizontal or vertical order, either in actuality or in potency.

To put it in a different way, the postmodern world-view entails the dissipation of objectivity. The element most conspicuously absent is a reference to the supracommunal, 'extraterritorial' grounds of truth and meaning. Instead, the postmodern perspective reveals the world as composed of an indefinite number of meaning-generating agencies, all relatively self-sustained and autonomous, all subject to their own respective logics and armed with their own facilities of truth-validation. Their relative superiority may be argued solely, if at all, in pragmatic and overtly self-referential mode, with no claim made to supracommunal authority. As the postmodern perspective, like its predecessor, has been developed within the western world, acceptance of plurality of sovereignties means first and foremost the surrender of the (diachronically and synchronically) dominant position of the west. What has been assumed to be the most accomplished, most advanced, pattern-setting formation of global social development (indeed, the only formation of universal significance) throughout the modern era – has been now reduced to the status of a mere one among the many. Its historicity has been extended from the admission of a fixed beginning to the anticipation of an impending end. And its once universalistic claims have been supplanted by the acceptance of a parochial significance and a purely local (both spatially and temporally) validity.

The above-mentioned 'dissipation of objectivity' does not end here, however. Dissolution of the universal authority on the global, ecumenical scale is paralleled by a similar tendency in intra-societal space. If the modern world-view theorized (both reflected and legitimized) the unificatory tendencies and uniformizing ambitions of state societies, the postmodern view shifts the focus on to the (admittedly underdefined) agency of community. More precisely, the focus shifts to communities; the most seminal distinction of the new framework of perception and analysis is precisely its plurality. If the concept of society was a device to 'erase' the 'outside' and reduce it at best to the status of environment (i.e. the 'goal-achievement' territory, and object, but not a subject of action), the concept of community as it appears in the postmodern discourse derives its essential meaning from the co-presence of other communities, all seen as agencies. The space in which the processes of meaning-generation and truth-validation are now set is not just confined in comparison with the setting distinctive of the modern world-view (one which, so to speak, filled the whole analytical space up to the horizon) – but also differs in quality. The old setting derived its solidity from the presence of mutually reinforcing, co-ordinated and overlapping agencies of integration. Even when not referred to explicitly, the totalizing impact of economic systemness, body politic, unified law, dominant value-cluster or ideology was tacitly assumed (indeed, it served as the very pre-condition of the possibility of discourse) and thus remained throughout the concealed, yet omnipotent guarantee of the authority of truth and meaning. The new, communal spaces (which bring instead into focus partiality, absence of autarky, and disunity) are grounded in their activities only, and so expose the absence of synchronization between the truth-and-meaning oriented action and other dimensions of social existence. Hence the endemic difficulties which the communal settings face in the course of their self-constitution. Indeed, the boundary-drawing now seems to be the paramount theoretical task, while the maintenance of spatial limits and divisions of authority projects itself as the most formidable among the practical issues.

François Lyotard (the person more than anybody else responsible for giving the new world-view its name, though also for obscuring, rather than clarifying, its sociological sense) has presented the communalization of truth and meaning as a by-product of the slow erosion of the dominance once enjoyed by science over the whole field of (legitimate) knowledge; this erosion being in its turn an effect of the gradual disintegration of science into the ever increasing number of separate, only formally interlinked discourses, and thus of the gradual collapse of the original prescriptive function. The vacated realm, now a no-man's land, has been filled by a multitude of discourses which can command only as much authority as they are able to generate themselves. What has happened, in Lyotard's words, is the '"atomization" of the social into flexible networks of language games'.[15] Glossing over the changes in the power structure and its imputed tendency, Lyotard prefers to refer the observed atomization to technological transformation, to new departures in information processing, which he holds directly responsible for the fact that the 'communication component is becoming more prominent day by day, both as a reality and as an issue'.[16] It is presumably this salience which leads to the constitution of social units which are grounded solely in language. The trouble with a communication-based morphology of the social is that it tends to be as fluid and processual as the communication itself. It lacks the comfort of clearly drawn, mutually agreed and effectively defended boundaries. The network is inherently flexible. Language games are burdened with an unenviable task of constituting the presence to be legitimized, rather than concerning themselves simply with the legitimizing of a presence already secured by other means. 'The limits are themselves the stakes and provisional results of language strategies.'[17]

Similarly, the sociopolitical phenomenon of the erosion of authority with ecumenical potential and pretension has been reduced in Lyotard to its linguistic-philosophical dimension: 'The grand narrative has lost its credibility.'[18] Having lost its discursive unity, science ceased to be such a grand narrative. It has been dethroned and demoted to a collection of language games none of which enjoys a privileged status or wields power to adjudicate in other games. Drawing on Wittgenstein's metaphor of language as a maze of little streets surrounded by solitary islands of orderly and planned suburbs, Lyotard questions the centredness of the emerging conurbation. But he also points to the autarky of the suburban sub-centres – they do not need to communicate with other suburbs, or for that matter with the 'old city' in the centre, to maintain a reasonably complete life. Visits between suburbs are rare, and no resident of the city has visited them all:

> Nobody speaks all of those languages, they have no universal metalanguage, the project of the system-subject is a failure, the goal of emancipation has nothing to do with science, we are all stuck in the positivism of this or that discipline of learning, the learned scholars have turned into scientists, the diminished tasks of research have become compartmentalized and no one can master them all. . . . That is what the postmodern world is all about. Most people have lost nostalgia for the lost narrative. It in no way follows that they are reduced to barbarity. What saves them from it is their knowledge that legitimation can only spring from their own linguistic practice and communicational interaction.[19]

In Lyotard's rendering, therefore, the advent of postmodernity is related to the dissipation of just one hierarchy: that of the language games. What has been left unexplored is the possibility that the collapse of this particular hierarchy might have been a manifestation (or a corollary) of a wider crisis, which involves many hierarchies which (jointly) supported the supreme adjudicating authority complete with the self-confidence it could and did inspire – a possibility, in other words, that the novel freedom and independence of language games is in itself an outcome of the decoupling of the communicative sphere from the structure of political and economic domination; and that such a 'decoupling' is in its turn the result of the decomposition of the hierarchy of systemic functions – in particular, of the erosion of the domination of economy over politics and the domain of ideas. It is possible that because of such erosion culture has become systemically irrelevant, shifting instead into the realm of social (as distinct from systemic) integration. Emancipation of culture from its previously performed systemic function made its disassembling into an aggregate of language games affordable. Emancipated from the co-responsibility for the reproduction of systemic domination, culture can joyously abandon that proselytizing, missionary fervour which marked the times of utopias and cultural crusades. Systematically irrelevant culture can do without a postmodern equivalent of, say, Weber's ideal type of rational behaviour, or Marx's project of universal emancipation – which in the preceding era were assigned the right to evaluate all varieties of social action and classify them as so many deviations from the unstoppably rising norm.

POSTMODERN SOCIOLOGY

At the threshold of postmodernity, sociology arrived in the form aptly called by Anthony Giddens the orthodox consensus. This form was constituted by the widely shared strategy of rational analysis of society, understood as a nation state; such a society, it was agreed, was subject to the processes of continuing rationalization, not necessarily free from contradictions and upsets (or, indeed, temporary retreats), yet sufficiently dominant to offer a safe frame against which information about social reality could be plotted. Constantly lurking behind the scene in the orthodox vision of social reality was the powerful image of the social system – this synonym of an ordered, structured space of interaction, in which probable actions had been, so to speak, pre-selected by the mechanisms of domination or value-sharing. It was a 'principally coordinated' space (in Talcott Parsons's rendition of Weber's imagery); one inside which the cultural, the political and the economic levels of supra-individual organization were all resonant with each other and functionally complementary. In Parsons's memorable phrase, sociology was best understood as an ongoing effort to solve the 'Hobbesian problem': the mystery of non-randomness, the regularity of behaviour of essentially free and voluntary subjects. The orthodox consensus focused accordingly on mechanisms which trimmed or eliminated the randomness and multidirectionality of human action and thus imposed co-ordination upon otherwise centrifugal forces; order upon chaos.

The first victim of advancing postmodernity was the invisibly present, tacitly assumed spectre of the system, the source and the guarantee of the meaningfulness of the sociological project and, in particular, of the orthodox consensus. The immediate outcome was a widespread feeling of unease and erosion of confidence. Well before the exact nature of postmodern change was articulated, the signs had appeared of growing disaffection with the way the business of sociology had been conducted in the era of orthodox consensus. Symbols of that era (Parsons's structural functionalism above all) came increasingly under attack, often for reasons only tenuously connected with the character of sensed change. Truly at stake was the overall de-legitimation of the orthodox consensus, rather than the ostensible topic of the assault; the replacement of specific theoretical assumptions or strategic principles. As T.H. Marshall wrote on a different occasion, sociologists knew what they were running from; they did not know yet where to.

At the time the rebellion started, there was little awareness of the link between the new spirit of theoretical and strategical restlessness and the changing social reality. The call to revise the practice of sociology was expressed in universalistic terms. It was not supposed that the orthodox consensus had outlived its usefulness and hence was ripe for reform; instead, the consensus was proclaimed wrong from the start; a sad case of error, of self-deception, or ideological surrender. Paradoxically (though not unexpectedly) the effort to discredit the modern view of the social world needed the thoroughly modern understanding of truth for self-validation. Without necessarily saying this in so many words, the rebels aimed at the substitution of the new consensus for the old (they often spoke of the search for a 'new paradigm'). In reality, their efforts led to the constitution of what one would best call a postmodern sociology (as distinct from the sociology of postmodernity).

Postmodern sociology received its original boost from Garfinkel's techniques conceived to expose the endemic fragility and brittleness of social reality, its 'merely' conversational and conventional groundings, its negotiability, perpetual use and irreparable underdetermination. Soon it adopted Alfred Schutz as its spiritual ancestor, with his contemplation of the marvel of social action and its self-propelling capacity, with his debunking of 'because-of' explanations as hidden 'in-order-to' motives, with his dissolution of systemic order into a plethora of multiple realities and universes of meaning. Shortly afterwards it turned to Wittgenstein and Gadamer for philosophical inspiration and the certificate of academic respectability. From Wittgenstein, the idea of language games was borrowed and skilfully adapted to justify the elimination of all 'tougher', extra-conversational constituents of social reality. From Gadamer came the vision of the life-world as a communally produced and traditionally validated assembly of meanings, and the courage to abandon the search for universal, supra-local, 'objective' (i.e. referring to none of the communally confined experiences) truth.

It was a postmodern world which lent animus and momentum to postmodern sociology; the latter reflects the former much in the same way the collage of the postmodern art 'realistically represents' (in the 'conceptual sense of realism')[20] randomly assembled experience of postmodern life. And yet postmodern sociology is distinguished by avoiding confrontation with postmodernity as a certain form of social reality, as a new departure set apart by new attributes. Postmodern sociology denies its kinship with a specific stage in the history of social life. In a curious way, this sociology which took impetus from dissatisfaction with visions born of the universalistic aspiration of the western, capitalist form of life, conceives of itself in universalistic, extemporal and exspatial, terms. It prefers to see its attainment as rectification of blunder, discovery of truth, finding of right direction, rather than as a self-adaptation to the transformed object of study. The attributes of social reality, made salient by the fading hopes of missionary culture and brought into relief by the postmodern world-view, postmodern sociology promoted to the status of perpetual (though heretofore overlooked) essences of social life in general.

One may say that postmodern sociology does not have the concept of postmodernity. One suspects that it would find it difficult to generate and legitimate such a concept without radically transforming itself. It is precisely because it is so well adapted to the postmodern cultural setting – that postmodern sociology (its tendency to argue the non-universality of truth in universalistic terms notwithstanding) cannot conceive of itself as an event in history. Indeed, it is singularly unfit to conceptualize the twin phenomena of the logic of historical succession and of the social embeddedness of ideas.

Postmodern sociology has responded to the postmodern condition through mimesis; it informs of that condition obliquely, in a coded way: through the isomorphism of its own structure, through commutation (Hjelmslev) between its structure and the structure of that extra-sociological reality of which it is a part. One can say that postmodern sociology is a signifier, with the postmodern condition as its signified. One can obtain a valid insight into the postmodern condition through the analysis of the practices of postmodern sociology. For the discursive knowledge of postmodernity as a type of social reality with a place in history and social space, one needs however to turn to other sociological responses.

I suggest that postmodern sociology can be best understood as a mimetic representation of the postmodern condition. But it can also be seen as a pragmatic response to this condition. Description of the social world is in it inextricably interwoven with praxeological choices. Indeed, the acceptance of communal sovereignty over meaning-production and truth-validation casts the sociologist, with no need of further argument, into the role of the interpreter,[21] of the semiotic broker with the function of facilitating communication between communities and traditions. A postmodern sociologist is one who, securely embedded in his own, 'native' tradition, penetrates deeply into successive layers of meanings upheld by the relatively alien tradition to be investigated. The process of penetration is simultaneously that of translation. In the person of the sociologist, two or more traditions are brought into communicative contact – and thus open up to each other their respective contents which otherwise would remain opaque. The postmodern sociologist aims at 'giving voice' to cultures which without his help would remain numb or stay inaudible to the partner in communication. The postmodern sociologist operates at the interface between 'language games' or 'forms of life'. His mediating activity is hoped to enrich both sides of the interface. The popularity of Clifford Geertz's strategic injunction of the 'thick description' (one which sums up anthropological practices distinguished by constituting their objects as culturally alien and thus in need of de-coding and translation) among contemporary sociologists is to a large extent due to its resonance with the postmodern world-view and the corresponding strategy of postmodern sociology. A typical exposition of such strategy, like that of Susan Heckman,[22] promotes a Karl Mannheim-style sociology of knowledge to the paradigm of total sociology (with, of course, the replacement of Mannheim's negative concept of ideology, as a distorting force and an enemy of truth, with the positive concept of ideology, or – better still – with the concept of communal tradition or linguistic community, as the sole framework, propagator and condition of truth).

SOCIOLOGY AGAINST POSTMODERNITY

Not all responses to the postmodern condition demand an equally radical revision of the orthodox model of sociological inquiry. Some of the most serious theoretical works of our time *deny the novelty of the present situation*; they deny, at least, that the novelty is radical enough to justify, let alone necessitate, abandonment of the model of modern (capitalist, industrial) society as the essential paradigm of social analysis.

Such works are *traditional* in a double sense: first, they deny the existential autonomy of postmodernity as a separate type of society, preferring to treat it as a variety, a stage, or a temporary aberration of a basically *continuous* modernity; second, they also deny the need for and legitimacy of the search for a *postmodern* sociology, as well as of the re-thinking of the role and the strategy of sociological theory and research.

What other sociologists tend to totalize as 'postmodernity', the traditional social theory of our time articulates as a manifestation of 'society in crisis'. The idea of crisis suggests that while society requires certain resources for its unhampered self-reproduction (and for retaining its identity over time), it is not, for one reason or another, capable of producing such resources, or of producing them in sufficient quantity. A more acute form of crisis would even imply that the society in question tends to produce *anti-resources* of a kind: phenomena which actively counteract its reproduction and threaten its identity. Description of a society as in crisis implies therefore that the society so described retains its identity and struggles to perpetuate it. By the same token, the appearance of phenomena resisting accommodation within known regularity can be only perceived as a case of 'malfunctioning': of a society diseased and in danger.

Such *doubly traditional* theories seek the roots of the crisis of modernity; in their most profound and sophisticated versions, they attempt to locate *endemic* sources of crisis, i.e. such structural features of modern society which bar it from behaving in a way necessary for its survival. By and large, they follow the time-honoured lines of theorizing the disruptive consequences of side-effects of societal reproduction in terms of *inner contradictions of capitalism, limits to rationalization*, or *civilization and its discontents*.

One category of crisis theories link the present change to the fading and eventual demise of the *Puritan personality* (and of the educational setting conducive to the upbringing of the Puritan, self-controlled, achievement-oriented personality, trained to delay gratification in the name of distant goals), believed to be an indispensable condition, as well as the major operating factor, of *modern* society. This theme had appeared relatively early in the period of post-war affluence and particular uncertainties brought forth by the cold war experience, and was approached simultaneously from a number of sides. There was David McClelland's suggestion of the cyclical rise and demise of *n-Achievement* (in itself an operationalized rendition of an older idea of Pitirim Sorokin, of the alternating *sensate* and *ideational* cultures). Riesman's discussion of a similar theme was conducted in terms of the rise of an other-directed man coming to replace the formerly dominant inner-directed personality – the one armed with an in-built 'gyroscope' which helped it resist cross-waves and keep it on course. Then came William W. Whyte Jr.'s well-rounded organization man, which triggered off an intense, though short-lived fashion to explore the anti-Puritan impact of the rapidly expanding 'white-collar' setting.

The 'demise of the Puritan personality' theme arguably found its fullest expression in the work of Richard Sennett, John Carroll and Christopher Lasch.[23] Whatever the differences between the three analyses, they converge on an imagery of the 'softening' civilization, where a sort of a *comfort principle* (if one is still allowed to talk about principles) has come to replace the *reality principle*, once promoted by the Puritan-inspired educational setting. Sennett lays the blame for the disastrously wrong turn at the door of the Puritan ethic itself: it contained, so he avers, the seeds of its own destruction, as it made its adherents painfully and interminably preoccupied with minute behavioural appearances serving as the only clue to individual fate and value, and thus warded off the very possibility of satisfying the lust for certainty. In Carroll, the passage from the Puritan to the present mixture of 'remissive' and paranoid personalities is abrupt and discontinuous, yet the outcome is similar: life reduced to an unceasing chase of ever elusive and never securely attainable pleasures. Other people become stepping stones for the unending climb to authenticity, happiness or whatever other names are given to the unachievable dream of restful self-confidence. All three authors stress the impact made by the personality change on the nature of human bonds. Interaction ceased to sediment *lasting* relations; inter-human networks and the institutions which once served to solidify them into structures turn brittle, fragile, lacking in all foundation except the intentions of the actors to continue. Human bonds are tentative, protean, and 'until further notice'.

The theories discussed so far present pictures of a *diseased society*; one in which 'the centre does not hold', one which has lost its determination and sense of direction; a 'softening' society, one which increasingly fails to harden its members and imbue them with a sense of purpose. Unlike in the case of postmodern sociology, the image of a society in the state of a constant Brownian movement, a society construed ever anew out of the flexible stuff of personal interaction, a society without a tough structure or firm developmental tendency – is here set firmly in historical times. The existential condition seen by postmodern sociology as the extemporal and universal truth of social reality, is perceived here as an eloquent testimony to the crisis of society. If asked, these authors would probably say that postmodern sociology is itself a symptom of the same disease; or, at least, the fact that it seems to many to be well geared to present-day society – is such a symptom.

The theorists discussed so far conceive of postmodernity (which, let us repeat, they theorize as the state of crisis of modernity 'as we know it', rather than a societal type in its own right), as essentially an event in culture; and they theorize it using the strategy of the once powerful culture-and-personality school. They locate their theory at the same level at which they have diagnosed the phenomena to be analysed. What is absent in these theories is an attempt to consider cultural manifestations of postmodernity as aspects of a wider, systemic, transformation, be it an emergence of a new type of social system, or a 'crisis' of the old one. It is the last possibility which has been explored by another, broad and influential category of crisis theorists, of whom Jurgen Habermas, Claus Offe, James O'Connor, and Andre Gorz may be named as the most sophisticated representatives.[24] What unites their theories (otherwise disparate in many important respects), is the assumption that the distinctiveness of contemporary society, elsewhere (but not in these theories) diagnosed as the advent of postmodernity, can be best understood as a deviation from the orthodox model of modern society; a deviation brought about by the present inability of the social system to *secure its own reproduction* in its old, 'classical' form.

For instance, in Habermas's view, capitalist society at its present stage finds it increasingly difficult to legitimize itself substantively (i.e. as a system which *secures* rationalization of economic activity, and *sustains* best allocation of resources and generation of constant economic growth). This remains the case, as the system-supportive function of the state (keeping the capital–labour relation alive and dominant) requires such transfers of resources as are bound radically to alter the setting of individual life-processes, and hence to undermine the *reproduction of motivations* indispensable for the smooth functioning of the capitalist economy. Among the motivations most painfully affected are the profit motive, the work ethic, familial privatism. In a truly dialectical way, attempts to sustain viability of the capitalist system cannot but erode the very conditions of its survival. Hence the *crisis of legitimation*; moral–political support for the system is not forthcoming in the required volume, and once-monolithic ideological domination gives way to heterogeneity of culture. Habermas's *Legitimation Crisis* was written virtually on the eve of the radical shift in the management philosophy of the capitalist system; a shift which revealed the orthodox method of servicing the capitalist economy as an, arguably, belated effort to respond to new economic realities with concerns generated by an earlier stage in capitalist history. It has been perhaps because of this unfortunate timing that Habermas failed to consider the possibility that the evident weakening of systemic legitimation could be a symptom of the *falling significance of legitimation* in integrating the system, rather than a manifestation of crisis. It could be for the same reason that Habermas theorized the decline of the work ethic as motivational crisis, rather than an outcome of a relative marginalization of the capital–labour relation inside the capitalist system in its present stage.

Such a marginalization did move into the focus of Offe's crisis theory. There, the *decentring* of the labour–capital conflict, and indeed of hired labour itself, is the main object of attention; the crisis of present-day capitalist society is ultimately traced back to the consistent and continuous dislodging of potential labour from the productive process. The rate of increase of labour productivity, Offe observes, exceeds that of production, which means that further technological advances (and further capital investment) result in growing redundancy of labour power.

Eviction of productive activities to a fast-shrinking segment of society rebounds on the structure of the life-world. *Orientation to work* rapidly loses its conduct-rationalizing capacity, as the traditional sociocultural 'proletarian' life-setting has all but dissipated, the perspective of 'life vocation' has lost its plausibility and, in general, the share of work-time in the whole of the life-process has drastically fallen.

Having diagnosed, in effect, the diminishing significance of exactly those social facts which formed the 'hard core' of the classical capitalist system and thus of the classical sociological theory, Offe moves further than any crisis theorist towards the inevitable conclusion: the extant sociological model of modern society is in urgent need of re-thinking, and possibly replacing.

> If we consider the answers given between the late eighteenth century and the end of the First World War to questions relating to the organising principles of the dynamics of social structures, we can safely conclude that labour has been ascribed a key position in sociological theorizing. . . . Can we still pursue this materialist preoccupation of the sociological classics? . . .

> It is precisely this comprehensive determining power of the social fact of (wage) labour and its contradictions which today has become sociologically questionable . . . .

> (L)abour and the position of workers in the production process is not treated as the chief organising principle of social structures; the dynamic of social development is not conceived as arising from conflicts over who controls the industrial enterprise; and . . . the optimization of the relations of technical–organisational or economic means and ends through industrial capitalist rationality is not understood in the form of rationality which heralds further social development.[25]

And yet, to Offe as to the rest of the crisis theorists, the identity of present-day society is fully negative; one describable in terms of absences, failures, declines, erosions – with the classical capitalist society, that archetype of modernity, serving as the benchmark and point of departure for all theorizing. Ours is a disorganized society; and a disorganized capitalism. It is, in other words, capitalism, or the capitalist form of modernity, in crisis. Being in crisis means that things that society needs, it does not have; institutions and processes which served its needs do not work any more or fail to maintain the required level of output. But being in crisis also means that the needs themselves have remained by and large unchanged; it is this circumstance, above all, which renders the failure of servicing mechanisms so critical. What makes the decentring of wage-labour look so dangerous and threatening to the administration of society, is the tacitly maintained perspective of the system organized first and foremost around its *productive* function, and hence engaging the society members in their role as the *producers*. With this role becoming scarce and marginal, the system becomes – wellnigh by definition – *disorganized*. It has lost its integrative principle, which once guarded the co-ordination between systemic reproduction, societal integration and the organization of the life-world.

As Offe does not believe in the possibility of healing the new wounds with old (and by now outdated) medicines, he feels obliged to suggest an unorthodox and truly revolutionary cure; a fully different 'logic of utilizing and maintaining labour power' – abandoning the 'fiscal linking of social security to revenues of employment', and replacing it with 'an egalitarian basic insurance scheme.[26] Offe admits that no social forces likely to promote the new principle of distribution are in sight, and thus acknowledges the theoretical and analytical, rather than empirical and processual, grounding of the suggested cure. Obliquely, the recourse to a solution of a *utopian* status re-confirms and re-states the initial assumption of Offe's theory: that the needs of present-day society are still the needs of a society organized around the *productive* function. It is this assumption which prevents one from focusing on already present new integrative principles (which cannot be recognized as such within the 'productive' perspective). And it is this assumption which inclines one to see various phenomena collectively named 'postmodernity' as symptoms of disease, rather than manifestations of new normality.

SOCIOLOGY OF POSTMODERNITY

Both basic types of crisis theories have been found wanting. The culture-and-personality type of crisis theory collapses manifestations of postmodernity with allegedly autonomous (i.e. subjected to its own logic, unrelated to that of the system as a whole) cultural dynamics; it leaves the central question of the validity of the orthodox sociological model, historically geared to 'classical' modernity, out of discussion. The system-in-crisis type of theory avoids such limitation and faces the central issue of sociological theory point-blank. And yet, having given priority to the theoretical redemption of the orthodox model, it finds itself bound to reduce the significance of the manifestations of postmodernity to that of clinical symptoms, and 'postmodernity' itself to that of a pathological aberration.

In this section, I propose to consider the possibility that the so-called postmodern phenomena combine into a cohesive aggregate of aspects of a new type of society, which differs from the orthodox model sufficiently to require a model of its own. In other words, I propose to consider whether postmodernity is a fully-fledged, comprehensive and viable type of social system; and whether – in consequence – the treatment of postmodern phenomena as dysfunctional, degenerative or otherwise threatening to the survival of society, is justified by anything but the pressure of historical memory, or an unwillingness to part with a theoretical model which served its purpose so well in the past.

The suggestion I propose to consider is the following: in present-day society, consumer conduct (consumer freedom geared to the consumer market) moves steadily into the position of, simultaneously, the cognitive and moral focus of life, the integrative bond of the society, and the focus of systemic management. In other words, it moves into the selfsame position which in the past – during the 'modern' phase of capitalist society – was occupied by work in the form of wage labour. This means that in our time individuals are engaged (morally by society, functionally by the social system) first and foremost as consumers rather than as producers.

Throughout the first (modern) part of its history, capitalism was characterized by the central position occupied by *work* simultaneously on the *individual*, *social* and *systemic* levels. Indeed, work served as the link holding together individual motivation, social integration and systemic reproduction, as the major institution responsible for their mutual congruence and co-ordination. It is from this central place that work is being gradually, though with an increasing speed, dislodged – as Claus Offe aptly demonstrated. And yet the room from which work is evicted has not remained vacant. Consumer freedom has moved in – first perhaps as a squatter, but more and more as a legitimate resident. It now takes over the crucial role of the link which fastens together the life-worlds of the individual agents and the purposeful rationality of the system. The assumption of such a role by consumer freedom seems to be the final outcome of the long process of displacement of the early-capitalist conflict focused on the issue of control, the right to management and to self-manage, from the productive to the distributive sphere; that displacement generated those 'ever rising expectations' which have become the basis for both the feasibility and inevitability of the selfsamerizing consumerism which came to be identified with capitalist economy.[27] It was this process which lay at the foundation of the decentring of work inside the life-world of the individual. The substitution of consumer freedom for work as the hub around which the life-world rotates may well change the heretofore antagonistic relation between the pleasure and reality principles (assumed by Freud to be extemporal). Indeed, the very opposition between the two may be all but neutralized.

In its present consumer phase, the capitalist system deploys the *pleasure principle* for its own perpetuation. *Producers* moved by the pleasure principle would spell disaster to a profit-guided economy. Equally, if not more disastrous, would be *consumers* who are not moved by the same principle.

Having won the struggle for control over production, and made its ascendancy in that sphere secure, capitalism can now afford the free reign of the pleasure principle in the realm of consumption – and it needs it more than anything else. As a matter of fact, the conquest of production remains secure precisely because a safe (and beneficial) outlet has been found for the potentially troublesome drive to pleasure.

For the consumer, reality is not the enemy of pleasure. The tragic moment has been removed from the insatiable drive to enjoyment. Reality, as the consumer experiences it, is a pursuit of pleasure. Freedom is about the choice between greater and lesser satisfactions, and rationality is about choosing the first over the second. For the *consumer system*, a spending-happy consumer is a necessity; for the *individual consumer*, spending is a duty – perhaps the most important of duties. There is a pressure to spend: on the *social level*, the pressure of symbolic rivalry, for the needs of self-construction through acquisition (mostly in commodity form) of distinction and difference,[28] of the search for social approval through lifestyle and symbolic membership; on the *systemic level*, the pressure of merchandising companies, big and small, who between themselves monopolize the definition of the good life, of the needs whose satisfaction the good life requires, and of the ways of satisfying them. These pressures, however – unlike the social and systemic pressures generated by the production-oriented system – are not entering life-experience as oppression. The surrender they demand promises mostly joy; not just the joy of surrendering to 'something greater than myself' (the quality which Emile Durkheim, somewhat prematurely, imputed to social conformity in his own, still largely pre-consumer, society, and postulated as a universal attribute of all conformity, in any type of society) – but a straightforward sensual joy of tasty eating, pleasant smelling, soothing or enticing drinking, relaxing driving, or the joy of being surrounded with smart, glittering, eye-caressing objects. With such duties, one hardly needs rights. Seduction, as Pierre Bourdieu intimated, may now take the place of repression as the paramount vehicle of systemic control and social integration.

From this re-arrangement, capitalism emerges strengthened. Excessive strain generated by the power contest has been channelled away from the central power structure and onto safer ground, where tensions can be unloaded without adversely affecting the administration of power resources; if anything, the tensions contribute now to its greater effectiveness. Deployment of energy released by free individuals engaged in symbolic rivalry lifts demand for the products of capitalist industry to ever higher levels, and effectively emancipates consumption from all natural limits set by the confined capacity of material or basic needs – those which require goods solely as utility values.

Last but not least, with consumption firmly established as the focus, and the playground, for individual freedom, *the future of capitalism looks more secure than ever*. Social control becomes easier and considerably less costly. Expensive *panoptical* methods of control, pregnant as they are with dissent, may be disposed of, or replaced by less ambivalent and more efficient methods of seduction (or, rather, the deployment of panoptical methods may be limited to a minority of the population; to those categories which for whatever reason *cannot be integrated through the consumer market*). The crucial task of soliciting behaviour functionally indispensable for the capitalist economic system, and at the same time harmless to the capitalist political system, may now be entrusted to the *consumer market* and its unquestionable attractions. Reproduction of the capitalist system is therefore achieved through individual freedom (in the form of consumer freedom, to be precise), and *not* through its suppression. Instead of being counted on the side of systemic overheads, the whole operation 'social control' may now be entered on the side of systemic assets.[29]

The consequence, most important for the emergence of the postmodern condition, has been the re-establishment of the essential mechanisms of systemic reproduction and social integration on entirely new grounds. Simultaneously, the old mechanisms have been either abandoned or devalued. To secure its reproduction, the capitalist system in its consumer phase does not need (or needs only marginally) such traditional mechanisms as *consensus-aimed political legitimation, ideological domination, uniformity of norms promoted by cultural hegemony.* Culture in general has lost its relevance to the survival and perpetuation of the system. Or, rather, it contributes now to such survival through its *heterogeneity and fissiparousness,* rather than the levelling impact of civilizing crusades. Once consumer choice has been entrenched as the point in which systemic reproduction, social integration and individual life-world are co-ordinated and harmonized – cultural variety, heterogeneity of styles and differentiation of belief-systems have become conditions of its success.

Contrary to the anguished forebodings of the 'mass culture' critics of the 1950s, the market proved to be the arch-enemy of uniformity. The market thrives on variety; so does consumer freedom and with it the security of the system. The market has nothing to gain from those things the rigid and repressive social system of 'classical' capitalism promoted: strict and universal *rules,* unambiguous criteria of *truth, morality and beauty,* indivisible *authority of judgement.* But if the market does not need these things, neither does the system. The powers-that-be lost, so to speak, all interest in universally binding standards, in the result, the standards lost the selfsame power-basis which used to give them credibility and sustained their never-ending pursuit as a worthwhile and attractive enterprise. To the authority of judgement disavowed by political powers, market forces offer the only alternative support. Cultural authorities turn themselves into market forces, become commodities, compete with other commodities, legitimize their value through the selling capacity they attain. Their habitual appeals to extraterritorial standards of judgement sound increasingly shallow and lose their cogency and attraction.

I suggest, in other words, that the phenomena described collectively as 'postmodernity' are not symptoms of systemic deficiency or disease; neither are they a temporary aberration with a life-span limited by the time required to rebuild the structures of cultural authority. I suggest instead that postmodernity (or whatever other name will be eventually chosen to take hold of the phenomena it denotes) is an aspect of a fully-fledged, viable social system which has come to replace the 'classical' modern, capitalist society and thus needs to be theorized according to its own logic.

Like all attempts to reveal the inner logic in the already-accomplished reality, the above analysis emphasizes the *systemness* of postmodern society: the *accuracy* with which individual life-world, social cohesiveness and systemic capacity for reproduction fit and assist each other. Consumption emerged from the analysis as the 'last frontier' of our society, its dynamic, constantly changing part; indeed, as the very aspect of the system which generates its own criteria of *forward movement* and thus can be viewed as *in progress*. It also appeared to play the role of an effective lightning-rod, easily absorbing excessive energy which could otherwise burn the more delicate connections of the system, and of an expedient safety-valve which re-directs the disaffections, tensions and conflicts continually turned out by the political and the social subsystems, into a sphere where they can be symbolically played out – and defused. All in all, the system appeared to be in good health, rather than in crisis. At any rate, it seemed to be capable of solving its problems and reproducing itself no less than other known systems could, and systems in general are theoretically expected to.

Let me add that the particular mode of problem-solving, conflict-resolution and social integration characteristic of the postmodern system tends to be further strengthened by the downright unattractiveness of what seems to be, from the perspective determined by the system itself, its only alternative. The system has successfully squeezed out all alternatives to itself but one: repression, verging on disenfranchisement, emerged as the *only realistic possibility* other than consumer freedom. The only choice not discredited by the system as *utopian* or otherwise unworkable, is one between consumer freedom and unfreedom; between consumer freedom and the dictatorship over needs (Feher, Heller and Markus's memorable phrase) – the latter practised on a limited scale towards the residue of *flawed consumers* inside a society organized around the commodity market, or on a global scale by a society unwilling, or incapable of providing the allurements of fully developed consumerism.

SOCIOLOGY AT THE AGE OF POSTMODERNITY

Constructing a new model of contemporary society, necessitated by profound changes in its organization and functioning, is but one task with which sociology has been confronted by the advent of postmodernity. Another, no less complex task, is that of rethinking major sociological categories shaped, as it were, under conditions now fast receding into the past.

From its birth, sociology was an adjunct of modernity. It took the accomplishment of modernity – the construction of the free individual through cutting him loose from visible, tangible 'pinpointable' bonds – for granted, and hence defined its task as the study and the service of unfreedom – all those processes of *socialization, cultural hegemony, control, power, culture, civilization,* which could account for the mystery of 'de-randomizing' the voluntary actions of free agents. It translated the 'rationalization spurt', the disciplinary practices, the uniforming ambitions of modernity from a normative project into the analytical framework for making sense of reality, and thus made the 'structure' those pre-individual forces which bring order into the otherwise chaotic and potentially damaging drives of the free agents – the pivot of its discourse. It drew its cognitive horizons with the leg of the compass placed firmly in the very spot from which the levelling, uniforming, proselytizing tendencies of modern times emanated – and thus identified 'society', the largest analytical totality meant to incorporate and accommodate all analysis – with the nation state.

Not only did sociology develop as a theory and a service discipline of modernity. Its underlying world-view, its conceptual apparatus, its strategy, were all geared to the latter's practices and declared ambitions. It seems unlikely, therefore, that with those practices and ambitions undergoing profound change, the business of sociology can go on 'as usual'. There seems to be little in the orthodox lore of sociology which can a priori claim exemption from re-thinking.

The first to have come under scrutiny is the very imagery of the social world as a *cohesive totality with a degree of stiffness and resilience against change, with a neatly arranged hierarchy of power and value prior to the interaction between individual and group agents.* Such an imagery was most conspicuously epitomized in the concept of structure, characterized first and foremost by the attributes of relative inflexibility and autonomy in relation to the level of interaction. No wonder it is the concept of structure which has been treated with most suspicion by the theorists seeking the 'new paradigm' for sociology – one better geared to the time of systemic indifference to cultural plurality and, indeed, to the waywardness of constitutive agencies. Previous emphasis on structurally determined constraints to interaction gives way to a new concern with the process in which ostensibly 'solid' realities are construed and reconstrued in the course of interaction; simultaneously, the ascribed potency of agency is considerably expanded, the limits of its freedom and of its reality-generating potential pushed much further than the orthodox imagery would ever allow. The overall outcome of such revisions is a vision of a fluid, changeable social setting, kept in motion by the interaction of the plurality of autonomous and unco-ordinated agents.

And so Alain Touraine promoted for more than a decade the substitution of the idea of social movement for that of the social class as the basic unit of societal analysis. The latter concept is most intimately related to the imagery of structure and structural constraints and determination. The first, in Touraine's rendering, implies a vision of pliable, under-determined, unfinished reality amenable to ideational and practical remoulding by motivated social actors. In a recent expression of this vision, Touraine rejects the idea of 'class in itself'; workers' action, he insists,

> is not a reaction to an economic and social situation; it is itself
> a blueprint which determines the state of social relations. . . .
> It follows from this that the working class cannot be defined
> 'objectively', and therefore that the concept governing the
> analysis is no longer one of class position, but of social
> movement.[30]

The most crucial attribute ascribed to a social movement is its *self-constituting* capacity: social movement is not an emanation, epiphenomenon, reflection of anything else; it is fully its own creation; it generates its own subject; it constitutes itself into a social agent.

Anthony Giddens directs his attention to the revisions which the teaching of the 'founding fathers' of sociology, and the concepts and visions they bequeathed, require in order to be of use in the analysis of contemporary society (though it is not entirely clear in Giddens's writings whether that 'contemporaneity' which makes revisions necessary, is one of *social theory*, or of the *social world* it theorizes). In the successive rewritings of his new theoretical synthesis, Giddens redefines structure as a process which incorporates motivated agents and their interaction as its, simultaneously, building material and operating force. Indeed, Giddens substitutes the concept of structuration for that of structure, rightly assuming that in this new, 'action-oriented' and 'action-expressive' form, the pivotal concept of social analysis is better geared to the task of theorizing an un-predetermined, flexible social reality which pre-empts none of its options, which is open to the influence of a plurality of only loosely co–ordinated power centres, and which emerges from an interaction between only partly translatable, communally grounded meanings.

A most important point has been promoted for some time by S.M. Eisenstadt in his seminal comparative study of civilizations. Eisenstadt insists that the very idea of the *social system* is in need of a radical reconsideration. He suggests that no human population is confined within a single system, 'but rather in a multiplicity of only partly coalescing organizations, collectivities and systems'.

> Unlike the view found in many sociological and anthropological studies – namely that social systems are natural or given, and that they change through internal processes of differentiation – we stress that these systems are constructed through continuous process and that this construction is always both there and very fragile. . . . These systems never develop as entirely self-enclosed ones. . . . Different structures evince differences in organization, continuity and change and, together with their patterns may change to different degrees or in different constellations within the 'same' society.[31]

Thus the current sociological theory (at least in its most advanced versions) takes cognizance of the increasingly apparent plurality and heterogeneity of the sociocultural world, and on the whole abandons the orthodox imagery of a co–ordinated, hierarchized, deviance-fighting social system in favour of a much more fluid, processual social setting with no clear-cut distinction between order and abnormality, consensus and conflict. There is, however, another large group of theoretical issues posited by the advent of postmodernity, which have not attracted as yet sufficient attention. These are issues related to the adequacy of the concept of 'society' as the horizon and the most inclusive category of social analysis.

For reasons which can be both understood and justified, the concept of 'society' has been historically cut to the measure of the nation state; however defined, this concept invariably carried ideas intimately associated with a situation which only a nation state (in its reality or in its promise) could bring about and sustain: a degree of normative – legal and moral – unity, an all-embracing system of classification which entailed and located every unit, a relatively unambiguous distribution of power and influence, and a setting for action sufficiently uniform for *similar actions* to be expected to bring *similar consequences* for the whole and thus to be interpreted in a similar way. Moreover, the nation state prototype for the concept of society endowed the latter with a visible *developmental tendency*; a self-sustained and self-propelled tendency, with all its relevant explanatory factors to be found *inside* the society in question – so that all *outside* factors could be theoretically reduced to the role of environment and accounted for, if at all, by the *caeteris paribus* formula.

Sociologists were always aware that the theoretical concept of society as a compact, sealed totality merely approximates the reality of any nation state, however large and justified in its ecumenical ambitions. In reality, the nation states, those prototypes of theoretical 'societies', were porous, and porous in a double sense; much of what went on inside could not be fully explained without a reference to factors uncontrolled by the inside authorities – and factors which had to be interpreted in terms of motives and agencies, not just in terms of the passive resistance of an environment treated solely as an *object* of action; and much of what was going on inside the nation states revealed its true significance only when traced through its consequences outside the boundaries of its home society – consequences which could look very different when seen in such a wider perspective. One could indeed find in sociological literature frequent warnings and rejoinders to this effect; yet few, if any, conclusions were drawn from them in sociological practice. It seems that most sociologists of the era of modern orthodoxy believed that – all being said – the nation state is close enough to its own postulate of sovereignty to validate the use of its theoretical expression – the 'society' concept – as an adequate framework for sociological analysis.

In the postmodern world, this belief carries less conviction than ever before. With the sovereignty of nation states vividly displaying its limitations in the 'input' as much as in the 'output' sense, the traditional model of society loses its credence as a reliable frame of reference, while the consequences of its persistent use in sociological analysis gain in gravity. Given the centrality of the notion of society in sociological analysis (indeed, its tacit presence in *all* sociological analysis, if only as the condition for the given space being an appropriate object of sociological treatment), this new situation confronts sociological theory with tasks whose total dimension it is too early to ascertain. Let us mention briefly, as illustration only, two among these tasks.

One is the issue of the *rationalizing tendency*. Its reliability as the frame of reference for processual analysis has come under suspicion even in application to inner-societal processes. The question is, however, to what extent one can retain the idea of rationality in its sociologically accepted form in view of the evident *porousness* of the state-based society. Can one ascertain the degree of rationality of action if the consequences of the action are traced *only as far as the boundaries of such a society*? More and more often we hear the opinion (though on the whole not from the professional sociologists) that it is precisely the enhanced rationality of arms production and strategic planning inside the state units of international conflicts which must be held responsible for constantly growing *irrationality* governing the *inter-state space*. Thus *rational* logic is deployed in order to create a situation in which the credibility of a threat will be guaranteed by the sheer irrationality of putting it into practice. In Philip Green's words, 'in deterrence theory, the general "assumption of rationality" takes the concrete form of the assumption that if policy-makers will only make correct choices (i.e., be "rational"), all-out nuclear war will be averted. . . .' Yet in order to make this assumption realistic, to wit credible, belief must be impressed upon the prospective enemy that the policy-makers will not try to avert it, i.e. that they will behave irrationally: 'It is . . . simply impossible to imagine circumstances in which an annihilatory counter-strike makes any sense at all, by any standards of "rationality"'.[32] Rational theorists of nuclear deterrence think therefore that an indispensable condition of rendering the deterrent force *rational*, that means goal-effective, is the deployment of 'no-retreat' devices, which will assure that once the war process has been triggered off, no last-moment rationality of political leaders would intervene to halt it.[33] Given that a 'highly motivated, technically competent and adequately funded team of research scientists will inevitably produce an endless series of brand new (or refined) weapon ideas',[34] and that 'armament firms are interested in fostering a state of affairs which will increase the demand for armaments',[35] it seems that at the far end of the long string of rational actions there is a world which (to quote, for a change, Woody Allen) 'is on a crossroads. One road leads to utter hopelessness and despair, the other road leads to utter destruction and extinction. God grant us the wisdom to use the right road.' It is high time for the sociologists to consider to what extent it is legitimate to go on testing Weber's 'rationalization hypothesis' against processes and trends confined to the inner-state space.

Another issue relates to the overall tendency of modernity (i.e.

the adequacy of the 'modernization' hypothesis, and – in view of considerations spelled out in the preceding section – of the idea of postmodernity as the destination of modernization logic). Recent reverses of the supposedly universal modernizing tendencies have been well noted, though their true significance (including their finality) is yet to be ascertained. What is, however, much less attended to, is the significance (and finality) of postmodern developments in view of the fact that they occur in a rather confined section of the globe, which cannot claim an ecumenical future with anything like the certainty and self-confidence typical of the past – modern – state of its history. If our suggestion of a close relation between the advent of postmodernity and advanced consumerism deserves credibility, it is necessary to ask to what extent postmodernity ought to be seen as a local event, a parochial phenomenon fully dependent on a temporary, and possibly transient, privilege of one group of states in the worldwide distribution of power and resources. Most of the current analyses of postmodernity do not admit the urgency of this question. Postmodernity is treated as the tendency of *contemporary culture* (without qualifications); if its causes are scrutinized at all, they are on the whole sought *inside* the society (or group of societies) in which postmodern phenomena are situated, with no reference to the unique position of such societies in global arrangements. There is, however, a distinct possibility that the advent of postmodernity in one part of the world is precisely the effect of such an unique position; both of the erosion of the universalistic ambitions that part of the world entertained in the past, and of the still considerable privilege this part enjoys in the world-wide distribution of resources. There is, in other words, a possibility that the phenomenon of postmodernity can be only sociologically interpreted as a Thelemic phenomenon (in François Rabelais' *Gargantua*, the imaginary Abbey of *Thélème* offers its inmates all the amenities of the 'good life' – strikingly similar to those offered today by the postmodern culture; this is achieved by locking out the impoverished providers of the insiders' luxury, outside thick and tall monastery walls. The inside and the outside determine and condition each other's existence.)

The problem is, however, that sociology so far is poorly equipped to treat the social space beyond the confines of the nation state as anything else but the analytically compressed 'environment'.

It is only now that we begin to understand to what extent all major categories of sociology are dependent for their meaning and practical usefulness on their relatedness to the typically inner-societal space, different from all other imaginable social spaces by being *held together by a universally* (i.e., within that space) *binding authority*. The society of which sociology has something to say is a 'principally co-ordinated' social space, with a unified, power-supported 'value-cluster' or a code of moral and behavioural norms, with a 'dominant' or 'hegemonic' culture, with a mechanism of tough or tender (depending on the emphasis of given theory) *control* which exerts a steady pressure towards *one* selected type of social relationship, simultaneously suppressing *alternative* types. The 'society' of sociologists is, by and large, a unified and organized space, a 'structured' space (i.e. a space within which probabilities are manipulated, so that some choices are more likely to occur than others). It is this theoretical selection which enables sociologists to speak of social laws of regularities, of the *normative regulation* of social reality, of *trends* and *developmental* sequences.

The fact that the social reality extending on the other side of the nation state boundaries is not such a space and hence should not be analytically treated as if it were was rarely noticed; when it was noticed, it was, explicitly or *de facto*, treated as a minor irritant. A minor irritant indeed it was, as long as sociologists spoke from *inside* such societies as legitimately considered themselves the avant-garde of the rest of the world, the civilizing or modernizing force of universal significance, the 'Yenan republic' of sorts, about to colonize the remaining part of mankind in order to remould it in its own likeness. At that time, sociologists spoke in unison with the *realities of power* in the world; that perspective from which other portions of mankind looked much as an environment, as a territory for action but not a source of action, was not of the sociologists' making or invention.

This is, however, not the case anymore. And so the irritant must seem anything but minor. There is hardly a power left in the world which can blithely entertain an ecumenically universalistic ambition. In our world, not just the 'Great Powers' set hard and fast limits to each other's dreams; there is more than ample evidence that the degree to which the more advanced societies can impose their versions of a *Pax Romana* on the lesser (and thus 'retarded') units of mankind is much smaller today than it was (or was hoped to be) when the 'white man' still carried his 'mission'. Societies whose 'agency' must be willy-nilly admitted, display in what seems to be a lasting plurality such an astounding variety of 'principal co-ordinations', of 'value-clusters' or 'dominant' cultures, that the *universality* of categories born out of experience of one, however privileged, 'modern' part of the world, can no longer be assumed as true either on a synchronic or a diachronic level.

We face, therefore, a social space populated by relatively autonomous agents who are entangled in mutual dependencies and hence prompted to interact. These agents, however, are not operating in anything like the 'principally co-ordinated' space, similar to that inside which all traditional sociological categories have been once securely allocated. It is becoming increasingly apparent, therefore, that even in those cases when the sociologists confine their research interests to the space safely enclosed by one well-structured nation state, their findings may claim no more than partial and provisional status – if the impact of a once comfortably inert, but now suddenly active 'environment' is left out of sight in the grey area of the *caeteris paribus*. . . . I suggest that the elaboration of categories appropriate to the analysis of dependencies and interactions in the 'non-societal' social space, a space without 'principal co-ordination', 'dominant culture', 'legitimate authority', etc., is now a most urgent task faced by sociology.

That this is a task at all, much less an urgent one, has not been generally recognized. The study of *international relations* (it is under this name that the interest in the 'inter-societal space' has been academically institutionalized) is a thriving discipline which has generated over the years an immense quantity of empirical findings and a rather large volume of theory. And yet, most of the conceptual apparatus deployed in the theorizing is vulnerable to Wittgenstein's critique of 'similarity' (the famous '5 pm on the Sun'); with concepts repeatedly used and tested in *one* context, their dependence on the peculiarities of this context is forgotten and their applicability is believed to be context-free. And so we read in a reputable study of international conflict that 'the definition of conflict can be extended from single people to groups (such as nations), and more than two parties can be involved in the conflict. The principles remain the same.'[36] The cognitive optimism notwithstanding, the fact that in the inter-societal space conflicts neither emerge, nor are resolved in a way 'similar' to that of inner-societal space, and that the very expectation of such similarity is responsible for their incomprehensibility, cannot be glossed over for long. And thus we read in the same study that the 'simple act of negotiation does not necessarily solve matters. It depends on how far each party to the negotiation believes that the other will carry out his promises.'[37] With such discovery comes realization that in the area of international relations, unlike in the inner-societal interactions, such certainty can be secured only by the superior force of one of the adversaries. As the alien context resists the analytical tool, response is radical and desperate; adversaries in the conflict abstain from cheating solely for the fear of force (and not for other reasons, like for instance the need for peace).

I believe that it was the conceptual bankruptcy, related to the frustrated expectation of similarity and the uncritical acceptance of the logic of '5 pm on the Sun' style of reasoning, which led to the resounding defeat of the 'international law and order' approach (dominant in political theory in the period immediately following the Second World War), by the 'Power Politics' school, best represented by Hans J. Morgenthau and George Schwarzenberg. In John W. Burton's description, that new school 'gave up any hope that an international system could be built in the image of a national community and settled for a system of anarchy in which relations would be determined by the relative power of states'.[38] This was, in Arnold Wolfer's expression, a 'billiard ball model' of social reality, long ago denigrated and rejected in sociological discourse; the ironic result of a false expectation of similarity was an emphatic denial of *any connection* between international relations and domestic politics.

In the last twenty years or so the 'Power Politics' approach has lost much of its original purity and self-confidence, and a slow and tortuous reverse movement has begun. Experts in international relations now pay attention to the fact that staving off 'enemy attack' is not the only motive for 'state behaviour'; that actors on the international stage pursue other benefits as well.

And yet the fateful discovery of the absence of shared normative organization in the field of interaction continues to haunt the analysis. Whatever the declared or imputed motives of action, their mutual impact is perceived as not too different from that elaborated upon by game theory: one which assumes that players do not behave randomly, but that they can behave rationally only in so far as they assume that their adversaries do behave at random and if they succeed in impressing upon the adversaries that they themselves are also capable of random conduct.

The regularity, the 'patterned character' of interaction, which made possible sociological theorizing and supplied the semantic field for sociological concepts – was an outcome of a historical process which occurred within certain parts of the world (and, as we suspect now, stopped short from embracing the totality of mankind). As Norbert Elias pointed out, the factor which stood behind this development of pattern and regularity (wherever they did develop) was that of power monopoly; more precisely, of the twin monopolies of violence (forcing people to behave in a specific way by acting upon their bodies) and taxation (forcing people to part with their products or possessions). With such monopolies, physical violence and its threat

> is no longer a perpetual insecurity that it brings into the life of the individual, but a peculiar form of security. . . . [A] continuous, uniform pressure is exerted on individual life by the physical violence stored behind the scenes of everyday life, a pressure totally familiar and hardly perceived, conduct and drive economy having been adjusted from earliest youth to this social structure.[39]

Rationality as sociologists came to define it, the very habit of connecting events in terms of cause and effect without which rational conduct is unthinkable – depends on that regularity of setting which only monopoly of power can bring about and make into a natural attribute of reality. The question is, to what extent the patterns of rational behaviour which have developed in such circumstances may turn into their opposite in a reality in which such natural attributes fail to appear; and to what extent analysis based on the expectation of rationality can becloud, rather than enlighten, the peculiarity of conditions radically different from the orderly inner-societal space.

The monopoly of violence and taxation had been, in Elias's view, a product of the long process of competition between roughly equal units; in the long run, such competition leads (through an *elimination contest*), to the concentration of power in ever fewer hands, up to the subordination of the whole space to one centre of power, and the monopolization of the use of power and of access to other people's surplus. This process, which has taken place in all societies passing from the state of feudal fragmentation to their modern, centralized form – *remains unfinished on the global scale*. Hence on the inter-state level 'the physically – or militarily – strongest group can impose their will on those who are weaker. In that respect not much has changed since humanity's earlier days.'[40] There is no immediate (and not much of the longer-term) hope of further elimination, and none of the units can realistically entertain ambitions to exclusivity. The long process of actual and projected universalization (the selfsame process which supplied epistemological ground for the modern world-view) has come abruptly to a halt. The postmodern acceptance of irreducible plurality followed. With it, however, came the necessity to revise the imagery of social reality which sustained the 'naturalness' of orthodox sociological categories. Hardly ever before did sociologists seriously confront the task of analysing conflicts, however violent, which took place in a setting other than the institutionalized, legally or morally unified context – existing, as it were, in the shadow of a superior, sanction-armed power. They must confront it now – as the enclaves answering the orthodox description become evidently too narrow and incomplete to accommodate a reliable analysis of the dynamics of the postmodern world.

FINAL REMARKS

This chapter has been intended as an inventory of topics to be researched and theoretical tasks to be undertaken; the topics and the tasks which the sociocultural transformations loosely aggregated in the emerging model of postmodernity put in front of sociology – that scholarly discipline which originated, and developed until recently, as an attempt to grasp the logic of modernity. The chapter lists questions and problems, while offering few solutions. It is not even a career report. Much more modestly, it intends to be an invitation to a debate.

The few positive ideas this chapter does offer can be summed up in the following way:

1 Postmodern phenomena, most commonly confined in their description to the cultural, or even merely the artistic level, can be viewed in fact as surface symptoms of a much deeper transformation of the social world – brought about by the logic of modern development, yet in a number of vital respects discontinuous with it.

2 These deeper transformations ought to be sought in the spheres of systemic reproduction, social integration and the structure of the life-world, as well as in the novel way in which these three spheres are linked and co-ordinated.

3 Proper analysis of the postmodern condition brings us, therefore, back into the orthodox area of sociological investigation (though an area now structured in an unorthodox way). This means that rather than seeking a new form of a postmodern sociology (a sociology attuned in its style, as 'an intellectual genre', to the cultural climate of postmodernity), sociologists should be engaged in developing a sociology of postmodernity (i.e. deploying the strategy of systematic, rational discourse to the task of constructing a theoretical model of postmodern society as a system in its own right, rather than a distorted form, or an aberration from another system).

4 This latter task differs from the past practice of sociology (that of constructing models of modern society) in one crucial respect, which renders the called-for operation not fully continuous with the orthodoxy: the model of postmodernity, unlike the models of modernity, cannot be grounded in the realities of the nation state, by now clearly not a framework large enough to accommodate the decisive factors in the conduct of interaction and the dynamics of social life. This circumstance makes the task particularly complex; the reality to be modelled is, both in its present shape and in its plausible prospects, much more fluid, heterogenous and 'under-patterned' than anything the sociologists tried to grasp intellectually in the past.

NOTES

1 Comp. Frederick Jameson, 'Postmodern and consumer society', in Hal Foster (ed.), *The Anti-Aesthetic, Essays in Postmodern Culture* (Port Townsend: Bay Press, 1983).
2 Comp. Kim Lewin, 'Farewell to modernism', in Richard Hertz (ed.), *Theories of Contemporary Art* (Englewood Cliffs: Prentice Hall, 1985), pp. 2–7.
3 Comp. Francis Picabia, in Lucy R. Lippard (ed.), *Dadas on Art* (Englewood Cliffs: Prentice Hall, 1971), p. 168.
4 Matei Calinescu, *Faces of Modernity: Avant-Garde, Decadence, Kitsch* (Indiana University Press, 1977), p. 147.
5 Peter Bürger, *Theory of the Avant-Garde*, tr. Michael Shaw (Manchester University Press, 1984), p. 87.
6 Quoted after Brian McHale, *Postmodernist Fiction* (London: Methuen, 1987), p. 3.
7 Ibid., p. 39.
8 Jean Baudrillard, *Les strategies fatales* (Bernard Gassett, 1983).
9 Martin Esslin, *The Age of Television* (San Francisco: W.H. Freeman, 1982), pp. 8, 22.

10 Quoted after Louis Banks, 'The rise of newsocracy', in Ray Eldon, Hiebert and Carol Reuss (eds), *Impact of Mass Media, Current Issues* (London: Longman, 1985), p. 31.

11 Daniel Dayan and Elihu Katz, 'Performing media events', in James Curan, Anthony Smith and Pauline Wingate (eds), *Impacts and Influences, Essays on Media Power in the Twentieth Century* (London: Methuen, 1987), pp. 175, 183.

12 Comp. Baudrillard, op. cit.

13 Mathew Arnold, *Culture and Anarchy* (Cambridge University Press, 1963), p. 50 (orig. 1869).

14 George Steiner, *Extraterritorial* (London: Atheneum, 1976).

15 Jean-François Lyotard, *The Postmodern Condition: A Report on Knowledge*, trans. by Geoff Bennington and Brian Marsuni (Manchester University Press, 1984), p. 17.

16 Ibid., p. 16.

17 Ibid., p. 17.

18 Ibid., p. 37.

19 Ibid., p. 41.

20 Comp. Rosalind E. Kraus, *The Originality of Avant-Garde and Other Modernist Myths* (MIT Press, 1985), pp. 52–4. The concept has been suggested by G.M. Luquet.

21 Comp. Zygmunt Bauman, *Legislators and Interpreters: On Modernity, Postmodernity and Intellectuals* (Cambridge: Polity Press, 1987), pp. 1–7, 143–5, 196–7.

22 Susan Heckman, *Hermeneutics and the Sociology of Knowledge* (Cambridge: Polity Press, 1986).

23 Richard Sennett, *The Fall of the Public Man* (Vintage Books, 1978); John Carroll, *Puritan, Paranoid, Remissive: A Sociology of Modern Culture* (Routledge, 1977); Christopher Lasch, *Culture of Narcissism* (Random Books, 1977).

24 Jurgen Habermas, *Legitimation Crisis* (Heinemann, 1976); Claus Offe, *Disorganised Capitalism: Contemporary Transformations of Work and Politics*, edited by John Keane (Polity Press, 1985); James O'Connor, *Accumulation Crisis* (Blackwell, 1984); Andre Gorz, *Path to Paradise: On the Liberation from Work* (Pluto Press, 1985).

25 Claus Offe, op. cit., pp. 129–32.

26 Ibid., pp. 63, 96–7.

27 This process has been discussed at length in Zygmunt Bauman, *Memories of Class: Essays in Pre-history and After-Life of Class* (Routledge, 1982), Chapters 3 and 4.

28 Cf. Pierre Bourdieu, *Distinction, A Social Critique of the Judgement of Taste* (Routledge, 1984).

29 More about deployment of market freedom in the service of social control – in Zygmunt Bauman, *Freedom* (Open University Press, 1988), Chapters 3 and 4.

30 Alain Touraine, Michel Wieviorka, Francois Dubet, *The Workers' Movement*, trans. by Ian Patterson (Cambridge University Press, 1987), pp. 20, 21.

31 S.N. Eisenstadt, *A Sociological Approach to Comparative Civilisation: The*

Development and Directions of a Research Program (Jerusalem: The Hebrew University, 1986), pp. 29–30.

32 Philip Green, *Deadly Logic, The Theory of Nuclear Deterrence* (Schocken Books, 1969), pp. 158–237.

33 Thomas C. Schelling, *Arms and Influence* (Yale University Press, 1976), p. 239.

34 Colin Gray, *The Soviet-American Arms Race* (Lexington: Saxon House, 1976), p. 40.

35 Salvador de Madariaga, *Disarmament* (New York: Coward-McLean, 1929), p. 11.

36 Michael Nicholson, *The Conflict Analysis* (The English University Press, 1970), p. 2.

37 Ibid., p. 68.

38 John W. Burton, *Global Conflicts: The Domestic Sources of International Crisis* (Wheatsheaf Books, 1986), p. 4.

39 Norbert Elias, *The Civilising Process: State Formation and Civilisation*, trans. by Edmund Jephcott (Blackwell, 1982), pp. 238–9.

40 Norbert Elias, *Involvement and Detachment*, trans. by Edmund Jephcott (Blackwell, 1987), p. 104.

3

THE CHANGING DISCURSIVE FORMATION OF SOCIOLOGY

There is little point, and still less hope of practical effect, in legislating for sociology; which means, as well, that there is little point in designing substantive definitions separating things sociological from those bound to remain outside the realm of sociological competence and concern. Definitions, like laws, are as good as the authority that backs them: no better and no worse. And authority is as good as the (physically or mentally) coercive forces at its disposal. The coercive capacity of such forces depends in turn on their exclusivity: on the degree to which their command is condensed and genuinely free from rivals.

The collective activity described or self-describing as sociology has met none of those conditions and is unlikely ever to meet them. Its authorities are plural and dispersed, and thus the coercive impact of each is countervailed and eroded by all the others. Each new attempt to legislate the proper realm and right strategy for sociology ends up, therefore, as a new addition to the extant variety. It splits instead of integrating. As a declaration of intent, it is self-defeating.

It is for this reason that professional sociologists proved to be the most avid admirers of Thomas Kuhn's narrative for *normal science*, least of all suitable for sociological applications. 'Paradigm' was exactly what the loose aggregate of chair-holders and lecturers of a discipline united by not much more than its name seemed to miss most spectacularly. Enthusiasm for the idea of the paradigm was beefed up by the hope that life without a paradigm is but a temporary and curable condition, the manifestation of a momentary crisis, and at any rate an abnormal state. It was also an expression of the belief that the missing unity could be achieved were only a unifying paradigm agreed upon, that such paradigm will be found sooner or later, and that once found, universally accepted on the strength of its self-evident cogency alone: an agreed set of ideas will, so to speak, have enough carrying power to sustain the otherwise brittle unity of sociological discourse. The hope was false, the belief misguided and misguiding.

A DISCOURSE THAT DREAMS ITSELF A FORMATION

Perhaps the nature of the sociological enterprise can be better grasped in terms of Michel Foucault's *discursive formation*. Confronted with 'large groups of statements' called respectively medicine, economics or grammar, Foucault tried to find out 'on what their unity' (that is, the quality that justified the use of a generic name) 'could be based'. He considered and rejected, one by one, all common answers to that question: 'on a full, tightly packed, continuous, geographically well-defined field of objects'; 'on a definite, normative type of statement'; 'on a well-defined alphabet of notions'; 'on the permanence of a thematic'. None of the traditional answers seemed to hold much water. What one was faced with instead was the reality of 'various strategic possibilities that permit the activation of incompatible themes, or, again, the establishment of the same theme in different groups of statement. Hence the idea of describing these dispersions themselves' – of reconstituting the *systems of dispersion* rather than, as has been commonly done in mainstream history of science or philosophy, tracing *chains of inference*.[1]

> We sought the unity of discourse in the objects themselves, in their distribution, in the interplay of their differences, in their proximity or distance – in short, in what is given to the speaking subject; and, in the end, we are sent back to a setting-up of relations that characterizes discursive practice itself; and what we discover is neither a configuration, nor a form, but a group of *rules* that are immanent in a practice. . . .

> It is not the objects that remain constant, nor the domain that they form; it is not even their point of emergence or their mode of characterization; but the relation between the surfaces on which they appear, on which they can be delimited, on which they can be analysed and specified.[2]

Areas of intellectual practice that we objectivize as *disciplines* and contemplate as entities with a certain degree of inner unity which we then (misguidedly) seek to found on things external to the discipline itself (most commonly on the properties of non-discursive reality, their ostensible 'object'), have nothing but the discourse to uphold them. They are, indeed, *discursive* formations. Their apparent unity is the constant activity of interwoven communicative practices. They are discursive *formations* in so far as 'one can show how any particular object of discourse finds in it its place and law of emergence; if one can show that it may give birth simultaneously or successively to mutually exclusive objects, without having to modify itself'.[3]

No discursive formation imposes itself upon non-discursive reality that waits for its court painter to be portrayed and thus have its obscure and elusive 'inner nature' fixed in an easily perceptible form and made readable. Neither, however, are the discursive formations territories on which non-discursive reality meets the narrating authority of reason, waiting to be let loose or deployed in the activity of discourse and thus to display its pre-existing and fully formed narrative potential. Discursive formations 'are not disturbing elements which, superimposing themselves upon its pure, neutral, atemporal, silent form, suppress its true voice and emit in its place a travestied discourse, but, on the contrary, its formative elements'.[4] Reason cannot legislate for discursive formation, being, as it were, formed by it much as the objects of its analysis and narration are. It is the incessant activity of discourse that spawns the narrated reality at one end and the narrating reason at the other. None of its twin products can claim an independent existence; none can boast the power to determine the flow of the discourse – and hence none can be legitimately construed as its *explanandum*.

Whatever authority presides over the delineation of the boundaries and the mechanisms that guard and secure their survival, must be found (if at all) *inside* the discursive practice. Its proper location hangs on the answers to such questions as: 'Who, among the totality of speaking individuals, is accorded the right to use this sort of language?' What are the *institutional sites* from which the use of such language is permitted, 'from which this discourse derives its legitimate source and point of application?' What are the situations 'in relation to the various domains or groups of objects' in which such 'institutional sites' are cast?[5] Let us note that among the questions to be answered the one most commonly asked by the standard history of science or philosophy – who are the individuals who in fact used the sort of language that makes the discourse, and to what effect? – is conspicuously absent. It is not the individuals, but the institutional sites from which they speak, that must be named if the discursive formation is to be properly described and its dynamism is to be adequately grasped. 'The subject of the statement' – Foucault insists – 'should not be regarded as identical with the author of the formulation.' What truly matters 'is a particular, vacant place that may in fact be filled by different individuals . . .':

> If a proposition, a sentence, a group of signs can be called 'statement', it is not because, one day, someone happened to speak them or put them into some concrete form of writing; it is because the position of the subject can be assigned. To describe a formulation *qua* statement does not consist in analysing the relations between the author and what he says (or wanted to say, or said without wanting to): but in determining what position can and must be occupied by any individual if he is to be the subject of it.[6]

Position implies a structure, structure implies a system, system implies boundaries: that is, the possibility of saying what belongs and what does not belong to the system; what does, and what does not is relevant to the determination of the position. Since it is not the personality and the will of the author of the statement, but the *possibility* of authoring a statement belonging to the discursive formation, that counts – the point of gravity of any description of sociology (or any other discipline, for that matter) lies in the mapping of its boundaries; a mapping that presupposes the reality of boundaries, that is the capacity of discursive formation to effectively draw and protect its boundaries – its only claim, as it were, to 'factual', objective existence.

In this vital respect, however, discursive formations vary. The boundary-drawing and boundary-defending capacity measures the degree of autonomy a given formation enjoys in relation to other discourses. Autonomy may be enhanced either by explicit or tacit, respectful or grudging acceptance by other discourses of the exclusive right of the given formation to draw its own boundaries (participants of any significant discourse would agree that only certified physicists can make statements belonging to physics; subjects of a totalitarian state would accept that only statements of the ruling party are properly political statements), or by rendering trespassing implausible by setting the formation outside the reach of other discourses (non-specialists would not challenge the statements of the physicists for lack of access to the events which they narrate; the subjects of an authoritarian government would not contest political pronunciations for lack of access to data guarded by the official secrets acts). More often than not, the two factors intertwine; they may well be seen on occasion as two formulations of the same state of affairs.

For instance, the matters dealt with by physics or astronomy hardly ever appear within the sight of non-physicists or non-astronomers. The non-experts cannot form opinions about such matters unless aided by – indeed, *instructed* – by the scientists of the field. The objects which sciences like these explore appear only under very special circumstances, to which no one else has access: on the screen of a multi-million-dollar accelerator, in the lens of a gigantic telescope, at the bottom of a thousand-foot deep shaft. Only the scientists can see them and experiment with them; these objects and events are, so to speak, a monopolistic possession of the given branch of science (or even of its selected practitioners); the monopoly has been assured by the fact that the objects and events in question would not occur if not for the scientists' own actions and the deployment of resources those scientists command; and thus the objects and events are, by the very nature of their appearance, a property unshared with anybody who is not a member of the profession. Monopoly of ownership has been guaranteed in advance by the nature of scientific practices, without recourse to legislation and law-enforcement (which would be necessary were the dealt-with objects and events in principle a part of a wider practice and hence accessible to outsiders). Being the sole owners of the experience which provides the raw material for their study, the scientists are in full control of the way the material is construed, processed, analysed, interpreted, narrated. Products of processing would have to withstand critical scrutiny of other scientists – but *their* scrutiny only. They will not have to compete with narratives construed outside the world limited by the walls of the laboratory or research institute; in particular, with no 'public' (read: non-specialist) opinion, no 'common' (read again: non-specialist) sense, or any other form in which the 'non-specialist' views may appear, for the simple reason that there is no 'public opinion' and no 'commonsensical' point of view in the matters they study and pronounce upon.

The privilege of discursive formations like physics or astronomy is not shared by such quasi-formations as are bound to exist parasitically upon objects and events already construed and pre-interpreted within other social discourses (that is, by virtually all formations that discursively process 'human made' realities, so called because of having been brought to the status of cognitive objects by the activities of men or women other than the self-proclaimed participants of the given formation; the latter, so to speak, arrive at the scene when the play is already in an advanced stage of the performance).

Sociology has been all along a foremost example of the discourses of the 'handicapped' category. Sociologists, as commentators on human experience, share their object with countless others, who may legitimately claim a first-hand knowledge of that experience. The object of sociological commentary is an already experienced experience, coming in the shape of a pre-formed narrative rather than a set of raw unnamed sensuous data waiting for a meaning to be offered by the subsequent commentary. Sociologists cannot even make a reasonable bid for the superiority, let alone exclusiveness, of their commentary over the interpretations produced incessantly by the direct 'owners' of experience and by other 'outside' commentators (writers, poets, journalists, politicians, religious thinkers) whose access to other people's experience is not dissimilar to that attained by the members of sociological profession and whose right to narrate the products of their interpretive work and to claim authority for them cannot be *proven* illegitimate, at least not off-hand. (To this plight, inferior and degrading when measured by the standards set by and for the 'better formatted' disciplines, sociologists striving for fully-fledged academic status may react, and did react, in a twofold way. They may simply deny the idiosyncrasy of their situation by treating its human subject matter as – in Kurt Wolff's apt metaphor – *puppets*: 'puppets mean nothing to themselves'; and they turn into puppets when sociology treats them 'as objects for its own [or somebody else's] purposes'. Or they may – with astoundingly similar consequences – simply surrender uncritically to the already 'accomplished' meanings entrenched in the social practices that parade as the 'objective reality'; to quote Kurt Wolff again, the human objects of sociological investigation may emerge as puppets merely as the side-effect of sociology trying diligently to 'account for social reality' which includes 'such features of our time and place as anonymity, loneliness, meaninglessness. In treating people as puppets, sociology repeats the treatment which many people more often than not experience and practice in our everyday world'.)[7]

One way or another, sociology fails the standards set by Foucault for discursive formations; sociological discourse is not a *formation* – as it has no authority over delineating its own boundaries, over setting the limits of the 'inside' from which valid or relevant statements can be made and distancing the 'outside' whose narrative products may be discarded as irrelevant. Any history of sociology that assumes otherwise and thus obliquely ascribes to sociological discourse a self-propelling autonomous logic it has not and could not possess, is misleading. Which does not mean, of course, that such history is likely to stop being written over again. It will be written as just one aspect of the unending war of independence, the discursive effort to promote the sociological commentary to the rank of autonomous or partly autonomous formation (alongside other efforts aimed at the same elusive goal – most prominently, the attempts to develop complex and sophisticated, specifically 'sociological' research methods, which, it is hoped, will remove the products of sociological commentary to a safe distance from lay scrutiny and, by the same token, assure their uncontested validity).

The fuzziness of boundaries is the major and decisive circumstance preventing the sociological discourse from ever turning into a fully-fledged formation. On the level of the narrative and its objects/products alike, sociological discourse is but a whirlpool in the incessant flow of human experience from which it draws and into which it discharges its material that, both before and after, is drawn into the orbit of countless other, similarly precarious and ill-defined quasi-formations. And yet the effort to elevate the discourse to the status of a formation cannot stop. Though the effort is bound to prove ineffective, it cannot be undertaken at all without a belief in the feasibility of success; discursive autonomy is the *focus imaginarius* that renders the blatantly non-autonomous discourse possible. The continuation of discourse in a recognizably sociological form, the maintenance of however counter-factual an appearance of continuity, the retention of a domain whose own logic of discourse may remain at least partly effective – all depend on the unrelenting drive towards autonomy. The drive may be self-defeating and doomed, but its relaxation, not to mention its end, would signal the dissipation and ultimately dismantling of the discourse.

This predicament of sociological discourse may be best grasped by the Kantian concept of *aesthetic community*, aptly described once by Jean-François Lyotard as 'escaping determination and arriving both too soon and too late'.[8] For Kant, the aesthetic community (that is, a territory defined by agreement inside well-protected boundaries) is and is bound to remain an *idea*: a promise, an expectation, a hope of unanimity that is not to be. Hope of unanimity brings the aesthetic community into being; unfulfilment of that hope keeps it alive. The aesthetic community owes its existence, so to speak, to a false promise. But individual choice cannot be committed without such promise.

> Kant uses the word 'promise' in order to point out the non-existent status of such a republic of taste (of the United Tastes?). The unanimity concerning what is beautiful has no chance of being actualized. But every actual judgment of taste carries with it the promise of universalization as a constitutive feature of its singularity.

> The community required as a support for the validity of such judgment must always be in the process of doing and undoing itself. The kind of consensus implied by such a process, if there is any consensus at all, is in no way argumentative but is rather allusive and elusive, endowed with a spiral way of being alive, combining both life and death, always remaining *in statu nascendi* or *moriendi*, always keeping open the issue of whether or not it actually exists. This kind of consensus is definitely nothing but a cloud of community.[9]

Sociological discourse sustains and reproduces such a 'cloud of community'; to be able to go on doing it with a measure of success, it must labour under the conviction that what is sustained and reproduced is not (or would not be eventually) a cloud but 'real community'. Yet were this belief ever to come true, discourse would fall apart. To remain alive, sociological discourse must aim at a goal which, if achieved, would mean its death.

SOCIAL LOCATIONS OF SOCIOLOGICAL DISCOURSE

Kurt Wolff's question, 'How can doing sociology be justified?' (at *this time of ours*, but for that matter at *any other* time) can be itself justified only within a discourse flawed as a formation. To a 'well formated' discipline, such a question would never occur or, if it perchance did, would be seen as meaningless. Only a discipline flawed as a discourse has to offer an apology, feels the need to justify its right to exist. If the existence follows rather than precedes the argument for need and pragmatic usefulness, a discourse lacking other (and presumably more solid) foundations would tend to measure the security of its existence by the persuasiveness of its case. Concern with self-justification has been, since the beginning, a conspicuous feature of sociological discourse.

'The beginning' was, of course, modern. Sociological discourse had been brought into being by the encounter between the awesome task of the management of social processes on a grand, societal scale and the ambitions of the modern state, made to the measure of such a task; it emerged to play the role of mediator between the two, to guide the engineering ambitions and to articulate the social condition as a collection of engineering *problems*.

American sociology was born in mid-western states in the heyday of the twin processes of urbanization and industrialization, massive immigration and new starts. That world was not only mysterious and unexplored, not to be trusted to follow the comfortingly familiar world; it was also poorly integrated and institutionalized, free from the constraining grip of cultural tradition and entrenched communal authorities, and for those reasons seemed utterly pliable – a grateful object for design and rational engineering. The universal modern tendency for social engineering found here the optimal, dreamt-of conditions: a *tabula rasa*, clean-slate situation in which everything seemed possible and nothing decent was likely to come about without the intervention and guidance of rational management.

Before they stormed the gates of universities and made their bid for the inclusion of sociology among the specialisms of university training, the founding fathers of American sociology shaped their world-view and sense of purpose in the ranks of 'social reformers'; people imbued with concern for law and order, or prompted to act by religious conscience and moral anxiety, but in each case convinced that conscious management of the human condition is a factor no complex society can do without. The 'science of society' was to be, in their view, first and foremost an instrument of social practice; and social practice was to be, first and foremost, aimed as the conscious 'solution' to spontaneously emerging 'problems'. The society they wished to study in a systematic and rational fashion was a *collection of problems* – and it ought to be systematically and rationally studied *because* it was a collection of problems. W. I. Thomas declared bluntly that the aim of sociology was 'the abolition of war, of crime, of drink, of abnormality, of slums, of this or that kind of unhappiness'.[10] The first university courses in sociology were 'predominantly oriented to social problems' and listed lectures and seminars in pauperism, charity, scientific philanthropy, private and public relief, unemployment, migratory labour, child labour, women wage-earners, labour movement, dependent children, insanity, illness, crime, juvenile delinquency, family instability, temperance, immigration, race relations, while Albion W. Small, in his Presidential Address of 1907, restated the thesis which had by then turned obvious by dint of constant repetition: that the investigation of social behaviour undertaken by sociology 'is not an end in itself', but must serve the ultimate realization of the highest 'spiritual possibilities of human beings' and the development of 'higher types of human association'.[11] Nowhere perhaps was the engineering-reformatory-managerial edge of the projected science of sociology protruding more sharply than in the *Prospectus* of the newly founded Chair of Sociology at Columbia, written in 1894 by Franklin H. Giddings:

> It is becoming more and more apparent that industrial and social progress is bringing the modern community face to face with social questions of the greatest magnitude, the solution of which will demand the best scientific study and the most honest practical endeavour. The term 'sociology', however it may be defined, includes a large number of subjects which are most seriously interesting men at the present time. The effective treatment of social problems demands that they be dealt with both theoretically and concretely.
>
> This newly established chair will provide for a thorough study of philosophical or general sociology and of the political or concrete social questions in their relation to sociological principles. By the term 'general sociology' is meant the scientific study of society as a whole, a search for its causes, for the laws of its structure and growth, and for a rational view of its purpose, function, meaning, or destiny. This will lead up to the more practical study of the phenomena of modern populations and their concentration in great cities. Of such phenomena none are of greater concern, from either

the theoretical or practical point of view, than the growth and characteristics of the dependent, defective, and delinquent classes. Special courses of instruction will, therefore, be offered on pauperism, poor laws, methods of charity, crime, penology, and social ethics.[12]

That sociology was hoped to be reformatory, and groomed to be managerial. The narrative of sociology was from the start (to use Bakhtin's term) *monological*[13] (more on this concept later); it construed populations it studied as *objects* moved by their proper constellations of external factors, much after the pattern of bodies shifted by the interplay of physical forces, and it denied or at least left out of the account the 'other' as another *consciousness*, as a partner in the dialogue. It was, to invoke once again Wolff's apt term, a 'sociology of puppets'. Aimed to be a tool of democratically conducted reform, it was not itself democratic. It took the accomplishment of the powers that be as the objectively given and non-negotiable 'facts of reality'. It knew in advance the meanings of 'defectiveness', 'delinquency' or 'socially ethical'. It accepted without questioning the right of the managers of social processes to determine the distinction between proper and improper, between norm and deviation; so much so that the fact that the distinctions are indeed *determined*, an outcome of management or a flawed dialogue, went on eluding attention. It staunchly remained a narrative resource, hardly ever turning itself (or the ontological status of its object – which amounted to the same) into an object of investigation. The very hope that the emerging sociology could serve the tasks of social improvement as defined by managerial purposes was founded in the imagery of 'tough reality' or 'natural laws of society'. The same imagery warranted the postulate of *objective* research and sustained the importance of methodological refinement and the obsessive attention paid to the development of research tools.

It was because 'social science developed largely as a way of perceiving, evaluating, and correcting the frictions and tensions generated by the high rate of individual mobility and institutional change in modernizing society' that it grew 'primarily as an empirical, quantitative, policy-related *method of inquiry* (not a system of beliefs)',[14] and that by 1959 a leading member of the sociological profession in the USA could observe that

contemporary sociology in America . . . is a discipline defined more by its special methods of research than by either its conclusions or its subject matter. . . . We will understand contemporary sociology better by considering the phenomenon of the men who wanted to measure everything than by remaining fixed on those who wanted to destroy or rebuild everything.[15]

There was, so to speak, an *elective affinity* between the scientifically objective ambitions of the rising sociology and its managerial involvement – on the latter's 'supply' as well as 'demand' side. The 'push' and the 'pull' factors reinforced each other; the more the sociologists stressed the fact-gathering, value-free, diagnostic quality of their work, the higher seemed the managerial potential of their services; the more the managers believed that this was the case, the more intense were the self-correcting and self-streamlining preoccupations of the sociologists. The fast sprawling and swelling New Deal state and federal bureaucracy provided the first powerful stimulus for the entrenchment of 'monologistic' sociological narrative. Then came big business, sensing in the impressively precise diagnostic capacities of sociologists a useful tool for resolving problems piling up on the way to the implementation of managerial tasks. It was through the influence of business-sponsored foundations that the pragmatics of sociology as, first and foremost, perhaps exclusively, a *behavioural science* (one aiming 'to understand, explain, and predict human behaviour in the same sense in which scientists understand, explain, and predict the behaviour of physical forces or biological entities or, closer still, the behaviour of goods and prices in the economic market' (Berelson) – an explicitly monologistic narrative, construing its object as a pliable or resistant focus of action whose meaning and purpose is invariably extrinsically determined. According to Bernard Berelson's testimony,

Although the phrase 'behavioural science' was used from time to time over a period of years it never caught on until about ten years ago when the Ford Foundation used the term as a shorthand description of its programme on Individual Behaviour and Human Relations. For about six years in the 1950s the Foundation operated a Behavioural Sciences Programme and supported this field in the amount of several millions of dollars. It was at this time that the term came into widespread use, and it was then that some people began to wonder whether they too were not behavioural scientists after all![16]

Once the whole impact of new and rising demand filtered through the academic profession, it could be observed, with no small satisfaction, that

> behavioural scientists are employed as such, and in increasing numbers, by governments, by business and industry, by hospitals and other agencies devoted to problems of health, by correctional institutions, by welfare agencies, by city commissions, by school systems, and by many, many other types of organizations and enterprises in which some systemic knowledge of human behaviour is required.[17]

In each case, let us comment, sociologists were employed for the same purpose of management and control. In Samuel S. Stouffer's view, 'the point, of course, is that research which is done to establish facts important for practical decisions needs to be searching and accurate and there is money to pay for it because so much depends on it'.[18] The growing obsession with the sharpening of research–diagnostic tools was justified in terms of the pragmatic, no–nonsense demands of the clients interested in effective control of the processes they managed. The argument that could not but expose and openly flout the subordination of social research to the power-holders' purposes opened sociology to the charge of exerting anti-democratic influence. It must be admitted that the charge was faced point-blank; the practitioners and defenders of monologistic sociology retorted that

> society can not survive without its many forms of social control, ranging from legislation and the policeman on the street to informal praise and mass ridicule, all capable of misuse. Improved understanding of human behaviour does no more than make possible improved utilization of the existing forms of social control for socially approved purposes, and, unfortunately, also for unconscionable human manipulation.[19]

At least in the USA the social location of sociology in its formative years and in the following period of affluence and self-importance was the public and private world of management. Its partners in discourse, often *the* significant partners, the chairpersons and the agenda-setters of the debate, were the designers and the administrators of social order on a macro- or micro-scale; the planners of New Deal or War on Poverty projects, the public relations and public opinion managers, executives of big companies, interested in a wide range of functionally distinct tasks that nevertheless had their common denominator in 'changing behaviour', stifling, neutralizing or bypassing the subjectivity of the human objects of purposeful action. The presence of such silent yet all-powerful partners of sociological discourse was felt in the sociologists' preoccupation with quantifying, 'statisticalizing', factor analysis; in the language of the discourse, articulating the universe under analysis into intrinsically asymmetrical processes like power, influence, socialization, deviation or control; in the widespread inclination for functional analysis, or for the principle that 'the whole is more than the sum of its parts' (this 'more' referring implicitly to the presence of the controlling agent) as the premise of the distinctly sociological theorization of human reality – both indicating the tendency to locate the meaning, and the interpretive ground, of action outside the life-world of the actors themselves. Sociological discourse was formed within the perspective of *managed social processes*, one that cast social reality as an object of a designed change and hence brought into relief aspects selected for their positive or negative relevance to practical success while *disarticulating* all other aspects. It was the design – any design, but always a design, always a prospect involving managerial action aimed at a behavioural change – that endowed human reality as construed in sociological discourse with (differentiated) meaning. As long as *both* the political state *and* private companies entertained designing-managerial ambitions and remained embarked on planned change in their respective, grand or confined, realms – a resonance of sorts could exist between macro-social models and micro-social practices of sociology, similarly informed by the managerial spirit: a unity that found in the end its programmatic expression in the daring totalistic project of Talcott Parsons; more tellingly still, in its inordinately enthusiastic reception.

This resonance has been undermined, weakened, perhaps broken altogether with the gradual retreat of the political state (its actual and aspiring ruling forces alike) from the programmes of grand social engineering and the ceding of the management of social processes as well as crucial tasks of overall social control to market mechanisms.

On the intellectual level, this rearrangement has been reflected in the unprecedented unpopularity of the 'social engineering mentality', the rejection of 'utopianism' and 'foundationalism' and the new sympathetic interest in the same spontaneity and 'messiness' of indigenous social processes that the modern project of managed society once set out to eliminate or tame. The two changes combine into what is often referred to as the advent of *postmodernity*: a bunch of intellectual attitudes ranging from the plaintive admission of the ultimate irreality of modern dreams of an orderly, rational society, to an angry rejection of modern ambitions as they stand charged with arrogance, inhumanity and unavoidably morbid consequences.

It is difficult to say what came first, what came second. Was it the erosion of ecumenical powers that rebounded in the intellectual devaluation of universalistic values? Or was it the gathering evidence of the 'sorcerer's apprentice' effect of the modern bid for control, and the revulsion it caused, that led to the refusal of co-operation with the tasks set by 'normalizing' powers? The second hypothesis, as more flattering to contemporary philosophers and sociologists, is clearly favoured by the writers of their autobiographies; its popularity notwithstanding, it remains less convincing, in view of the fact that for almost half a century that has passed since Auschwitz and Hiroshima the social sciences have failed spectacularly to revise their understanding of the world and of their place in it,[20] and that still in 1982 one could write that 'much of life and thought as it is still carried on now is based on the assumption that Auschwitz and Hiroshima never happened, or, if they did, then only as mere events, far away and long ago, that need not concern us now'.[21] Without deciding between the rival hypotheses, we can still agree that much as there was an intimate link between universal ambitions of legislative powers and the unchallenged domination of legislative reason in philosophical and social-scientific discourses, there is more than coincidence in the simultaneous erosion of the two.

FROM MONOLOGUE TO DIALOGUE

Commenting on the work of Richard Rorty (that by far the most symptomatic expression of the current intellectual re-orientation), David R. Hiley suggests that

in so far as philosophy has a unique role in the conversation, it is not to secure the foundations of inquiry for the rest of culture or to serve as a tribunal of reason before which the rest of inquiry is to be judged. Its role is merely to prevent the partners of the conversation from the self-deception of thinking that momentary agreement is the whole truth for time and eternity. The end of philosophy is not to achieve the truth about ourselves but to keep the conversation going by constantly calling current agreement into question and sending the conversation off in new directions.[22]

This seems to be a recipe for an obstreperous, irreverent philosophy, one that makes an avocation out of the melting of solids and profaning the sacred, that cares little about the solemnity of chairpersons, the dull routine of rule-governed debate and the stultifying grip of agendas. It comes close to Foucault's description of critical thought as consisting in 'the endeavour to know how and to what extent it might be possible to think differently, instead of legitimizing what is already known';[23] Rorty himself describes the philosophy he promotes as *abnormal discourse*:

Normal discourse is that which is conducted within an agreed-upon set of conventions about what counts as a relevant contribution, what counts as answering a question, what counts as knowing a good argument for that answer or a good criticism of it. Abnormal discourse is what happens when someone joins in the discourse who is ignorant of these conventions or who sets them aside.[24]

Once again, philosophy becomes the pastime of Mannheimian *strangers*; but this time not in their capacity of courtly jesters or royal advisors, but of rebels disdainful of the courtly etiquette, or self-appointed Parsifals making a point of remaining naively unaware of the power-assisted ways and means of the world. Foucault's critical thought and Rorty's abnormal discourse (named in other contexts the *edifying philosophy*) confine their ambitions to the corrosion of universalistic, legislative pretences; they derive their determination not from the desire to 'correct', to standardize, to 'normalize', to 'rationalize' – but from an overwhelming feeling of solidarity with other human beings; a solidarity threatened by the very prospect of 'setting things right' disguised as a promise of liberation; by the thrust toward omnipotence of the species-Man, bought at the expense of the powerlessness of the men and women that make the species.

From the vantage point of this new sensibility, both modern philosophy and modern sociology (now turned into a *yesterday* philosophy and sociology) are accused of pursuing, through thick and thin, the elusive target of the purely *monologistic* discourse (in Bakhtin's memorable rendering, 'monologism ideally denies the presence – outside its own realm – of the other as an equal, answering consciousness, as another legally endowed "I" (*thou*). For the monologistic attitude, in its liminal or pure form, the *other* remains solely an *object* of consciousness – it never becomes another consciousness').[25] Two prominent Soviet philosophers, Gozman and Etkind, suggested recently an intimate link between the intellectual strategy of monologism and the class of political programmes they dubbed *monophilic*[26] – one entailing totalitarianism as its most vivid, liminal specimen yet accommodating the intentions and hidden tendencies, if not always practices, of all typically modern regimes. 'Monophilia' is marked by the belief in a simple and essentially atemporal structure of the world (or at least an essential reducibility of the world to simple factors and indivisible units), by the conviction that the 'proper world' (just society, good life, rational conduct, etc.) can be constituted by a thorough application of one dominant and decisive standard, and that extraordinary rupture of continuity originated and managed by a condensed effort of will (Gozman and Etkind call it 'belief in miracles') may secure the passage from one class of uniform phenomena to another. The monologistic mind faithfully reflected, and in its turn informed, the reality administered by monophilic power. The two were born together and since their birth shared victories and defeats; they sustained each other, exchanging confidence-inspiring formulae for the conjured-up proofs of their realism. It is their fate to remain united in the midst of the current crisis, the time when monologism retreats before the advancing (welcomed or enforced) dialogue, while monophilia surrenders to the ever more evident resilience of pluralism.

Kurt Wolff's question ('How can doing sociology be justified at this time?') conveys the sense we all share: that of standing on a uniquely confusing crossroads. There is no way back, and the experience distilled from past wanderings cannot be trusted to guide us unambiguously in the choice of a path still to be made. The awkward and unwieldy concept of postmodernity was coined to account for this kind of feeling: the thrust that brought us here is to be discarded, but what is bound to be discarded with it is precisely that confidence and self-assurance that we most badly need to make the choice we cannot but make.

And yet the condition is less dramatic than it seems to be when viewed in the light of the now ostensibly abandoned modernist conviction that only the decisions standing up to the test of universal, objective reason are likely to lead to consequences both useful and desirable. We still wish to be guided by principles that we would like others to accept; but we may resign ourselves to the possibility (even the likelihood) that others may not accept them, and then refrain from efforts to force them to do so, and rejoice in their ability to resist such efforts if made. We may, in other words, retain our hope for a better world that could be, as well as a commitment to disaffection with the world that is and to its critical *Aufhebung*, while abandoning the role of the tribunal and the ultimate sanction of the prison network, let alone Auschwitz, the Gulag and Hiroshima.

From the lofty heights of modernist ambitions, this programme looks unforgivably modest. It contains no reference to legislative entitlements, to the correction of common sense, to obligatory truth and universally binding norms (no wonder that it begets the all-too-predictable reaction of the bureaucratic mind, trained to think in terms of instrumental utilities: 'Just why do you think the taxpayer should finance this sort of useless self-indulgence?'). It tells us instead of the universal ungroundedness of all and any form of life, and warns of the harm that comes from all attempts to compensate for existential weakness and diversified and contingent human reality with the strength of coercive uniformity.

And it can hardly tell us anything else. This is, after all, a programme articulated within a discursive formation strikingly different from the one that accommodated sociological discourse throughout the modern era. From this discursive formation the power-holders, the managers of social processes, the dreamers of artificial order have all but opted out. With them, off went the demand for the legislative services of sociology and the self-authenticating potential of the sociologists' normative zeal. The vacated place need not remain vacant, though. For critical and emancipatory sociology, this departure may mean liberation as much as it spells bereavement for the legislative and normative one. A new discursive formation (of a *dialogical*, not *monological*, sociology) may well be sustained and kept alive by the spirit of loyalty and solidarity with fellow humans faced with the implacable reality of their contingency and the horrors of freedom and responsibility of choice. Existence that knows of its ungroundedness and that no longer believes in promises to supply concrete foundations needs, more than at any other time, a reflective, critical self-understanding; it may even – who knows? – come to know that it needs it. Sociology may then come to fulfil, at long last, the Enlightenment dream of the meeting of rational minds – without recourse to the post-Enlightenment subterfuges of blind alleys or twisted roads to Auschwitz, masquerading as short-cuts to a world without problems, conflicts and change.

SOCIOLOGIA DUPLEX

Pascal commented on Plato and Aristotle, that 'if they wrote on politics, it was as if laying down rules for a lunatic asylum'. Hannah Arendt unpacked Pascal's quip: 'Plato clearly wrote the *Republic* to justify the notion that philosophers should become kings . . . because . . . it would bring about in the commonwealth that complete quiet, that absolute peace, that certainly constitutes the best condition for the life of the philosophers.'[27] It is the philosophers who wove the canvas of imaginary bliss, who told the story of the good society that was not yet and the bad society that was; predictably, philosophers could not conceive of good society otherwise than in the shape of a world made to their own measurements; a world that takes it to be its major (perhaps only) task to permit the philosophers to do undisturbed what they intend to do anyway and what, being philosophers, they cannot but go on doing. The world forgetful of such task is, truly, a lunatic asylum. To make it into a livable world, one needs to lay down rules, and make the inhabitants doggedly observe them: if called to be kings, philosophers intended to do just that. Or, rather, this is what they expected a king to do were he to be conferred the honorific title of philosopher. And yet – if philosophers hailed absolute peace for its service to philosophy, the kings listened to philosophers (if they did) and tolerated philosophy (if they did) for the services they hoped would be rendered to assist their efforts to make peace absolute.

The pattern first seen in the *Republic* survived into the modern age when, finally, it could become more than a literary device; when kings did appear who could contemplate absolute peace as a *practical* task: they had the resources, the tools, and thus also the will. Legislative reason met with the practice of legislators, ideas turned into a material force. It might have seemed that the marriage thus consummated was preordained and that the couple was bound to remain united in wedlock forever: that philosophy and its social-scientific, 'applied' extensions were meant by nature to serve the designers and guardians of order. That this is not the case (not now), that it is not easy to make it a case (for now), has become increasingly obvious as modernity progressed and its postmodern destination became discernible. The question is, however, whether this *was ever the case* – even at a time when it was earnestly wished to be and seemed to be.

The latter doubts arise out of the inherent and irreparable duality (two-facedness, two-functionality) of the social-scientific enterprise. On the one hand, sociology in all forms and independently of its specific school loyalty must always start from an already-present society; even in its nominalistic version, it deals with individuals in their social habitat, individuals already 'made human', i.e. *socialized*, trained, cultured. A non-social or pre-social human being cannot be spoken of in the language of sociology (not seriously, not as anything but polemical construct), as this language is formed precisely to articulate 'the social' in the individual and to construe the rest as either a raw material for social processing or unmanageable ('sociopathic') residue. Sociology, therefore, willynilly accepts socially produced existence as 'objective reality', and admits its authority to set apart the real and realistic from the unreal and irrealistic; it accepts it as the rule of its grammar well before any of its positive statements will have been made. On the other hand, however, sociology cannot but represent this objective reality of the human as a *social accomplishment*: as an artifice, as something 'less-than-absolute', something inherently and irremediably brittle, relative, questionable and challengeable, produced by society and sustained solely by the work and the vigilance of society (by socially constructed and controlled norms and values). Society, in other words, is simultaneously *promoted* by sociology to the status of the ultimate standard of sociologically produced knowledge and *demoted* as a factor which inevitably temporalizes and localizes all standards of valid knowledge.

The two messages of sociology can be no more set apart and separated than the two faces of a coin. Each is possible only thanks to the presence of another; each sustains and reinforces the other.

Thus sociology can 'side with' the designers and guardians of social order only on its own terms – the terms which the power-holding recipients of its services must find uncomfortable and potentially threatening, whatever the verbal zeal with which the alliance is offered. However keen is the assertion of the present naturalness of the social order, it cannot be delivered without rousing the spectre of its past artificiality (and thus questioning a priori the identity of the presently-natural order as 'order as such', as the only form which 'the other of chaos' may take). Sociology, one may say, can assist the extant order of society only by sapping it: by inviting and legitimizing its critique and spreading the message (short of an explicit message, a suspicion) of its non-invincibility.

The inherent duality of the sociological enterprise has been grasped and expressed in a number of different ways. More often than not, as the alleged choice between a 'conservative' and a 'progressive' engagement; between a commitment to the tightening of external, socially managed conditions of individual life and thus making individual conduct more regular and predictable (thereby protecting the social order at the expense of individual freedom), and the commitment to the widening of individual self-knowledge and conscious choice and thus making individual conduct more voluntaristic and unpredictable (thereby promoting individual freedom at the expense of the manageability of the social order). But sociology does not have such a choice – not in relation to the 'society as a whole', society as a global, administered and managed system. It cannot perform one of the two jobs without spawning knowledge which can be, at least potentially, deployed in the performance of the other. To put it yet more bluntly, critical theory and practice is not one of the strategies sociology can embrace or reject at will. Sociology cannot help but be critical; that is, to supply material amenable to critical uses. And the reverse is true as well: it is hard to imagine a sociological critique that could not in principle be deployed to tighten the grip of the extant or future social institutions.

The slow decline and rapid discrediting of global-engineering projects, traditionally entertained by the national state bent on the installing and servicing of a global social order, may well defuse the 'conservative–radical' controversy. The two functions of sociology now have fields of application that do not come into direct contact. Large-scale organizations (still the potential recipients of sociology's managerial wisdom), emphatically disown responsibility for the management of the social order, happy as they are with 'rationalizing' their own internal and strictly confined environment. The global order has split into many local, partial, functionally specific and privately policed mini-orders. This leaves individuals, conducting their life-business in the interstices of such partial orders, with the *chance* of self-construction and self-management (yet a chance that must be *necessarily* embraced). However tightly administered is each of the many mini-orders that combine in the setting of the individual life-process, this setting (for the lack of global co-ordination expressible in a unifying, *Weltanschauung*-type formula) appears to the individual incurably contingent; an arena of freedom and uncertainty, choice and inconclusiveness. Managerial interests in the streamlining of their own enclaves of order and the self-monitoring interests of the individuals (that is, outside the subordinate roles the latter may play part-time in one or another of the mini-orders) are not in competition and are not bent on extinguishing or even constraining each other. On the contrary – they are tied together in a relationship of mutual dependency and reinforcement.[28]

Thus the two faces of sociology are not turned now in opposite and mutually hostile directions, and this new situation rebounds in reducing the inner tension which plagued the sociological enterprise for the duration of the modern age. The two messages/services of sociology do not seem to clash as jarringly and fatally as they once did. Since the modern 'state vs individual' contention that cast it as such has subsided and lost part of its past venom, sociology itself begins to look much less demonic than it used to. No more is it an object of contradictory territorial claims; such claims as are still made are more a tribute to the memory of past battles than fruits of current concerns. They incite but a half-hearted, lackadaisical opposition.

The guardians of mini-orders and the individuals abandoned to the tasks of self-construction alike have developed vested interests in *managerial services*; in a kind of reliable, practically useful knowledge that could be deployed in designing realistic projects and making them effective. The two demands cast the sociologists, as the self-proclaimed purveyors of such services, in a similar field of expertise. The two applications of expert knowledge (in management and in self-management) may differ in scale, but not in substance. They are not at cross-purposes, as the tasks on which they are targeted are mutually functional and complementary. Moreover, the nature of service has undergone a profound change. The knowledge expected to be delivered is not to be made after the pattern of legislative reason. It is to be rather an *interpretive*, a 'sense-making', a 'world-mapping' knowledge, that results in a mental setting in which decisions are taken and freedom of choice is exercised.

In other words, the door through which sociology enters the social and individual life alike is that of self-monitoring. Ours is a self-reflexive world (as Anthony Giddens has demonstrated to great effect);[29] self-reflection, monitoring the outcome of past action, revising the plan according to the result of the reflection, re-drawing the map of the situation as the latter keeps changing in the course and under the influence of action, re-evaluation of the original purposes and adequacy of the originally selected means, and above all an ongoing reassessment of the plural and uncoordinated values and strategies, have replaced to great extent the deterministic push of tradition both on the organizational and the individual level. The new situation shapes its own demands for a social-scientific expertise. It calls for a sociology resonant with its own structure: that is, a sociology as a flexible and self-reflective activity of interpretation and reinterpretation, as an on-going *commentary* on the many-centred process of interplay between relatively autonomous yet partially dependent agents (dependency and autonomy being themselves important stakes of the game). Self-reflexivity and the ensuing flexibility of sociological commentary by itself facilitates the activity of self-monitoring – as it demonstrates in practice (even if not in theory) the *non-exclusiveness* of any of the competing interpretations, the absence of a single *authoritative* standpoint from which unambiguous and universally binding pronouncements can be made, and the mutual interpenetration and inter-feeding of interpretations and their ostensible objects which they generate while pretending to reflect.

One may say that the interweaving, simultaneity (rather than opposition and functional – as well as temporal – separation) of Elias's 'detachment and involvement', or Wolff's 'surrender and catch' has become now a more realistic prospect for sociology than at any other time of its history. It is because of that interweaving that sociology, for once, does not need *protreptics*; that it need neither apologize for its presence in the world nor justify its right to remain there.

NOTES

1 Michel Foucault, *The Archeology of Knowledge,* trans. by A.M. Sheridan Smith (London: Tavistock, 1974), p. 37.
2 Ibid., pp. 46, 47.
3 Ibid., p. 44.
4 Ibid., p. 68.
5 Ibid., pp. 50–2.
6 Ibid., pp. 95–6.
7 Kurt H. Wolff, *Survival and Sociology* (New Brunswick: Transactions, 1991), pp. 103–4.
8 Jean-François Lyotard, *Peregrinations: Law, Form, Event* (Columbia University Press, 1988), p. 32.
9 Ibid., p. 38.
10 Quoted in Leon Bramson, *The Political Context of Sociology* (Princeton University Press, 1961), p. 90.
11 Quoted in Roscoe C. Hinkle and Gisela J. Hinkle, *The Development of Modern Sociology: Its Nature and Growth in the USA* (New York: Doubleday & Co., 1954), pp. 4, 9.
12 Quoted in Howard W. Odum, *American Sociology: The Story of Sociology in the USA through 1950* (New York: Columbia University Press, 1951), pp. 60–1.
13 M. Bakhtin, Estetika slovesnovo trorchestra (*Aesthetics of Verbal Creativity*) (Moscow: Nauka, 1986), p. 336.
14 Daniel Lerner, *The Human Meaning of the Social Sciences* (New York: Meridian Books, 1959), pp. 8, 19.
15 Nathan Glazer, 'The rise of social research in Europe', in: ibid., pp. 43, 45.
16 Bernard Berelson, *Introduction to the Behavioural Sciences,* The Voice of America Forum Lecture, pp. 1, 2–3.
17 John W. Riley, *Some Contributions of Behavioural Science to Contemporary Life,* The Voice of America Forum Lecture, p. 1.
18 Samuel S. Stouffer, *Methods of Research Used by American Behavioural Scientists,* The Voice of America Forum Lecture, p. 2.
19 Donald R. Young, *Behavioural Science Application in the Professions,* The Voice of America Forum Lecture, p. 7.
20 Cf. Zygmunt Bauman, *Modernity and the Holocaust* (Cambridge: Polity Press, 1989).
21 Harry Redner, *In the Beginning was the Deed; Reflections on the Passage of Faust* (University of California Press, 1982), p. xi.
22 David R. Hiley, *Philosophy in Question; Essays on a Pyrrhonian Theme* (University of Chicago Press, 1988), p. 145.
23 Michel Foucault, *The Use of Pleasure,* vol. 2 (New York: Pantheon Books, 1985), p. 9.
24 Richard Rorty, *Philosophy and the Mirror of Nature* (Princeton University Press, 1979), p. 320.
25 M. Bakhtin, Estetika slovesnovo trorchestra p. 336.
26 L. Gozman and A. Etkind, 'Kult vlasti', in *Osmyslitkult Stalina* (Moscow:

Progress, 1989), pp. 365ff.

27 Hannah Arendt, *Lectures on Kant's Political Philosophy*, ed. by Ronald Beiner (Brighton: Harvester, 1982), p. 22.

28 As Peter F. Drucker recently observed, management has become now 'all-pervasive', penetrating every nook and cranny of social and individual life and turning into *the* way of acting and doing. Under these conditions, 'the truly important problems managers face do not come from technology or politics. They do not originate outside management and enterprise. They are problems caused by the very success of management itself' (*The New Realities*, London: Mandarin, 1990, p. 214 ff).

29 Comp. particularly Anthony Giddens's *Consequences of Modernity* (Cambridge: Polity Press, 1990), but also his forthcoming *Modernity and Self-identity*.

4

IS THERE A
POSTMODERN SOCIOLOGY?

Why do we need the concept of 'postmodernity'? On the face of it, this concept is redundant. In so far as it purports to capture and articulate what is novel at the present stage of western history, it legitimizes itself in terms of a job which has been already performed by other, better established concepts – like those of the 'post-capitalist' or 'post-industrial' society. Concepts which have served the purpose well: they sharpened our attention to what is new and discontinuous, and offered a reference point for counter-arguments in favour of continuity.

Is, therefore, the advent of the 'postmodernity' idea an invitation to rehash or simply replay an old debate? Does it merely signify an all-too-natural fatigue, which a protracted and inconclusive debate must generate? Is it merely an attempt to inject new excitement into an increasingly tedious pastime (as Gordon Allport once said, we social scientists never solve problems; we only get bored with them)? If this is the case, then the idea of 'postmodernity' is hardly worth a second thought, and this is exactly what many a seasoned social scientist suggests.

Appearances are, however, misleading (and the advocates and the detractors of the idea of 'postmodernity' share the blame for confusion). The concept of 'postmodernity' may well capture and articulate a quite different sort of novelty than those the older, apparently similar concepts accommodated and theorized. It can legitimize its right to exist – its cognitive value – only if it does exactly this: if it generates a social-scientific discourse which theorizes different aspects of contemporary experience, or theorizes them in a different way.

I propose that the concept of 'postmodernity' has a value entirely of its own in so far as it purports to capture and articulate the

93

novel experience of just one, but one crucial social category of contemporary society: the intellectuals. Their novel experience – that is, their reassessment of their own position within society, their reorientation of the collectively performed function, and their new strategies.

Antonio Gramsci called the 'organic intellectuals' of a particular class the part of the educated elite which elaborated the self-identity of the class, the values instrumental to the defence and enhancement of its position within society, an ideology legitimizing its claims to autonomy and domination. One may argue to what extent Gramsci's (1971) 'organic intellectuals' did in fact answer this description; to what extent they were busy painting their own idealized portraits, rather than those of their ostensible sitters; to what extent the likenesses of all other classes represented (unknowingly, to be sure) the painters' cravings for conditions favourable and propitious for the kind of work the intellectuals had been best prepared, and willing, to do. In the discourse of 'postmodernity', however, the usual disguise is discarded. The participants of the discourse appear in the role of 'organic intellectuals' of the intellectuals themselves. The concept of 'postmodernity' makes sense in so far as it stands for this 'coming out' of the intellectuals.

The other way of putting it is to say that the concept of 'postmodernity' connotes the new self-awareness of the 'intellectuals' – this part of the educated elite which has specialized in elaborating principles, setting standards, formulating social tasks and criteria of their success or failure. Like painters, novelists, composers, and to a rapidly growing extent the scientists before them, such intellectuals have now come to focus their attention on their own skills, techniques and raw materials, which turn from tacitly present means into a conscious object of self-perfection and refinement and the true and sufficient subject-matter of intellectual work.

This implosion of intellectual vision, this 'falling upon oneself', may be seen as either a symptom of retreat and surrender, or a sign of maturation. Whatever the evaluation of the fact, it may be interpreted as a response to the growing sense of failure, inadequacy or irrealism of the traditional functions and ambitions, as sedimented in historical memory and institutionalized in the intellectual mode of existence. Yet it was this very sense of failure which rendered the ambitions and the functions visible.

'Postmodernity' proclaims the loss of something we were not aware of possessing until we learned of the loss. This view of past 'modernity' which the 'postmodernity' discourse generates is made entirely out of present-day anxiety and uneasiness, as a model of a universe in which such anxiety and uneasiness could not arise (much like the view of 'community', of which Raymond Williams (1975) said that it 'always has been'). The concept of 'modernity' has today a quite different content from the one it had before the start of the 'postmodern' discourse; there is little point in asking whether it is true or distorted, or in objecting to the way it is handled inside the 'postmodern' debate. It is situated in that debate, it draws its meaning from it, and it makes sense only jointly with the other side of the opposition, the concept of 'postmodernity', as that negation without which the latter concept would be meaningless. The 'postmodern' discourse generates its own concept of 'modernity', made of the presence of all those things for the lack of which the concept of 'postmodernity' stands.

The anxiety which gave birth to the concept of 'postmodernity' and the related image of past 'modernity' is admittedly diffuse and ill-defined, but nevertheless quite real. It arises from the feeling that the kind of services the intellectuals have been historically best prepared to offer, and from which they derived their sense of social importance, are nowadays not easy to provide; and that the demand for such services is anyway much smaller than one would expect it to be. It is this feeling which leads to a 'status crisis'; a recognition that the reproduction of the status which the intellectuals got used to seeing as theirs by right, would now need a good deal of rethinking as well as the reorientation of habitual practices.

The services in question amount to the provision of an authoritative solution to the questions of cognitive truth, moral judgment and aesthetic taste. It goes without saying that the importance of such services is a reflection of the size and importance of the demand for them; with the latter receding, their *raison d'être* is eroded. In its turn, the demand in question draws its importance from the presence of social forces, which need the authority of cognitive and normative judgments as the legitimation of their actual, or strived-for domination. There must be such forces; they must need such legitimation; and the intellectuals must retain the monopoly on its provision. The 'status crisis', or rather that vague feeling of anxiety for which it can serve as a plausible interpretation, can be made sense of if account is taken of the undermining of the conditions of intellectual status in at least three crucial respects.

First of all, the advanced erosion of that global structure of domination, which – at the time the modern intellectuals were born – supplied the 'evidence of reality' of which the self-confidence of the west and its spokesmen has been built. Superiority of the west over the rest remained self-evident for almost three centuries. It was not, as it were, a matter of idle comparison. The era of modernity had been marked by an active superiority: part of the world constituted the rest as inferior – either as a crude, still unprocessed 'raw material' in need of cleaning and refinement, or a temporarily extant relic of the past. Whatever could not be brought up to the superior standards, was clearly destined for an existence of subordination. Western practices defined the rest as a pliable or malleable substance still to be given shape. This active superiority meant the right of the superior to proselytize, to design the suitable form of life for the others, to refuse to grant authority to the ways of life which did not fit that design.

Such superiority could remain self-evident as long as the denied authority showed no signs of reasserting itself, and the designs seemed irresistible. A historical domination could interpret itself as universal and absolute, as long as it could believe that the future would prove it such; the universality of the western mode (the absoluteness of western domination) seemed indeed merely a matter of time. The grounds for certainty and self-confidence could not be stronger. Human reality indeed seemed subject to unshakeable laws and stronger ('progressive') values looked set to supersede or eradicate the weaker ('retrograde', ignorant, superstitious) ones. It was this historically given certainty, grounded in the unchallenged superiority of forces aimed at universal domination, which had been articulated, from the perspective of the intellectual mode, as universality of the standards of truth, judgment and taste. The strategy such articulation legitimated was to supply the forces bent on universal and active domination, with designs dictated by universal science, ethics and aesthetics.

The certitude of yesteryear is now at best ridiculed as naïvety, at worst castigated as ethnocentric. Nobody but the most rabid of the diehards believes today that the western mode of life, either the actual one or one idealized ('utopianized') in the intellectual mode, has more than a sporting chance of ever becoming universal. No social force is in sight (including those which, arguably, are today aiming at global domination) bent on making it universal. The search for universal standards has suddenly become gratuitous; there is no credible 'historical agent' to which the findings could be addressed and entrusted. Impracticality erodes interest. The task of establishing universal standards of truth, morality, taste does not seem so important. Unsupported by will, it appears now misguided and unreal.

Second, even localized powers, devoid of ecumenical ambitions, seem less receptive to the products of intellectual discourse. The time modern intellectuals were born was one of the great 'shake-up': everything solid melted into air, everything sacred was profaned. . . . The newborn absolutist state did not face the task of wrenching power from old and jaded hands; it had to create an entirely new kind of social power, capable of carrying the burden of *societal* integration. The task involved the crushing of those mechanisms of social reproduction which had been based in communal traditions. Its performance took the form of a 'cultural crusade'; that is, practical destruction of communal bases of social power, and theoretical delegitimation of their authority. Faced with such tasks, the state badly needed 'legitimation' (this is the name given to intellectual discourse when considered from the vantage point of its power-oriented, political application).

Mais où sont les croisades d'antan? The present-day political domination can reproduce itself using means more efficient and less costly than 'legitimation'. Weber's 'legal–rational legitimation' – the point much too seldom made – is, in its essence, a declaration of the redundancy of legitimation. The modern state is effective without authority; or, rather, its effectiveness depends to a large extent on rendering authority irrelevant. It no longer matters, for the effectiveness of state power, and for the reproduction of political domination in general, whether the social area under domination is culturally unified and uniform, or how idiosyncratic are the values sectors of this area may uphold.

The weapon of legitimation has been replaced with two mutually complementary weapons: this of *seduction* and that of *repression*. Both need intellectually trained experts, and indeed both siphon off, accommodate and domesticate an ever growing section of the educated elite. Neither has a need, or room, for those 'hard-core' intellectuals whose expertise is 'legitimation', i.e. supplying proof that what is being done is universally correct and absolutely true, moral and beautiful.

Seduction is the paramount tool of integration (of the reproduction of domination) in a consumer society. It is made possible once the market succeeds in making the consumers dependent on itself. Market-dependency is achieved through the destruction of such skills (technical, social, psychological, existential) as do not entail the use of marketable commodities; the more complete the destruction, the more necessary become new skills which point organically to market-supplied implements. Market-dependency is guaranteed and self-perpetuating once men and women, now consumers, cannot proceed with the business of life without tuning themselves to the logic of the market. Much debated 'needs creation' by the market means ultimately creation of the need of the market. New technical, social, psychological and existential skills of the consumers are such as to be practicable only in conjunction with marketable commodities; rationality comes to mean the ability to make right purchasing decisions, while the craving for certainty is gratified by conviction that the decisions made have been, indeed, right.

Repression stands for 'panoptical' power, best described by Foucault (1977). It employs surveillance, it is aimed at regimentation of the body, and is diffused (made invisible) in the numerous institutionalizations of knowledge-based expertise. Repression as a tool of domination-reproduction has not been abandoned with the advent of seduction. Its time is not over and the end of its usefulness is not in sight, however overpowering and effective seduction may become. It is the continuous, tangible presence of repression as a viable alternative which makes seduction unchallengeable. In addition, repression is indispensable to reach the areas seduction cannot, and is not meant to, reach: it remains the paramount tool of subordination of the considerable margin of society which cannot be absorbed by market dependency and hence, in market terms, consists of 'non-consumers'. Such 'non-consumers' are people reduced to the satisfaction of their elementary needs; people whose business of life does not transcend the horizon of survival. Goods serving the latter purpose are not, as a rule, attractive as potential merchandise; they serve needs over which the market has no control and thus undermine, rather than boost, market dependency. Repression reforges the market unattractiveness of non-consumer existence into the unattractiveness of alternatives to market dependency.

Seduction and repression between them make 'legitimation' redundant. The structure of domination can now be reproduced, ever more effectively, without recourse to legitimation; and thus without recourse to such intellectuals as make the legitimation discourse their speciality. Habermas's (1976) 'legitimation crisis' makes sense, in the final account, as the intellectual perception of 'crisis' caused by the ever more evident irrelevance of legitimation.

The growing irrelevance of legitimation has coincided with the growing freedom of intellectual debate. One suspects more than coincidence. It is indifference on the part of political power which makes freedom of intellectual work possible. Indifference, in its turn, arises from lack of interest. Intellectual freedom is possible as political power has freed itself from its former dependence on legitimation. This is why freedom, coming as it does in a package-deal with irrelevance, is not received by the intellectuals with unqualified enthusiasm. All the more so as the past political patronage made a considerable part of intellectual work grow in a way which rendered it dependent on the continuation of such a patronage.

What, however, more than anything else prevents the intellectuals from rejoicing is the realization that the withdrawal of government troops does not necessarily mean that the vacated territory will become now their uncontested domain. What the state has relinquished is most likely to be taken over by powers over which the intellectuals have even less hold than they ever enjoyed in their romance with politics.

The territory in question is that of culture. Culture is one area of social life which is defined (cut out) in such a way as to reassert the social function claimed by the intellectuals. One cannot even explain the meaning of the concept without reference to human 'incompleteness', to the need of teachers and, in general, of 'people in the know' to make up for this incompleteness, and to a vision of society as a continuous 'teach-in' session. The idea of culture, in other words, establishes knowledge in the role of power, and simultaneously supplies legitimation of such power. Culture connotes power of the educated elite and knowledge as power; it denotes institutionalized mechanisms of such power – science, education, arts.

Some of these mechanisms, or some areas of their application, remain relevant to the repressive functions of the state, or to the tasks resulting from the state role in the reproduction of consumer society (reproduction of conditions for the integration-through-seduction). As far as this is the case, the state acts as the protector-cum-censor, providing funds but reserving the right to decide on the tasks and the value of their results. The mixed role of the state rebounds in a mixed reaction of the educated elite. Calls for more state resources intermingle with protests against bureaucratic interference. There is no shortage of the educated willing to serve; neither is there a shortage of criticisms of servility.

Some other mechanisms, or some other areas of their application, do not have such relevance. They are, as a rule, 'underfunded', but otherwise suffer little political interference. They are free. Even the most iconoclastic of their products fail to arouse the intended wrath of the dominant classes and in most cases are received with devastating equanimity. Challenging capitalist values stirs little commotion in as far as capitalist domination does not depend on the acceptance of its values. And yet freedom *from* political interference does not result in freedom *for* intellectual creativity. A new protector–cum–censor fills the vacuum left by the withdrawal of the state: the market.

This is the third respect in which intellectual status is perceived as undermined. Whatever their other ambitions, modern intellectuals always saw culture as their private property; they made it, they lived in it, they even gave it its name. Expropriation of this particular plot hurts most. Or has it been, in fact, an expropriation? Certainly intellectuals never controlled 'popular' consumption of cultural products. Once they felt firmly in the saddle, they saw themselves as members of the circle of 'culture consumers', which, in the sense they would have recognized, was probably significant, if small. It is only now that the circle of people eager to join the culture consumption game has grown to unheard of proportions – has become truly 'massive'. What hurts, therefore, is not so much an expropriation, but the fact that the intellectuals are not invited to stand at the helm of this breath-taking expansion. Instead, it is gallery owners, publishers, TV managers and other 'capitalists' or 'bureaucrats' who are in control. The idea has been wrested out of the intellectual heads and in a truly sorcerer's apprentice's manner, put to action in which the sages have no power.

In another sense, however, what has happened is truly an expropriation, and not just 'stealing the profits'. In the early modern era intellectual forces had been mobilized (or self-mobilized) for the gigantic job of conversion – the culture crusade which involved a thorough revamping or uprooting of the totality of heretofore autonomously reproduced forms of life. The project was geared to the growth of the modern absolutist state and its acute need of legitimation. For reasons mentioned before, this is no longer the case. Native forms of life have not, however, returned to autonomous reproduction; there are others who manage it – agents of the market, this time, and not of academia. No wonder the old gamekeepers view the new ones as poachers. Once bent on the annihilation of 'crude, superstitious, ignorant, bestial' folkways, they now bewail the enforced transformation of the 'true folk culture' into a 'mass' one. The mass culture debate has been the lament of expropriated gamekeepers.

The future does not promise improvement either; the strength of market forces continues to grow, their appetite seems to grow even faster and, for an increasing sector of the educated élite, the strategy 'if you cannot beat them, join them' gains in popularity. Even the areas of the intellectual domain still left outside the reach of market forces are now felt to be under threat. It was the intellectuals who impressed upon the once incredulous population the need for education and the value of information. Here as well their success turns into their downfall. The market is only too eager to satisfy the need and to supply the value. With the new DIY (electronic) technology to offer, the market will reap a rich crop from the popular belief that education is a human duty and (any) information is useful. The market will thereby achieve what the intellectual educators struggled to attain in vain: it will turn the consumption of information into a pleasurable, entertaining pastime. Education will become just one of the many variants of self-amusement. It will reach the peak of its popularity and the bottom of its value as measured by original intellectual-made standards.

The three developments discussed above go some way, if not all the way, towards explaining this feeling of anxiety, out-of-placeness, loss of direction which, as I propose, constitutes the true referent of the concept of 'postmodernity'. As a rule, however, intellectuals tend to articulate their own societal situation and the problems it creates as a situation of the society at large, and its systemic or social problems. The way in which the passage from 'modernity' to 'postmodernity' has been articulated is no exception. This time, however, those who articulate it do not hide as thoroughly as in the past behind the role of 'organic intellectuals' of other classes; and the fact that they act as 'organic intellectuals of themselves' is either evident or much easier to discover. Definitions of both 'modernity' and 'postmodernity' refer overtly to such features of respective social situations as have direct and crucial importance for the status, role and strategy of the intellectual.

The main feature ascribed to 'postmodernity' is thus the permanent and irreducible *pluralism* of cultures, communal traditions, ideologies, 'forms of life' or 'language games' (choice of items which are 'plural' varies with theoretical allegiance); or the awareness and recognition of such pluralism. Things which are plural in the postmodern world cannot be arranged in an evolutionary sequence, or be seen as each other's inferior or superior stages; neither can they be classified as 'right' or 'wrong' solutions to common problems. No knowledge can be assessed outside the context of the culture, tradition, language game, etc. which makes it possible and endows it with meaning. Hence no criteria of validation are available which could be themselves justified 'out of context'. Without universal standards, the problem of the postmodern world is not how to globalize superior culture, but how to secure communication and mutual understanding between cultures.

Seen from this 'later' perspective, 'modernity' seems in retrospect a time when pluralism was not yet a foregone conclusion; or a time when the ineradicability of pluralism was not duly recognized. Hence the substitution of one, 'supracommunal', standard of truth, judgement and taste for the diversity of local, and therefore inferior, standards, could be contemplated and strived for as a viable prospect. Relativism of knowledge could be perceived as a nuisance, and as a temporary one at that. Means could be sought – in theory and in practice – to exorcize the ghost of relativism once and for all. The end to parochialism of human opinions and ways of life was nigh. This could be a chance – once real, then lost. Or this could be an illusion from the start. In the first case, postmodernity means the failure of modernity. In the second case, it means a step forward. In both cases, it means opening our eyes to the futility of modern dreams of universalism.

The reader will note that I am defining 'modernity' from the perspective of the experience of 'postmodernity', and not vice versa; all attempts to pretend that we proceed in the opposite direction mislead us into believing that what we confront in the current debate is an articulation of the logic of 'historical process', rather than re-evaluation of the past (complete with the imputation of a 'telos' of which the past, as long as it remained the present, was not aware). If the concept of 'postmodernity' has no other value, it has at least this one: it supplies a new and external vantage point, from which some aspects of that world which came into being in the aftermath of the Enlightenment and the Capitalist Revolution (aspects not visible, or allotted secondary importance, when observed from inside the unfinished process) acquire saliency and can be turned into pivotal issues of the discourse.

The reader will note also that I am trying to define both concepts of the opposition in such a way as to make their mutual distinction independent of the 'existential' issue: whether it is the 'actual conditions' which differ, or their perception. It is my view that the pair of concepts under discussion is important first and foremost (perhaps even solely) in the context of the self-awareness of the intellectuals, and in relation to the way the intellectuals perceive their social location, task and strategy. This does not detract from the significance of the concepts. On the contrary, as far as the plight of 'western culture' goes, the way the two concepts are defined here presents them as arguably the most seminal of oppositions articulated in order to capture the tendency of social change in our times.

The change of mood, intellectual climate, self-understanding, etc. implied by that vague, but real anxiety, the proposition of the 'advent of postmodernity' attempts to capture, has indeed far-reaching consequences for the strategy of intellectual work in general – and sociology and social philosophy in particular. It does have a powerful impact even on 'traditional' ways of conducting the business of social study. There is no necessity whatsoever for the old procedures to be rescinded or to grind to a halt. One can easily declare the whole idea of 'postmodernity' a sham, obituaries of 'modernity' premature, the need to reorient one's programme non-existent – and stubbornly go where one went before and where one's ancestors wanted to go. One can say that finding the firm and unshakeable standards of true knowledge, true interpretation, defensible morality, genuine art, etc. is still a valid one, and the major task. There is nothing to stop one from doing just that. In the vast realm of the academy there is ample room for all sorts of specialized pursuits, and the way such pursuits have been historically institutionalized renders them virtually immune to pressures untranslatable into the variables of their own inner systems; such pursuits have their own momentum; their dynamics subject to internal logic only, they produce what they are capable of producing, rather than what is required or asked of them; showing their own, internally administered measures of success as their legitimation, they may go on reproducing themselves indefinitely. This is particularly true regarding pursuits of a pronouncedly philosophical nature; they require no outside supply of resources except the salaries of their perpetrators, and are therefore less vulnerable to the dire consequences of the withdrawal of social recognition.

Even with their self-reproduction secure, however, traditional forms of philosophizing confront today challenges which must rebound in their concerns. They are pressed now to legitimize their declared purpose – something which used to be taken (at least since Descartes) by and large for granted. For well-nigh three centuries relativism was the *malin génie* of European philosophy, and anybody suspected of not fortifying his doctrine against it tightly enough was brought to book and forced to defend himself against charges, the horrifying nature of which no one put in doubt. Now the tables have been turned – and the seekers of universal standards are asked to prove the criminal nature of relativism; it is they now who are pressed to justify their hatred of relativism, and clear themselves of the charges of dogmatism, ethnocentrism, intellectual imperialism or whatever else their work may seem to imply when gazed upon from the relativist positions.

Less philosophical, more empirically inclined varieties of traditional social studies are even less fortunate. Modern empirical sociology developed in response to the demand of the modern state aiming at the 'total administration' of society. With capital engaging the rest of the society in their roles of labour, and the state responsible for the task of 're-commodifying' both capital and labour, and thus ensuring the continuation of such an engagement, the state needed a huge apparatus of 'social management' and a huge supply of expert social-management knowledge. The methods and skills of empirical sociology were geared to this demand and to the opportunities stemming from it. The social-managerial tasks were large-scale, and so were the funds allotted to their performance. Sociology specialized, therefore, in developing the skills of use in mass statistical research; in collecting information about 'massive trends' and administrative measures likely to redirect, intensify or constrain such trends. Once institutionalized, the skills at the disposal of empirical sociologists have defined the kind of research they are capable of designing and conducting. Whatever else this kind of research is, it invariably requires huge funds – and thus a rich bureaucratic institution wishing to provide them. Progressive disengagement of capital from labour, falling significance of the 're-commodification' task, gradual substitution of 'seduction' for 'repression' as the paramount weapon of social integration, shifting of the responsibility for integration from the state bureaucracy to the market – all this spells trouble for traditional empirical research, as state bureaucracies lose interest in financing it.

The widely debated 'crisis of (empirical) sociology' is, therefore, genuine. Empirical sociology faces today the choice between seeking a new social application of its skills or seeking new skills. The interests of state bureaucracy are likely to taper to the management of 'law and order', i.e. a task aimed selectively at the part of the population which cannot be regulated by the mechanism of seduction. And there are private bureaucracies in charge of seduction management, who may or may not need the skill of empirical sociology, depending on the extent to which the latter are able, and willing, to reorient and readjust their professional know-how to the new, as yet not fully fathomed, demand.

To sum up: if the radical manifestos proclaiming the end of sociology and social philosophy 'as we know them' seem unfounded, equally unconvincing is the pretence that nothing of importance has happened and that there is nothing to stop 'business as usual'. The form acquired by sociology and social philosophy in the course of what is now, retrospectively, described as 'modernity' is indeed experiencing at the moment an unprecedented challenge. While in no way doomed, it must adjust itself to new conditions in order to self-reproduce.

I will turn now to those actual, or likely, developments in sociology which do admit (overtly or implicitly) the novelty of the situation and the need for a radical reorientation of the tasks and the strategies of social study.

One development is already much in evidence. Its direction is clearly shown by the consistently expanding assimilation of Heideggerian, Wittgensteinian, Gadamerian and other 'hermeneutical' themes and inspirations. This development points in the direction of sociology as, above all, the skill of interpretation. Whatever articulable experience there is which may become the object of social study, it is embedded in its own 'life-world', 'communal tradition', 'positive ideology', 'form of life', 'language game'. The names for that 'something' in which the experience is embedded are many and different, but what truly counts are not names but the inherent pluralism of that 'something' which all the names emphasize more than anything else. Thus there are *many* 'life-worlds', *many* 'traditions' and *many* 'language-games'. No external point of view is conceivable to reduce this variety. The only reasonable cognitive strategy is therefore one best expressed in Geertz's (1973) idea of 'thick description': recovery of the meaning of the alien experience through fathoming the tradition (form of life, life-world, etc.) which constitutes it, and then translating it, with as little damage as possible, into a form assimilable by one's own tradition (form of life, life-world, etc.). Rather than proselytizing, which would be the task of a cross-cultural encounter in the context of 'orthodox' social science, it is the expected 'enrichment' of one's own tradition, through incorporating other, heretofore inaccessible, experiences, which is the meaning bestowed upon the exercise by the project of 'interpreting sociology'.

As interpreters, sociologists are no longer concerned with ascertaining the 'truth' of the experience they interpret – and thus the principle of 'ethnomethodological indifference' may well turn from the shocking heresy it once was into a new orthodoxy. The only concern which distinguishes sociologists-turned-interpreters as professionals is the correctness of interpretation; it is here that their professional credentials as experts (i.e. holders of skills inaccessible to the lay and untrained public) are re-established. Assuming that the world is irreducibly pluralist, rendering the messages mutually communicable is its major problem. Expertise in the rules of correct interpretation is what it needs most. It is badly needed even by such powers as are no longer bent on total domination and do not entertain universalistic ambitions; they still need this expertise for their sheer survival. Potential uses are clear; the users, so far, less so – but one may hope they can be found.

As all positions, this one has also its radical extreme. The admission of pluralism does not have to result in an interest in interpretation and translation, or for that matter in any 'social' services sociology may offer. Release from the often burdensome social duty sociology had to carry in the era of modernity may be seen by some as a relief – as the advent of true freedom of intellectual pursuits. It is, indeed, an advent of freedom – though freedom coupled with irrelevance: freedom *from* cumbersome and obtrusive interference on the part of powers that be, won at the price of resigning the freedom to influence their actions and their results. If what sociology does does not matter, it can do whatever it likes. This is a tempting possibility: to immerse oneself fully in one's own specialized discourse inside which one feels comfortably at home, to savour the subtleties of distinction and discretion such discourse demands and renders possible, to take the very disinterestedness of one's pursuits for the sign of their supreme value, to take pride in keeping alive, against the odds, a precious endeavour for which the rest, the polluted or corrupted part of the world, has (temporarily, one would add, seeking the comfort of hope) no use. It is one's own community, tradition, form of life, etc. which commands first loyalty; however small, it provides the only site wherein the intrinsic value of the discourse can be tended to, cultivated – and enjoyed. After all, the recognition of futility of universal standards, brought along by postmodernity, allows that self-centred concerns treat lightly everything outside criticism. There is nothing to stop one from coming as close as possible to the sociological equivalent of *l'art pour l'art* (the cynic would comment: nothing, but the next round of education cuts).

The two postmodern strategies for sociology and social philosophy discussed so far are – each in its own way – internally consistent and viable. Looked at from inside, they both seem invulnerable. Given their institutional entrenchment, they have a sensible chance of survival and of virtually infinite self-reproduction (again, barring the circumstances referred to by the cynic). Whatever critique of these strategies may be contemplated, it may only come from the outside, and thus cut little ice with the insiders.

Such a critique would have to admit its allegiance to ends the insiders are not obliged to share. It would have to cite an understanding of the role of sociology the insiders have every reason to reject, and no reason to embrace. In particular, such a critique would have to declare its own value preference, remarkable above all for the supreme position allotted to the *social relevance* of sociological discourse.

The critique under consideration may be launched in other words only from the intention to preserve the hopes and ambitions of modernity in the age of postmodernity. The hopes and ambitions in question refer to the possibility of a reason-led improvement of the human condition; an improvement measured in the last instance by the degree of human emancipation. For better or worse, modernity was about increasing the volume of human autonomy, but not autonomy which, for the absence of solidarity, results in loneliness; and about increasing the intensity of human solidarity, but not solidarity which, for the absence of autonomy, results in oppression. The alternative strategy for a postmodern sociology would have to take as its assumption that the two-pronged ambition of modernity is still a viable possibility, and one certainly worth promoting.

What makes a strategy which refuses to renounce its modern ('pre-postmodern'?) commitments a 'postmodern' one, is the bluntness with which its premises are recognized as assumptions; in a truly 'postmodern' vein, such a strategy refers to values rather than laws; to assumptions instead of foundations; to purposes, and not to 'groundings'. And it is determined to do without the comfort it once derived from the belief that 'history was on its side', and that the inevitability of its ultimate success had been guaranteed beforehand by inexorable laws of nature (a pleonasm: 'nature' *is* inexorable laws).

Otherwise, there is no sharp break in continuity. There is a significant shift of emphasis, though. The 'meliorative' strategy of social science as formed historically during the era of modernity had two edges. One was pressed against the totalistic ambitions of the modern state; the state, in possession of enough resources and goodwill to impress a design of a better society upon imperfect reality, was to be supplied with reliable knowledge of the laws directing human conduct and effective skills required to elicit a conduct conforming to modern ambitions. The other was pressed against the very humans modernity was bent on emancipating. Men and women were to be offered reliable knowledge of the way their society works, so that their life-business might be conducted in a conscious and rational way, and the causal chains making their actions simultaneously effective and constrained become visible – and hence, in principle, amenable to control. To put the same in a different way: the 'meliorative' strategy under discussion was productive of two types of knowledge. One was aimed at rationalization of the state (more generally: societal) power; the other at rationalization of individual conduct.

Depending on the time and the location, either one or the other of the two types of knowledge was held in the focus of sociological discourse. But both were present at all times and could not but be co-present, due to the ineradicable ambiguity of ways in which any information on social reality can be employed. This ambiguity explains why the relations between social science and the powers that be were at best those of hate–love, and why even during the time-spans of wholehearted co-operation there was always more than a trace of mistrust in the state's attitude toward sociological discourse; not without reason, men of politics suspected that such a discourse may well undermine with one hand the selfsame hierarchical order it helps to build with the other.

Inside the postmodern version of the old strategy, however, the balance between the two types of knowledge is likely to shift. One circumstance which makes such a shift likely has been mentioned already: the drying up of state interest in all but the most narrowly circumscribed sociological expertise; no grand designs, no cultural crusades, no demand for legitimizing visions, and no need for models of a centrally administered rational society. Yet the effect of this factor, in itself formidable, has been exacerbated further by the gradual erosion of hope that the failure of the rational society to materialize might be due to the weaknesses of the present administrators of the social process, and that an alternative 'historical agent' may still put things right. More bluntly, the faith in a historical agent waiting in the wings to take over and to complete the promise of modernity using the levers of the political state – this faith has all but vanished. The first of the two types of knowledge the modern sociological discourse used to turn out is, therefore, without an evident addressee – actual or potential. It may be still used: there are, after all, quite a few powerful bureaucracies which could do with some good advice on how to make humans behave differently and in ways more to their liking. And they will surely find experts eager to offer such advice. We did discuss such a possibility in the context of strategies which refuse to admit that 'postmodernity' means a new situation and calls for rethinking and readjustment of traditional tasks and strategies. For the strategy aimed at the preservation of modern hopes and ambitions under the new conditions of postmodernity, the question *who* uses the administrative knowledge and for what *purpose* is not, however, irrelevant. It would recognize such knowledge as useful only if in the hands of a genuine or putative, yet rationalizing agent. From the vantage point of the political power all this reasoning is redundant anyway. Having lost interest in its own practical application of sociological knowledge, the state will inevitably tend to identify the totality of sociological discourse with the second of its traditional edges, and thus regard it as an unambiguously subversive force; as a problem, rather than a solution.

The expected state attitude is certain to act as a self-fulfilling prophecy; rolling back the resources and facilities the production of the first type of knowledge cannot do without, it will push sociological discourse even further toward the second type. It will only, as it were, reinforce a tendency set in motion by other factors. Among the latter, one should count an inevitable consequence of the growing disenchantment with societal administration as the carrier of emancipation: the shifting of attention to the kind of knowledge which may be used by human individuals in their efforts to enlarge the sphere of autonomy and solidarity. This looks more and more like the last chance of emancipation.

So far, we have discussed the 'push' factors. There is, however, a powerful 'pull' factor behind the shift: a recognition that the task of providing men and women with that 'sociological imagination' for which C. W. Mills (1959) appealed years ago, has never been so important as it is now, under conditions of postmodernity. Emancipation of capital from labour makes possible the emancipation of the state from legitimation; and that may mean in the long run a gradual erosion of democratic institutions and the substance of democratic politics (reproduction of legitimation having been the major historical function of political democracy). Unlike the task of reproducing members of society as producers, their reproduction as consumers does not necessarily enlarge the political state and hence does not imply the need to reproduce them as citizens. The 'systemic' need for political democracy is thereby eroded, and the political agency of men and women as citizens cannot count for its reproduction on the centripetal effects of the self-legitimizing concerns of the state. The other factors which could sponsor such reproduction look also increasingly doubtful in view of the tendency to shift political conflicts into the non-political and democratically unaccountable sphere of the market, and the drift toward the substitution of 'needs creation' for 'normative regulation' as the paramount method of systemic reproduction (except for the part of the society the market is unable or unwilling to assimilate). If those tendencies have been correctly spotted, knowledge which provides the individuals with an accurate understanding of the way society works may not be a weapon powerful enough to outweigh their consequences; but it surely looks like the best bet men and women can still make.

Which leads us into an area not at all unfamiliar; some would say traditional. The third of the conceivable strategies of sociology under the postmodern condition would focus on the very thing on which the sociological discourse did focus throughout its history:

on making the opaque transparent, on exposing the ties linking visible biographies to invisible societal processes, on understanding what makes society tick, in order to make it tick, if possible, in a more 'emancipating' way. Only it is a new and different society from the one which triggered off the sociological discourse. Hence 'focusing on the same' means focusing on new problems and new tasks.

I suggest that a sociology bent on the continuation of *modern* concerns under *postmodern* conditions would be distinguished not by new procedures and purposes of sociological work, as other postmodern strategies suggest, but by a new *object* of investigation. As far as this strategy is concerned, what matters is that the society (its object) has changed; it does not necessarily admit that its own earlier pursuits were misguided and wasted, and that the crucial novelty in the situation is the dismissal of the old ways of doing sociology and 'discovery' of new ways of doing it. Thus to describe a sociology pursuing the strategy under discussion one would speak, say, of a 'post-full-employment' sociology, or a 'sociology of the consumer society', rather than of a 'post-Wittgensteinian' or 'post-Gadamerian' sociology. In other words, this strategy points toward a sociology of postmodernity, rather than a postmodern sociology.

There are number of specifically 'postmodern' phenomena which await sociological study. There is a process of an accelerating emancipation of capital from labour; instead of engaging the rest of society in the role of producers, capital tends to engage them in the role of consumers. This means in its turn that the task of reproducing the capital-dominated society does not consist, as before, in the 're-commodification of labour', and that the non-producers of today are not a 'reserve army of labour', to be tended to and groomed for a return to the labour market. This crucial fact of their life is still concealed in their own consciousness, in the consciousness of their political tutors, and of the sociologists who study them, by a historical memory of a society which is no more and will not return. The new poor are not socially, culturally or systemically an equivalent of the old poor; the present 'depression', manifested in massive and stable unemployment, is not a latter day edition of the 1930s (one hears about the poor losing their jobs, but one does not hear of the rich jumping out of their windows). 'The two nations' society, mark two, cannot be truly understood by squeezing it into the model of mark one.

'The two nations, mark two' society is constituted by the opposition between 'seduction' and 'repression' as means of social control, integration and the reproduction of domination. The first is grounded in 'market dependency': replacement of old life-skills by the new ones, which cannot be effectively employed without the mediation of the market; in the shifting of disaffection and conflict from the area of political struggle to the area of commodities and entertainment; in the appropriate redirecting of the needs for rationality and security; and in the growing comprehensiveness of the market-centred world, so that it can accommodate the totality of life-business, making the other aspects of systemic context invisible and subjectively irrelevant. The second is grounded in a normative regulation pushed to the extreme, penetration of the 'private' sphere to an ever growing degree, disempowering of the objects of normative regulation as autonomous agents. It is important to know how these two means of social control combine and support each other; and the effects their duality is likely to have on the tendency of political power, democratic institutions and citizenship.

One may guess – pending further research – that while control-through-repression destroys autonomy and solidarity, control-through-seduction generates marketable means serving the pursuit (if not the attainment) of both, and thus effectively displaces the pressures such a pursuit exerts from the political sphere, at the same time redeploying them in the reproduction of capital domination. Thus the opposite alternatives which determine the horizon and the trajectory of life strategies in the postmodern society neutralize the possible threat to systemic reproduction which might emanate from the unsatisfied ambitions of autonomy and solidarity.

Those alternatives, therefore, need to be explored by any sociology wishing seriously to come to grips with the phenomenon of postmodernity. Conscious of the postmodern condition it explores, such a sociology would not pretend that its preoccupations, however skilfully pursued, would offer it the centrality in the 'historical process' to which it once aspired. On the contrary, the problematics sketched above are likely to annoy rather than entice the managers of law and order; it will appear incomprehensible to the seduced, and alluring yet nebulous to the repressed. A sociology determined to tread this path would have to brace itself for the uneasy plight of unpopularity. Yet the alternative is irrelevance. This seems to be the choice sociology is facing in the era of postmodernity.

REFERENCES

Foucault, Michel (1977) *Discipline and Punish,* Harmondsworth, Allen Lane.

Geertz, Clifford (1973) *The Interpretation of Culture,* New York, Basic Books.

Gramsci, Antonio (1971) *Selections from the Prison Notebooks,* London, Lawrence & Wishart.

Habermas, Jürgen (1976) *Legitimation Crisis,* London, Heinemann.

Mills, C. Wright (1959) *The Sociological Imagination,* Oxford, Oxford University Press.

Williams, Raymond (1975) *The Country and the City,* St Albans, Paladin.

5

PHILOSOPHICAL AFFINITIES OF POSTMODERN SOCIOLOGY

The debate on the relationship between sociology and philosophy is as sociologically understandable as it is philosophically inconclusive.

Looked upon sociologically, the debate is easily explained as an expression of natural concern with boundary-drawing: two intellectual traditions, two wide-open discursive formations that draw upon each other, feed each other, intertwine and live through joint history, need to guard their precarious institutional autonomy within the academic world of departmental divisions and specializations. The passion and ferocity of the battle reflect the elusiveness of its objective; the two discursive formations staunchly resist administrative attempts at separation and stay alive only in so far as the artificially erected dams are far too low and porous to resist overflowing. One can usefully think of the two discourses as two eddies inside one river. The same fluid matter passes through them incessantly; the eddies exist solely as conductors. For each of the two, to keep its respective identity means drawing in ever new matter and letting out the processed one.

Looked upon philosophically, the debate reveals its futility. It makes philosophical sense only in so far as it assumes, counterfactually, that institutional separation has indeed led to (or, more fallaciously yet, that it 'expressed') the substantive segregation of the subject-matter; and in so far as it assumes that the institutional boundaries that guard the integrity of – respectively – philosophy and sociology against external intrusion, circumscribe internally unified entities. In other words, in the generalized form in which it normally appears, the debate makes sense only after a tacit acceptance that philosophy and sociology are two separate and integrated, self-contained totalities that can enter into contractual agreements, negotiate compromise or declare wars on each other. This is, however, manifestly not the case. Philosophy and sociology as modes of intellectual activity are not separated in a way even remotely reminiscent of the tight departmental segregation of academic philosophers and sociologists guarded by appointments committees and professional guilds. As intellectual activities, neither philosophy nor sociology are integrated to an extent that would enable them to confront each other as homogeneous subjects, each marked by a distinctive profile and defined purpose.

It is on that latter point that this paper will dwell. The choice is not a matter of accident; the postmodern era, here understood as the era of re-evaluation of modernity (and, by the same token, of a retrospective *condensation* of the modern mode of existence into a 'project of modernity', whose imputed intentions and ascribed consequences are thereby exposed to examination), has focused attention on internal splits which cut, in strikingly similar ways, through the bodies of philosophy and sociology. Though the split is often represented as one between *modern* and *postmodern* mentalities (attitudes, perspectives, frames of thought), treating the two philosophical or sociological modes as remaining in a relation of historical succession means courting an unproductive and in the end superfluous contention: it would be pointed out immediately that 'postmodern' practices can be easily traced far back, right to the heart of the modern era, while the advent of postmodernity need not mean at all that characteristically 'modern' forms of philosophical and sociological practice are about to be replaced and leave the stage forever. The alleged historical succession is but an illusion fed by the construction of the 'other' of the self-consciously postmodern philosophy and sociology as a matter of 'the past' to be transcended and left behind (a bid for hegemony, accomplished through the well-tried expedient of temporalizing a spatial relationship, substituting a temporal hierarchy for spatial coexistence, much as in the case of the 'primitivization' of alien cultures).

I suggest that the two distinct and alternative modes of philosophical and sociological practice recently classified as 'modern' and 'postmodern' are best described as *legislative* and *interpretive*.[1] What we witness today is, first, the rising relative weight of the interpretive mode among philosophical and sociological practices, and second, the rising militancy of its foremost practitioners aimed at discarding the alternative as either outdated or misguided from the start.

POLITICS OF LEGISLATIVE REASON

The philosopher, Kant[2] insisted in the *Critique of Pure Reason*, 'is not merely an artist – who occupies himself with conceptions, but a law-giver – legislating for human reason'. The task of reason, for which the philosopher acts as the supreme spokesman, is 'to establish a tribunal, which may secure it in its well-grounded claims, while it pronounces against all baseless assumptions and pretensions, not in an arbitrary manner, but according to its own eternal and unchangeable laws'. The idea of the philosopher's 'legislative power resides in the mind of every man, and it alone teaches us what kind of systematic unity philosophy demands in view of the ultimate aims of reason' (*teleologia rationis humanae*).

Philosophy cannot but be a legislative power; it is the task of good philosophy, of the right type of metaphysic to serve the men who require 'that knowledge which concerns all men should transcend the common understanding'. 'Reason cannot permit our knowledge to remain in an unconnected and rhapsodistic state, but requires that the sum of our cognitions should constitute a system'. The kind of knowledge that may indeed transcend the common understanding, composed of mere opinions and beliefs (*opinion*: judgment insufficient both subjectively and objectively; *belief*: the most perfidious sort of judgment, one 'recognized as being objectively insufficient', yet subjectively accepted as convincing), could and should only 'be revealed to you by philosophers'. In performing this task, metaphysics would be 'the completion of the *culture* of human reason'; it will raise that reason from the raw and disorderly state in which it is naturally given, to the level of orderly system. Metaphysics is called upon to *cultivate* harmonious perfection of thought.

> The supreme office of censor which it occupies, assures to it the highest authority and importance. This office it administers for the purpose of securing order, harmony, and well-being to science, and of directing its noble and fruitful labours to the highest possible aim – the happiness of all mankind.

Adjudicating on the matter of human happiness is the philosopher's prerogative, and his duty. Here Kant merely re-states the centuries-long tradition of the sages, originating at least with Plato. In the Seventh Book of Plato's *Republic*, Socrates advised Glaucon that once he had visited the realm of 'true philosophy', and thus ascended 'into real being' ('turning of a soul round from a day which is like night to a true day'), he must return to those who did not follow him on his expedition (sages who never return from their escapade to the world of eternal truths are as wrong as the ordinary men and women who never embarked on the journey; in addition, they are guilty of the crime of lost opportunity and unfulfilled duty). Then he 'will see a thousand times better than those who live there' – and this advantage will give him the right and the obligation to pass judgments and enforce obedience to truth. One needs to proclaim the philosopher's duty 'the care and guardianship of other people'.

> Then it is the task of us founders . . . to compel the best natures to attain the learning which we said was the greatest, both to see the good, and to ascend that ascent; and when they have ascended and properly seen, we must never allow them what is allowed now.

'It is more likely that the truth would have been discovered by few than by many' – declared Descartes in the third rule of the *Rules for the Direction of the Mind*. Knowing the truth, knowing it with such certainty as can withstand the cross-currents of vulgar experience and stay immune to the temptations of narrow and partial interests, is exactly the quality that sets the few apart from the many – and makes them stand above the crowd. To legislate and to enforce the laws of reason is the *burden* of those few, the knowers of truth, the philosophers. They are called to perform the task without which the happiness of the many will never be attained. The task would require sometimes a benign and clement teacher; at some other time it would demand the firm hand of a stern and unyielding guardian. Whatever the acts the philosopher may be forced to perform, one element will remain – cannot but remain – constant: the philosopher's unchallenged prerogative to decide between true and false, good and evil, right and wrong; and thus his license to judge and authority to enforce obedience to the judgment. Kant had little doubt as to the nature of the task; to explain it, he drew his metaphors profusely from the vocabulary of power. Metaphysics was 'the queen', whose 'government' could 'under administration' of dogmatists turn into despotism, but still remain indispensable to hold in check 'nomadic tribes, who hate permanent habitation and settled mode of living' and hence attack 'from time to time those who had organized themselves into civil communities'. The specific service metaphysics is called upon to render is criticism of reason;

> to deny the positive advantage of the service which this criticism renders us, would be as absurd as to maintain that the system of police is productive of no positive benefit, since its main business is to prevent the violence which citizen has to apprehend from citizen, that so each may pursue his vocation in peace and security.

One may be easily tempted to play down these or similar tropes drawn from the rhetoric of power as a predictable part of all *protreptics* – the habitual laudatory preambula to philosophical treatises meant to ingratiate the subject with the prospective readers, and particularly with the powerful and resourceful among them. Yet the case for *legislative* reason was addressed to a special kind of reader, and thus the language in which the bid for attention and favours was couched was one familiar to such a reader and resonant with his concerns. This reader was first and foremost the government of the day, the despot approached with an offer of enlightenment – of a means to do more effectively the very thing he declared himself to be after. Like the earthly rulers, critical philosophy braced itself to 'strike a blow' 'at the root'. The enemies such philosophy was particularly apt to transfix and overpower were those of the 'dogmatic schools' of Materialism, Fatalism, Atheism, Free-thinking, Fanaticism and Superstition 'which are universally injurious'. It had to be shown then that these adversaries threaten mundane and intellectual orders alike; that their annihilation is attuned to the interest of the powers that be in the same measure as it conforms to those of critical philosophy; that therefore the task of Royal legislators overlaps with the aim of legislative reason.

> If governments think proper to interfere with the affairs of the learned, it would be more consistent with a wise regard for the interests of science, as well as for those of society, to favour a criticism of this kind, by which alone the labours of reason can be established on a firm basis, than to support the ridiculous despotism of the schools, which raise a loud cry of danger to the public over the destruction of cobwebs, of which the public has never taken any notice, and the loss of which, therefore, it can never feel.

Yet there was more to Kant's choice of metaphors than consideration of expediency in the bid for Royal sponsorship. There was a genuine affinity between the legislating ambitions of critical philosophy and the designing intentions of the rising modern state; as there was a genuine symmetry between the tangle of traditional parochialisms the modern state had to uproot to establish its own supreme and uncontested sovereignty, and the cacophony of 'dogmatic schools' that had to be silenced so that the voice of universal and eternal (and hence *one* and uncontested: 'nothing will be left to future generations except the task of illustrating and applying it *didactically*') reason could be heard and its '*apodectic certitude*' could be appreciated. Modern rulers and modern philosophers were first and foremost *legislators*; they found chaos, and set out to tame it and replace with order. The orders they wished to introduce were by definition artificial, and as such had to rest on designs appealing to the laws that claimed the sole endorsement of reason and by the same token de-legitimized all opposition to themselves. The designing ambitions of modern rulers and modern philosophers were meant for each other and, for better or worse, were doomed to stay together, whether in love or in war. As in all marriages between similar rather than complementary spouses, this one was destined to sample delights of passionate mutual desire alongside the torments of all-stops-pulled rivalry.

Securing supremacy for a designed, artificial order is a two-pronged task. It demands the unity and integrity of the realm; and the security of its borders. Both sides of the task converge on one effort: that of separating the 'inside' from the 'outside'. Nothing left inside may be irrelevant to the total design or preserve autonomy *vis-à-vis* the exceptionless rulings of the order ('valid for every rational being'). 'For pure speculative reason is an organic structure in which there is nothing isolated or independent, but every single part is essential to all the rest; and hence, the slightest imperfection, whether defect or positive error, could not fail to betray itself in use' – just as in the case of political reason of the state. In the intellectual and political realms alike, the order must be both exclusive and comprehensive. Hence the two-pronged task folds into one: that of making the boundary of the 'organic structure' sharp and clearly marked, which means 'excluding the middle', suppressing or exterminating everything ambiguous, everything that sits astride the barricade and thus compromises the vital distinction between *inside* and *outside*. Building and keeping order means making friends and fighting enemies. First and foremost, however, it means purging *ambivalence*.

In the political realm, purging ambivalence means segregating or deporting strangers, sanctioning some local powers and delegalizing the unsanctioned ones, filling the 'gaps in the law'. In the intellectual realm, purging ambivalence means above all de-legitimizing all grounds of knowledge philosophically uncontrolled or uncontrollable. More than anything else, it means decrying and invalidating 'common sense' – be it 'mere beliefs', 'prejudices', 'superstitions', or sheer manifestations of 'ignorance'. It was Kant's crowning argument in his devastating case against extant dogmatical metaphysics that 'this so–called queen could not refer her descent to any higher source than that of common experience'. The duty of philosophy Kant set out to establish was, on the contrary, 'to destroy the illusions which had their origin in misconceptions, whatever darling hopes and valued expectations may be ruined by its explanations'. In such a philosophy, *'opinion* is perfectly inadmissible'. The judgments admitted into the philosophical tribunal of reason are *necessary* and carry 'strict and absolute universality', that is they brook no competition and leave outside nothing that may claim any recognized authority. For Spinoza, the only knowledge deserving of this name is one that is certain, absolute and *sub specie aeternitatis*. Spinoza divided ideas into strictly separate categories (leaving no room for 'the middle case') of such as constitute knowledge and such as are false; the latter were flatly denied all value and reduced to pure negativity – to the absence of knowledge ('False or fictitious ideas have nothing positive . . . through which they may be called false or fictitious; but only from the want of knowledge they are so called'). In Kant's view, the speculative philosopher is 'the sole depositor of a science which benefits the public without its knowledge' (the public awareness of being benefited is irrelevant to the validity of the benefits; it is the warranty of the philosopher that counts). Kant repeats: 'in the judgments of pure reason, opinion has no place. . . . For the subjective grounds of a judgment, such as produce beliefs, cannot be admitted in speculative inquiries.' Descartes would readily concur: 'A man who makes it his aim to raise his knowledge above the common should be ashamed to derive the occasion for doubting from the forms of speech invented by the vulgar' (*Second Meditation*); intuition and deduction, both systematically deployed by philosophers,

are the most certain routes to knowledge, and the mind should
admit no others. All the rest should be rejected as suspect of
errors and dangerous. . . . We reject all such merely probable
knowledge and make it a rule to trust only what is completely
known and incapable of being doubted.

(*Rules for the Direction of Mind*)

These are, in an outline, the main characteristics of what Richard
Rorty was to dub *foundational philosophy* – having first charged
Kant, Descartes and Locke with joint responsibility for imposing
the model on the following two hundred years of philosophical
history.[3] As I have implied above, such foundational philosophy
had its correlate in what may be called the *foundational politics* of
the rising modern state; there was a striking symmetry of declared
ambitions and practised strategies, as well as a similar obsession
with the question of sovereignty of legislative power expressed as
the principle of universality of legal or philosophical principles.

In a curious way, both sides of the symmetrical relationship
came to be incorporated in the self-image and strategy of
modern sociology (that is in the kind of social study that was
prevalent and academically dominant throughout the modern
period); the philosophical and state-political versions of the
modern project found their equivalents in the two aspects of
sociological practice. First, sociology set itself up as the critique
of common sense; second, it undertook to design foolproof
frames for social life that could effectively put paid to deviation,
unauthorized forms of conduct and everything else that, from
the systemic perspective, had been construed as manifestation
of social dis-order. In the first capacity, it offered itself to the
public as the adjudicator and umpire in the struggle between
rival conceptions of the human condition, as the supplier of
truth about the 'real springs' of human conduct and fate, and
thus a guide to genuine freedom and rational living, identified
with goal-implementation and effectiveness of action. In the
second capacity, it offered its services to the power-holders
of every level as the designer of conditions that would secure
predictable, patterned human behaviour – and thus deploy precepts
of rationality in the service of power-promoted social order through
defusing and neutralizing the consequences of individual freedom.

Both functions of modern social science converged, again, on the
supreme objective of fighting ambivalence: the scandal of mind

which cannot be recognized as reason, of consciousness that cannot be granted the vaunted human ability of truth-knowing, of knowledge that should not be permitted to aver that it grasps, exhausts and masters its object in the way *real* knowledge was promised to do. In other words, they converged on the task of demoting, exprobrating and de-legitimizing 'merely appearential' – spontaneous, home-made, autonomous manifestations of human consciousness and self-consciousness. They led inexorably to the denial of the human capacity for generating adequate self-knowledge (or, rather, they defined all self-knowledge, for the fact of being *self*-knowledge, as inadequate). Much as the Church must have defined its flock as a gathering of sinners, modern social sciences had to define their wards as a collection of ignoramuses.

'The social structure and the state continually evolve out of the life-processes of definite individuals, but individuals not as they may appear in their own or other people's imagination but rather as they really are . . .'[4] wrote Marx and Engels in the famous sentence that for the intellectual practice that followed paved the way to the two-tier world, inhabited by the ignorant and the duped at the base level of the mundane, and by the sharp-eyed social scientists at the lofty summit of objective truth; as it paved the way in political practice for the denigration of popular opinions and wishes as so many symptoms of 'false consciousness' and the dismissal of all views originating outside the established hierarchy of power as 'a mere trade-union mentality'. As Alvin Gouldner would write later, Marx's focus on 'true consciousness' as the gap that ought to be filled to bridge the way to the good society 'tends to transform the proletariat into political raw material, to be assembled and reprocessed by the Party organization, which justifies its leadership precisely in the name of its possession of theory and consciousness'.[5]

Durkheim demanded that

the sociologist put himself in the same state of mind as physicists, chemists, or physiologists, when they enquire into a hitherto unexplored region of the scientific domain. When he penetrates the social world, he must be aware that he is penetrating the unknown. He must feel himself in the presence of facts whose laws are as unsuspected as were those of life before the development of biology . . . .

This is a bold statement in view of the fact that the 'human units' of the social world, unlike the cells or the minerals investigated by biologists and physicists, have a well formed opinion of themselves and their actions; and yet, Durkheim is adamant, this fact is no objection to his postulate: things we encounter in our daily life give us only

> confused, fleeting, subjective impressions . . . but no scientific notions or explanatory concepts. . . . We can only with difficulty obtain a very confused and a very distorted perception of the true nature of our action and the causes which determined it. . . . We believe ourselves disinterested when we act egoistically; we think we are motivated by hate when we are yielding to love, that we obey reason when we are the slaves of irrational prejudices, etc.[6]

What Durkheim's argument discloses is truly illuminating: it shows that in order to sustain the scientificity of sociological practice, the authority of lay judgment (indeed, lay access to truth, the capacity of ordinary members of society to form adequate knowledge of themselves and their circumstances) must be denied. Durkheim's rules of sociological method establish, first and foremost, the superiority of the professional over the lay interpretation of reality and the professional's right to *correct*, *declare out of court* or downright abrogate the non-professional judgment. They belong to the rhetoric of power – to the politics of legislative reason.

So do the methodological principles of Max Weber, however distant the German *Kulturwissenschaften* tradition seemed to be from French positivism, and however indifferent the two 'founding fathers' of modern sociology were to each other's work. Like Durkheim, Weber argues the case for the truth of the sociologist through denigrating the cognitive value of lay knowledge:

> In the great majority of cases actual action goes on in a state of inarticulate half-consciousness or actual unconsciousness of its subjective meaning. The actor is more likely to 'be aware' of it in a vague sense than he is to 'know' what he is doing or be explicitly self-conscious about it. . . . The ideal type of meaningful action where the meaning is fully conscious and explicit is a marginal case.[7]

In a remarkable inversion of the asymmetry of initiative, the assumed inherent haziness and non-reliability of the actor's awareness is invoked to argue the imperative of the sociologist's intervention.

In the very first section of *Wirtschaft und Gesellschaft*, Weber declares that 'the present work departs from Simmel's method . . . in drawing a sharp distinction between subjectively intended and objectively valid "meanings"; two different things which Simmel not only fails to distinguish but often deliberately treats as belonging together'. The difference between the two kinds of meaning, as later reasoning amply documents, is one between untrustworthy accounts of motives, heavily influenced by non-rational and irrational (unconscious) factors, and the logically coherent explanations constructed by the rational analyst. In the course of arriving at such an explanation, the question of what the actor actually thought and felt when acting is the least of the analyst's worries – the 'theoretically conceived *pure type* of subjective meaning' is *attributed* to the *hypothetical* 'actor or actors in a given type of action'. It is enough that the explanation 'makes sense' once the actor 'can be said' to have been aware of a given motive, 'even though it has not actually been concretely part of the conscious "intention" of the actor; possibly not at all, at least not fully'. The actor's unawareness of the motives imputed to him by the sociologist does not detract from the truth-value of the explanation. Emphatically, it need not be considered as that truth's indispensable condition.

> For the purposes of a typological scientific analysis it is convenient to treat all irrational, affectually determined elements of behaviour as factors of deviation from a conceptually pure type of rational action. . . . The construction of a purely rational course of action . . . serves the sociologist as a type ('ideal type') which has the merit of clear understandability and lack of ambiguity[8]

– the features which the self-consciousness of the actor cannot boast by definition. Rationality of the actor remains mostly wanting, always suspect. The actor needs the rational scientist to make sense of her action, the sense of which – when left to her own flawed rationality – she would hardly account for.

The arguments differ, yet the cause persists: lay knowledge of society members cannot be trusted as representation of truth. To put it bluntly, people on the whole do not know what they are doing and why are they doing it. The knowledge of the lay member and that of the scientist differ in their quality; their difference is narrated by the scientist's side of the opposition as one between truth and falsity, but whatever the name, the essence of the difference is hierarchy and subordination.

The 'orthodox consensus' (the term proposed by Anthony Giddens) of modern sociology was founded on the shared assumption of *false consciousness* (wrongly supposed to be the distinctive property of post-Lukacsian Marxists – only because they theorized overtly what the rest of sociological practice assumed, or rather construed, tacitly). Most of the refined practices of sociologists, like factor analysis and statistical tabulations, derived their *raison d'être* from a common agreement that the objects of investigation are incapable of explaining their conduct causally; they do whatever they do for wrong reasons, or at any rate because of factors of which they are but vaguely (if at all) aware. In its totality, the research-and-diagnostic strategy of modern sociology served to perpetuate the state of intellectual disendowment in which common sense and lay knowledge in general had been cast.

This side of legislative reason displayed by modern sociology chimed in well with the other side: the promise of the rational organization of the human condition. As it has been already assumed (and continuously corroborated by sociological practice) that adequate knowledge of determinants (causes or reasons) is not a necessary condition of any conduct being effectively determined, this promise could be dissociated from the Enlightenment function sociology had claimed to perform. The design and implementation of rational order could involve, but did not require in principle the dissemination of truth or, for that matter, any sort of indoctrination. It could be conducted solely through the manipulation of outer environment known to induce the desirable kind of actions (discipline – or, in Weber's formulation, 'the probability that the command will be obeyed') in disregard or defiance of the accompanying thoughts of the actors. Denial of authority to lay knowledge implied the legalization of coercive order. It wedded the project of rationality to the exercise of force. It also represented this marriage as something people need without knowing that they need it (particularly *because* they do not know it), thereby effectively protecting the practice from moral reprobation.

THE STRATEGY OF INTERPRETIVE REASON

Interpretive reason is to legislative what *sophrosyne* is to *hubris*. Though it wants to capture and possess 'the other' (as all reason must want), it does not assume that the act of appropriation ennobles the object of possession, makes it better than it was in its unpossessed state. It assumes instead either that the object has been transformed in the course of appropriation, so that its appropriated form does not invalidate the original one and does not make it obsolete, or that the act of appropriation is a productive act, in which a new object comes into being which supplements rather than displaces the object that triggered off the effort of appropriation. Interpretive reason is engaged in dialogue where legislative reason strives for the right to soliloquy. Interpretive reason is interested in continuation of the dialogue that legislative reason wants to foreclose or terminate. Interpretive reason is unsure when to stop, treating each act of appropriation as an invitation to further exchange. Legislative reason, on the contrary, values all accretions only in so far as they promise to advance toward the end. To simplify somewhat, one may say that while legislative reason services the structure of domination, interpretive reason gears itself to the process of reciprocal communication. All in all, one is tempted to say that while interpretive reason is guided by *libido*, legislative reason is the work of *thanatos*.

The strategy of interpretive reason has been elaborated in various forms by Freud, Heidegger, late Wittgenstein, Gadamer, Ricoeur and Derrida; it finds today arguably its most radical, uncompromising expression in the work of Richard Rorty. Its growing audibility is more than contingently coincidental with the crisis and slow decomposition of the modern project and the falling from grace of the central modern values[9] – the process that in its turn tends to render the services of legislative reason in both its philosophical and sociological garbs increasingly redundant while generating growing demand for cultural mediation and brokerage.

Whenever the historical pedigree of interpretive reason is explored, the tradition of hermeneutic inquiry is the favourite choice. More often than not hermeneutics is identified with interpretive reason as such: or, rather, whatever may be the distinctive trait of interpretive reason is imputed to hermeneutics as, undoubtedly, its major tool. This identification, however, is fraught with the twin dangers of diluting the specificity of interpretive strategy (not a necessary condition of the practice of hermeneutics), and of promoting an illusion that the divorce between hermeneutics and legislative reason is principal and absolute. However central is the role played by hermeneutical practice in interpretive strategy, hermeneutics does not exhaust the idea of interpretive reason; most certainly and more importantly still, not all hermeneutics abides by that reason's rules.

To make the point clear: under the influence of Wilhelm Dilthey (and, more recently, Hans Gadamer), the work of Schleiermacher is most often referred to as the starting point of contemporary hermeneutics. Yet Schleiermacher's hermeneutics was originated, informed and moved by the erstwhile concerns of legislative reason; Schleiermacher's most pressing worry was not the lack of understanding, and the passage from the absence of understanding to its presence, but the danger of *misunderstanding*: the suspicion (indeed, an unchallenged assumption) that without systematically codified *methods* of interpretation a *false* understanding may, and in all probability will result. The founding axiom of Schleiermacher's project was the unreliability and thus inferiority of understanding unaided by expert guidance. Hence Schleiermacher's major purpose was to establish grounds for the *true* representation of meaning; obversely, for de-legitimation or refutation of all competitive interpretations. Most conspicuously, the notorious ambition of legislative reason found its expression in Schleiermacher's well-nigh obsessive concern with demonstrating the superiority of the methodical interpreter over the producer of the object of interpretation. Schleiermacher strived to prove that the understanding of the interpreter is better than that of the author of the text; that the author is not a trustworthy judge of the meaning of his own creation; and this despite the the fact that the proclaimed purpose of hermeneutic investigation was the *recreation* of the act of creation, the retrieval of something that had been known already but been forgotten or beclouded with the passage of time, or become poorly visible because of the distance in space.

Efforts to deploy hermeneutics as a weapon of legislative reason never truly stopped. They were salient among the concerns of Dilthey, and in the very conception of the *hermeneutic circle* that depicted the process of understanding as gradual, yet relentless distancing of the interpreter from the idea once residing in the creator's mind, and emphatically asserted the correlation between that distance and the quality of comprehension (indeed, the closeness of interpretation to the sought truth). For Dilthey, the chance of true interpretation *grows* instead of *diminishing* with the passage of time and the growth of geographical distance, that is with the deepening of cultural difference (an idea avidly adopted later by Claude Lévi-

Strauss in one of the most influential among recent attempts to establish the practice of interpretation as the servant of legislative reason). Dilthey tried to ground that intellectual superiority of the interpreter as, so to speak, a law of history: through its inherent trend towards universalizing the human condition and fusing cultural perspectives, history in each successive stage widens the cognitive horizons of the interpreters. Readers located in a historically superior culture are superior interpreters thanks to the superiority of their culture; a characteristically modern variety of confidence, one that blended the right to intellectual adjudication with the axiom of the peak location of modern civilization in the temporal and spatial hierarchy of social forms. The same intention shows through another of Dilthey's decisions – to focus the labour of interpretation on art and philosophy, as allegedly the 'high points' of any civilization, in which the spirit of a given culture comes into full blossom and hence can be best found and most completely grasped. Hermeneutics turns, therefore, into a family affair of sorts: an ongoing conversation between intellectuals as cultural creators, with each successive generation wiser ('by the logic of historical universalization') than the preceding one (the assumption that serves no purpose better than the reaffirmation of the inherently progressive nature of intellectual history).

Toward the end of his life, however, Dilthey came close to the critique and rejection of legislative ambitions. His belief in the superiority of a historically privileged interpreter became more a hope (a methodological postulate rather) than a certainty. What is worse, it could no more become certainty through the interpreter's own efforts: only the end of history (that is, the unlikely and at any rate distant moment of universality so complete that it excludes the possibility of further extension) could have brought an interpretation comprehensive and evident enough to be acknowledged as the final truth and stay uncontested. In late Dilthey one finds the seeds of that doubt that later overwhelmed the hermeneutical philosophers and prompted them to shift their practices from the realm of legislative to that of interpretive reason.

The seeds planted by Dilthey came into full fruition in Hans Gadamer's work (ironically called *Truth and Method*) and thus attracted the wrath of the spokesmen of legislative reason led by Betti. Gadamer spelled out the inevitable conclusion that 'the discovery of true meaning of a text or a work of art is never finished; it is in fact an infinite process'. This was bad enough as the ambitions of legislative reason go, but still a minor offence when compared with Gadamer's really unforgivable sin: his denial of the special privilege claimed by professional hermeneutics (or, rather, by the part of the knowledge class that claimed hermeneutics as its exclusive property, an unshared field of expertise):

> It follows from this intermediate position in which hermeneutics operates that its work is not to develop a procedure of understanding, but to clarify the conditions in which understanding takes place. But those conditions are not of the nature of a 'procedure' or a method, which the interpreter must of himself bring to bear on the text, but rather they must be given. The prejudices and fore-meanings in the mind of the interpreter are not at his free disposal . . . .
>
> Understanding is not, in fact, superior understanding. . . . It is enough to say that we understand in a different way, if we understand at all. [10]

From the point of view of legislative reason such statements must sound like heresy and abomination. They are not thoughts one can forgive and live in peace with. The *raison d'être* of the legislative project was the possibility of a *method* – that is, of a procedure that guarantees the validity of the result by the sheer fact that it has been scrupulously followed; and the principle that the findings at the end of the methodical procedure carry superior validity no non-methodical effort can claim. These are the canons that Gadamer explicitly or implicitly denied, suggesting instead that the lay and professional understanding cannot but be ascribed identical noological status, as each has been made possible by (and stays enclosed in) its own specific variety of *Vorurteil*; and that, while remaining (possibly forever) different from each other, neither can claim superiority.

Only at this point does hermeneutics emancipate itself from the supremacy (factual or intentional) of legislative reason and become instead a practice of interpretive reason. Whatever Gadamer did say about the ultimate convergence between the activity of interpretation and the truth, looks far from satisfactory when measured by the aims of legislative reason and thus justly dismissed as no more than lip-service paid to philosophical nostalgia: the notorious suggestion of 'fusion of horizons' points clearly beyond the confines of the kind of practice philosophers may hope ever to administer and control. Given the uninvited and unavoidable precedence of prejudice over all perception and understanding, fusion of horizons cannot be an outcome of thought processes alone. The prospect is more in the nature of consolation rather than a practical advice that can be with due effort re-forged into a method – and action.

The spokesmen for interpretive reason grew bolder by the year. Roland Barthes made Nietzsche's aphorism about the truth being 'only the solidification of old metaphors' into the principle of his own, highly influential, theory of interpretation:

> *Text* means *Tissue*; but whereas hitherto we have always taken this tissue as a product, a ready-made veil, behind which lies, more or less hidden, meaning (truth), we are now emphasizing, in the tissue, the generative idea that the text is made, is worked out in a perpetual interweaving; lost in this tissue – this texture – the subject unmakes himself, like a spider dissolving in the constructive secretions of its web. Were we fond of neologisms, we might define the theory of the text as an *hyphology* (*hyphos* is the tissue and the spider's web).[11]

From there, there was but a small step to Jacques Derrida's *intertextuality* (an endless conversation between the texts with no prospect of ever arriving at, or being halted at an agreed point) and his defiant maxim *'there is nothing outside the text'* (that is: anything we can possibly know is a text; the only thing a text can refer us to in our effort to grasp its meaning is another text; nothing we can possibly know of may claim a status better, more solid, or in any other way different from that of the text).

Derrida's philosophy is one of a contingent world and contingent knowledge; and one in which the dividing line between the world and the knowledge is no longer clear or hoped to be clear or wished to be clear. With that dividing line, off go all other sacred boundaries of the 'Platonic discourse': those between subject and object, inside and outside, meaning and nonsense, knowledge and opinion, certainty and contingency, truth and error. The impossibility of drawing and protecting such boundaries, we are told, lies in the very impulse and effort to mark them; all systems of marks (language most prominent among them) contain an inner tendency to multiply the chance-like and the contingent while striving to contain and eliminate it: they produce ambivalence on the way pointing to the well marked and transparent universe of meanings. One of the most important boundaries that cannot be drawn clearly and that generate ambiguity in the very process of being compulsively drawn is that between the text and its interpretation. The central message of Derrida is that interpretation is but an extension of the text, that it 'grows into' the text from which it wants to set itself apart, and thus the text expands while being interpreted which precludes the possibility of the text ever being exhausted in interpretation. Derrida's philosophy of deconstruction asserts the inescapability of multiple meaning and the endlessness of the interpretive process[12] – not because of the impotence of the cognizing mind, but as the result of the awesome potency of cognitive capacity to regenerate the very text it aims to tame, arrest and ossify; to expand the world it strives to confine and enclose. The work of interpretation spawns metonymical *supplements* while determined to gestate metaphorical *substitution*.

While Derrida's hermeneutics challenged the whole idea that logical consistency and a specifically scientific method can lead to conclusive and *apodictic* truth inaccessible in any other way (an idea constitutive of legislative reason), its arguably most seminal precept is 'the methodological necessity of including itself in the issue and the problem, accepting responsibility for its own reflexivity of error'. This hermeneutics, which the authors of these words[13] treat as identical with *postmodernist discourse*,

> wants to field its rebound – to abandon a tradition of self-certainty, to stand aside from the conditions of sense defined in this tradition, without lapsing into mere unintelligibility. The outsider's accusation of massive contradiction ('What you say refutes what you say') is an ancient *topos* of philosophical argument. . . . But in postmodernism the rebound of statement upon itself is not suffered passively or received in embarrassment, as somehow silencing, but actively embraced. Discourse has been reconstituted about precisely this instability.

The activity of interpretation is thereby 'absorbed into the activity of the text',[14] and spawns ever new tasks for itself while busy resolving them. Such a self-distending quality of all hermeneutical labour rebounds as the undecidability and inconclusiveness of all interpretation, each supplementing instead of replacing the interpreted text and opening up a new demand for yet more complex interpretation. One could say that the hermeneutic circle of legislative reason is broken up and stretched into a spiral with (to paraphrase Pascal) its centre everywhere, its circumference nowhere; a spiral that points towards infinity.

What follows is that for interpretive reason its own work is the main cause of the impossibility of its task (the *focus imaginaire*, to borrow Rorty's expression, that guides its pursuits) ever being fulfilled. *First*, if legislative reason is energized by the overwhelming desire 'to complete the job', interpretive reason labours while aware of the infinity and perpetuity of the task. Not the truth, but its search is now unbound by space and time. It is in view of that infinity that the power-hierarchies crumble (all power, as an effort to subsume and foreclose, is tied to temporality), differences in status between coexisting and rival interpretations are dwarfed and become insignificant, and the very idea of a 'privileged knowledge' (that is, a 'true' interpretation entitled to declare its alternatives invalid) loses sense. *Second*, the plurality of interpretations (coexistence of rival knowledges) ceases thereby to be seen as a regrettable yet temporary and in principle rectifiable inconvenience (as it was for legislative reason), becoming instead the constitutive feature of being as such. In other words, interpretive reason takes off from the moment of reconciliation with the intrinsically pluralist nature of the world and its inevitable consequence: the ambivalence and contingency of human existence. This armistice with the contingency of the world and all knowledge interpretive reason would not admit to be sign of weakness and surrender; above all, this reason will stubbornly refuse to consider seriously the charge of relativism (or, rather, to consider relativism as a serious charge). Rorty's response is typical of the normal reaction:

> Only the image of a discipline – philosophy – which will pick out a given set of scientific or moral views as more 'rational' than the alternatives by appeal to something which forms a permanent neutral matrix for all inquiry and all history, makes it possible to think that such relativism must automatically rule out coherence theories of intellectual and practical justification. One reason why professional philosophers recoil from the claim that knowledge may not have foundations, or rights and duties on ontological ground, is that the kind of behaviourism which dispenses with foundations is in a fair way toward dispensing with philosophy[15]

– with the philosophy of legislative reason, to be precise. Interpretive reason refuses to legislate, and this refusal makes it criminal from the vantage point of legislative strategy. This crime cannot be repented nor forgiven. The two philosophies cannot be reconciled.

Neither can the two sociologies whose mutual relationship replicates the chasm dividing legislative and interpretive reason. In defiance of the modern strategy, *postmodern* (interpretive) sociology refuses to adjudicate on the matter of lay knowledge and in particular refrains from the task of 'correcting' common sense. It is also unwilling to position itself outside the (inevitably particular and 'local') discourse and thus to seek grounds other than those such a discourse may provide. It accepts as a fate its own 'insidedness' and tries to re-forge its *fate* into *destiny* – into a position one may choose in full awareness, in order to explore and utilize the chances it contains. It sets out thereafter to clarify the conditions under which knowledge (all knowledge, including itself) is formed and socially sustained, all along remaining conscious of its own work as an activity that adds to, rather than replacing and displacing, the interpretations woven into reality it wishes to interpret. It aims not so much at the *fusion of horizons*, as at the *widening of horizons* through exposition of their inherent plurality and their mutually *supplementary*, rather than mutually *exclusive*, character.

LEGISLATIVE REASON AS HISTORICAL MEMORY

In his recent book of essays Martin Jay offered his own version of the widespread post-Heideggerian intellectual concerns. He suggested as the formula for social-scientific (and, more generally, philosophical) strategy to 'combine hermeneutics of suspicion with recollected meaning' – the first part standing for the acceptance of plurality of truths in the hopelessly plural postmodern world, the second for the perpetuation of the traditional – modern, legislative – role by the intellectuals turned perforce into interpreters. He insists on the need to maintain the hierarchy of cultural values and artistic taste, and offers an updated version of the old Schleiermachian principle of the interpretative authority of the critic and cultural historian over that of the artist or, more generally, the lay member of a cultural community.[16] What Jay and many others for whom he acts as the spokesman have not done, is to lay bare the sociological essence of such concerns that shows through the acute preoccupation with the distinction between horizons to be fused and the people expected or claiming to fuse them, between 'suspect interpretations' and 'suspicious interpreters', between distorted communication violating its 'regulative principles' and the guardians and umpires of principles.

With modernity gradually coming to terms with its own predicament (the only habitat it can live in while remaining itself), the ultimate solitude and irreducible sovereignty of the thinking subject has become apparent, thus throwing the 'collective security' arrangements of intellectual work into disarray. With the new awareness that 'the discourse is intended to *constitute* the ground whereon to decide *what should count as a fact* in the matters under consideration and to determine *what mode of comprehension* is best suited to the understanding of the facts thus constituted',[17] or that 'every social scientist (as an individual repository of the sphere of social science) must deal with his or her own hermeneutic spiral. . . . The only thing that determines the point at which a social scientist should cease the quest for understanding is his or her good judgement . . .'[18] – the questions repeatedly raised by Jay must have been asked with growing anxiety. By all standards inherited from the long rule of legislative reason, good judgement, strong will and a lot of daring needed to determine what would be judged as 'the facts of the matter' seemed to offer hopelessly inadequate grounds for sustaining the social standing of social thought.

Thus postmodernity, the age of contingency *für sich*, of self-conscious contingency, is for the thinking person also the age of community: of the lust for community, search for community, invention of community, imagining community. The nightmare of our contemporary – writes Manning Nash[19] – 'is to be deracinated, to be without papers, stateless, alone, alienated, and adrift in a world of organized others'; to be, in other words, *denied* identity by those who, being others (that is, different from ourselves), always *seem* at a distance enviably 'well settled', 'integrated', 'organized' and sure of their own identity. Nash is concerned with only one, ethnicity-type, response to this fear – but this response can stand as a pattern for all the others:

> The identity dimension of ethnicity (whatever its deep psychological roots) rests on the fact that fellow members of the ethnic groups are thought to be 'human' and trustworthy in ways that outsiders are not. The ethnic group provides a refuge against a hostile, uncaring world.

Community – ethnic or otherwise – is thought of as the uncanny (and in the end incongruous and unviable) mixture of difference and company: as uniqueness that is not paid for with loneliness, as contingency with roots, as freedom with certainty; its image, its allurement are as incongruous as that world of universal ambivalence from which – one hopes – it would provide a shelter.

The real reason for the specifically intellectual variety of the universal (though by and large unrequited) love for community is seldom spelled out. More often than not it is given away unintentionally, as in a recent phrase of Chantal Mouffe:[20]

> it is always possible to distinguish between just and unjust, the legitimate and the illegitimate, but this can only be done from within a given tradition. . . . In fact, there is no point of view external to all tradition from which one can offer a universal judgement.

This sentence was intended as a polemic against the false pretences of impersonal, supra-human objectivism that guided modern strategies aimed at the suppression of contingency; as another salvo in the unrewarding but on the whole pleasurable skirmishes against 'positivistic science',[21] against the pious hope that one can be 'in the right' for all times, places, and *for everybody*. In fact, Mouffe's message is that – even with absolute truth defunct and universality dead and burried – some people at least can still have what their past (legislatively predisposed) benefactors, now decried as deceitful, promised to give: the joy of being 'in the right' – though now perhaps not at all times, not in all places at the same time, and only for certain people.

'Tradition' (it could be in other texts 'community' or a 'form of life') is the answer to Richard Bernstein's anxiety expressed in his rejoinder to Rorty's treatment of contingency – one that many found too radical to elicit popular enthusiasm, and certainly calling for too much heroism to seriously anticipate a massive following. Having conceded to Rorty the lack of universal foundations for any belief or value locally upheld, Bernstein[22] could not deny himself asking

> How are we to decide who are the rational discussants and in what sense they are 'rational'? . . . Sorting out rational discussants from those who are judged to be irrational is precisely the type of issue that needs to be 'hammered out'. . . . There are plenty of questions concerning justification, objectivity, the scope of disciplines, the proper way of distinguishing rational from irrational discussants, and *praxis* that are answerable and demand our attention'.[23]

All right – so Bernstein seemed to be saying – one cannot establish authoritative rules stretching beyond the confines of a given community of meaning or tradition; but surely this need not mean that the game of rules is over? Surely the referees and their decisions, which the players are not allowed to appeal against, are still in place and needed, though with a somewhat smaller 'area of catchment', narrower area of jurisdiction? The 'distinguishing between just and unjust' that is 'always possible' is precisely the purpose for which Mouffe postulates 'tradition'. The need of the '*objective* demand for our attention', of the grounding of the right to set us, the *rational* subjects, apart from those who we are allowed to dismiss as *irrational*, is Bernstein's motive to do the same. The anguish of the contingent person seeking affirmation of her personal truth is aided and abetted by the anxiety of an intellectual seeking reaffirmation of her legislative rights and leadership role.

Michel Maffesoli has recently suggested a highly suggestive concept of *neo-tribalism*[24] to describe the world like ours: a world that contains, as its conspicuous feature, the obsessive search for community. Ours, Maffesoli suggests, is a *tribal* world, one that admits of but tribal truths and tribal decisions about right and wrong or beauty and ugliness. Yet this is also a *neo*-tribal world, a world different in most vital aspects from the original tribal antiquity.

The tribes, as we know them from ethnographic reports and ancient accounts, were tightly structured bodies with controlled membership. Gerontocratic, hereditary, military or democratic agencies, invariably armed with effective powers of inclusion and exclusion, monitored the traffic (limited as it was) over the boundary of the group. Remaining inside or outside the tribe was seldom a matter of individual choice; indeed, this kind of fate was singularly unfit to be re-forged into destiny. The neo-tribes – the tribes of contemporary world, are on the contrary formed – as concepts rather than integrated social bodies – by the multitude of individual acts of *self-identification*. Such agencies as might from time to time emerge to hold the faithful together have limited executive power and little control over co-option or banishment. More often than not, 'tribes' are oblivious of their following, and the following itself is cryptic and fickle. It dissipates as fast as it appears. 'Membership' is relatively easily revocable, and it is divorced from long-term obligations; this is a kind of 'membership' that does not require an admission procedure or authoritative rulings, and that can be dissolved without permission or warning. Neo-tribes 'exist' solely by individual decisions to sport the symbolic tags of tribal allegiance. They vanish once the decisions are revoked or the zeal and determination of 'members' fades out. They persevere only thanks to their continuing seductive capacity. They cannot outlive their power of attraction.

Neo-tribes are, in other words, the vehicles (and imaginary sediments) of individual self-definition. The efforts of self-construction generate them; the inevitable inconclusiveness and frustration of such efforts leads to their dismantling and replacement. Their existence is transient and always in flux. They inflame imagination most and attract most ardent loyalty when they still reside in the realm of hope. They are much too loose as formations to survive the movement from hope to practice. They seem to illustrate Jean-François Lyotard's description of being as 'escaping determination and arriving both too soon and too late'.[25] They seem also to fit very closely the Kantian concept of *aesthetic community*.

For Kant, the aesthetic community is and is bound to remain an *idea*; a promise, an expectation, a hope of unanimity that is not to be. Hope of unanimity brings aesthetic community into being; unfulfilment of that hope keeps it struggling for life, and thus alive. The aesthetic community owes its existence, so to speak, to a false promise. But individual choice cannot be committed without such promise.

> Kant uses the word 'promise' in order to point out the non-existent status of such a republic of taste (of the United Tastes?). The unanimity concerning what is beautiful has no chance of being actualized. But every actual judgement of taste carries with it the promise of universalization as a constitutive feature of its singularity. . . .

> The community required as a support for the validity of such judgment must always be in the process of doing and undoing itself. The kind of consensus implied by such a process, if there is any consensus at all, is in no way argumentative but is rather allusive and elusive, endowed with a spiral way of being alive, combining both life and death, always remaining *in statu nascendi* or *moriendi*, always keeping open the issue of whether or not it actually exists. This kind of consensus is definitely nothing but a cloud of community.[26]

Those among us who – prompted by memories of the legislative era – wish a situation in which 'it is always possible to distinguish legitimate and illegitimate' to hold, are bound to be disappointed. The best they can obtain to support such a possibility under present postmodern conditions are but such aesthetic communities – *clouds of communities*. Such communities will never be anything like Tönnies's cosy and unreflective (cosy *because* unreflective) homes of unanimity. Tönnies-style communities fall apart the moment they know of themselves as communities. They vanish (if they have not evaporated before) once we say 'how nice it is to be in a community'. From that moment on, community is not a site of secure settlement; it is all hard work and uphill struggle, a constantly receding horizon of the never ending road; anything but natural and cosy. We console ourselves and summon our wilting determination by invoking the magic formula of 'tradition' – trying hard to forget that tradition lives only by being recapitulated, by being construed as *heritage*; that it appears, if at all, only at the end, never at the beginning of agreement; that its retrospective unity is but a function of the density of today's communal cloud . . . .

Given our knowledge of contingency – now spilling over from the idea of the beautiful to that of the being itself, to its truth and its *reason* – we cannot abandon our search for consensus: we know after all that agreement is not pre-determined and is not guaranteed in advance, that it has nothing but our argument to stand on. Ours is the courage of despair. We cannot but redouble our efforts while going from defeat to defeat. The Kantian antinomy of the judgment of taste showed that disputation was as much unavoidable as in the end inconclusive and irrelevant – a circumstance that both Habermas and his detractors lose sight of. Habermas, in so far as he presents the model of undistorted communication as a realistic prospect of truth-consensus; and his critics, when they try to disavow the adequacy of such model, accusing it of not offering a firm enough ground for agreement, and so tacitly implying that some other, presumably firmer grounds, ought to be sought and can be found.

Under these circumstances, the foremost paradox of the frantic search for communal grounds of consensus is that it results in more dissipation and fragmentation, more heterogeneity. The drive to synthesis is the major factor in producing endless bifurcations. Each attempt at convergence and synthesis leads to new splits and divisions. What purported to be the formula for agreement to end all disagreement – proves to be, the moment it has been formulated, an occasion for more disagreement and new need of negotiation. All efforts to solidify loose life-world structures prompt more fragility and fissiparousness. The search for community turns into a major obstacle to its formation. The only consensus likely to stand a chance of success is the acceptance of heterogeneity of dissensions.

For the intellectual, such a prospect is hard to live with. It means a realm of authority as frail and friable as the current capacity to impress one's 'regulative principles' upon some others who (as long as they abide by those principles, but hardly a minute longer) form 'the community' for which a joint 'tradition' can be then retrospectively put together, and commonality of language construed through inclusive/exclusive practices. No wonder intellectuals dream of something more solid. Being intellectuals, they must believe that the sought-after solidity may be only a function of theoretical practice; that their juridical authority over communities may be only made permanent and secure through enforcing their version of intellectual law and order. Hence attempts like Jay's will be made over and over again. They will hardly ever stop, as each attempt to draw up firm borders of another communal consensus (in so far as it remains unsupported by institutionalized coercion) would itself become one more ingredient of that pluralism it purported to abolish or at least qualify. Once communally grounded (and reconciled to such grounding) rather than seeking supracommunal, species-wide or even *apodictic* guarantees, the standard of truth poorly serves the ambition of expanding authority. Whatever remains of the strategies of legislative reason turns out to be counterproductive: it defies its purpose.

PYRRHONIAN CRISIS, MARK TWO

Just before the spectacular rise of 'foundational philosophy', in the sixteenth century, European metaphysics went through a brief, yet dramatic period of *Pyrrhonian crisis*.[27] The unclouded rule of the Aristotelian paradigm seemed to come to an end when the arguments of the sworn enemies of Aristotelian 'dogmatism' among the ancient philosophers were unearthed, rehashed and turned against contemporary seekers of truth, now redefined as latter-day dogmatists.

The critics reached for the legacy of the long line of sceptics – from Pyrrhon to Sextus Empiricus – who in the Hellenic and Roman worlds successfully played the role of 'bad conscience' (for some)

or the 'sober voice' (for others) of philosophy until banished by
the ascending Christian truth of the Revelation. Sceptics doubted
that truth was possible; they doubted that if truth were possible,
we would know it; they doubted that if we knew the truth, we
would be able to convince ourselves and the others that we did.
One by one, the Sceptics took apart all criteria advanced by the
Aristotelians for telling true from false beliefs; no criterion stood
up to their scrutiny, and – by induction – the Sceptics concluded
that no such criterion can be ever found, and thus the beliefs we
hold will never ascend to the level of truth, and doubt will never
stop haunting our knowledge.

In particular, ancient Sceptics declared suspect the two pillars of
dogmatic certainty: the 'evidence of senses' – the reliability of
human sensual impressions, and the 'evidence of clarity' – the
human critical faculty to tell apart the 'obviously true' from false
convictions. However clear and obvious our representations, we
would not know whether they are true, as the senses on which
we rely keep supplying fickle and contradictory information.
And there was no way of setting apart true from false ideas,
as both appeared to us with similar strength, 'obviousness' and
degrees of clarity. The Sceptic case had been summed up and
codified in the course of the second century by Ainesydemos
in the form of ten arguments (*tropoi*), focusing on the frailty
of the knowing subject's cognitive faculties. Thus the second
trope pointed to the differences in the impressions received by
individual subjects; the fourth argument referred to the change
of impressions depending on the state of the subject – age, health
or mood, while several following *tropoi* considered the changing
shape of the objects depending on the external circumstances of
perception, like the position occupied by the object or its distance
from the observer. Finally, the last argument raised the issue of
the subject's inability to set apart the evidence of senses from the
representations induced by customs, laws, legendary beliefs or,
indeed, dogmatic theories themselves.[28] As no knowing subject
could insist on the truthfulness of his impressions and ideas, no
one could claim the kind of certainty that would ground a universal
validity of his knowledge. No opinion could be accepted with full,
unqualified confidence; there was no way to measure in advance the
error of any view, as no standards permitted the selection from the
multitude of impressions and ideas the ones that could be assigned
the attribute of truth.

The arguments of the Sceptics, relegated first to the margins of Greek philosophy, rapidly gained in strength, influence and audience with the growing cultural pluralism of the Hellenistic world and expanding *oikoumene* opened up by the spread of Roman rule. With the prospect of the 'fusion of horizons' or any other form of 'melting pot' rather distant if not altogether irrealistic, what inspired the efforts of Sceptic philosophers more than any purely philosophical question was a thoroughly practical issue: is it possible to live reasonably (indeed, successfully) under conditions of lasting and irreparable uncertainty, and if so, how? Sceptics were not prophets of despair, as their critics tried to insinuate; neither did they advise resignation and retreat from active life (in which they differed from Cynics and, to an extent, from Stoics). What they did suggest was that philosophical equanimity (a state of mind they compared to *galene* – the smooth surface of a bottomless sea), the abandonment of vain efforts to separate the grains of truth from the chaff of illusions, was needed the better to concentrate on the practical business of life; an art that could be practised effectively without the certainty countersigned and vouched for by dogmatic philosophers. According to Pyrrhon, withdrawal from worldly affairs would be an act of rebellion, a conduct utterly at odds with the sceptical doctrine that advised reconciliation and humility. Resignation from universally valid truth did not mean rejection of the evidence offered by representation; it only suggested the need for caution and careful application of reason to the planning and the execution of action. Having rejected all dogmatic criteria of truth, another Sceptic, Carneades, insisted on the practical criteria of proper (effective) behaviour. For the latter, he suggested, one did not need the truth. One could rely on trustworthy representations; better still, on representations unquestioned and unchallenged by others and thus enjoying the tacit support of general agreement; best of all, on representations checked and tested as thoroughly as could be done in given circumstances.

The power-assisted truth of Christian Revelation silenced for a time sceptic voices; they became audible again once the ecclesiastic version of the power/knowledge package fell apart at the threshold of the modern era. Thus the *Pyrrhonian crisis* took off, playing havoc, for a time, with the philosophical establishment suddenly deprived of the protective cover of the universal Church. Soon, however, the power/knowledge syndrome was reassembled again, this time thanks to the increasingly ambitious and potent secular state. With a new universal order becoming once more a plausible prospect, philosophical certainty was reassembled again through the work of Spinoza, Descartes or Kant. This time, however, it was Reason and not Revelation that served as the guarantee of the confidence called truth: *legislative* reason was now taking over the world-creating potency once accredited only to God. The universal order of the future, after all, was to be *made*; it could only be a *human* work and could count only on earthly powers.

The falling credibility of the project of modernization as the royal road to new pan-species universality, coupled with the falling dependency of the now well established modern state on *ideological* (legitimational) grounding of administrative discipline and social integration, once more weakened the conviction and resolve of legislative reason and the verisimilitude of its promise. Difference has been revealed for what it was throughout the modern adventure: the existential condition rather than a temporary irritant, and so was the existential foundation of disagreement and undecideability. Sceptical doubts, never fully extinguished, surfaced again. Pyrrhonian Crisis Mark Two began. It constitutes the philosophical folklore of postmodernity.

As each of two crises responded to the collapse of a specifically grounded certainty, the Mark Two differs somewhat from its three-centuries-old predecessor. Instead of dwelling on the *weakness* of the cognitive subject and its inability to make a good choice among the cacophony of contradictory pretences (suddenly exposed once the protective cover of religious authority had been withdrawn), it focuses on the *strength* of community; on its ability to *make* choices good. Instead of calling individuals, bereaved by the withdrawal of supra-human guarantees of truth, to distrust promises of faultless wisdom and fall back on the faculties of their own good sense, it exhorts them, now liberated from coercive practices of truth-definers, to huddle in the warm embrace of community.

Community, present only marginally if at all in the deliberations of the Pyrrhonians of the sixteenth and the seventeenth centuries (mostly negatively, as the habitat of the sinister idols of tribe or the marketplace), figures most prominently in the very centre of the scepticism of present-day interpretive reason. Conversation and agreement-seeking – the defining traits of the community – serve as the arch-metaphor of this reason as against the command-issuing, order-guarding powers favoured by its legislative opponent.

RE-NEGOTIATING THE PHILOSOPHY/ SOCIOLOGY RELATION

The current crisis of legislative reason and the ascent of its interpretive alternative has a profound impact on the relationship between philosophy and sociology. For sociologists, it means much more than switching allegiances and affiliations from one type of philosophical doctrine and strategy to another. It means nothing less than the revision of the very relationship between sociology and philosophy established and rarely questioned throughout the modern era.

The declaration of intent associated with philosophy impelled and agitated by legislative reason was, overtly or implicitly, an anti-sociological manifesto. The pronounced (even if unintended) *relativizing* edge of sociological reason was anathema to the legislating project aiming at the universal grounds of truth. The localized sources of beliefs sociology was adept in documenting (and willy-nilly playing with the danger of legitimizing) were precisely the obstacles to truth that legislative philosophy was determined to disempower. The last great act of legislative reason, Husserl's phenomenology, listed socially and culturally induced representations (the very subject-matter of sociological inquiry) as the first among the impurities destined to fall under the blade of transcendental reduction and to be 'bracketed away' from the field of philosophical relevance. Philosophy inspired by legislative reason left sociology a choice between the role of a handmaiden, keeping clean the analytical cutlery in the home of good knowledge owned by philosophers, or facing the prospect of dishonourable discharge without references.

With interpretive reason's discovery of communal bases of knowledge and the selection of communication-servicing as the major task of philosophers, the traditional figuration has been drastically changed. Deprecated and more often than not suppressed inclinations inherent in sociological practice have been rehabilitated while their detractors have been discredited. Moreover, inquiry into the bases of knowledge in general, good knowledge included, turned out to be first and foremost a *sociological* enterprise, once it has been accepted that the 'goodness' of knowledge is socially (communally) determined and cannot be otherwise arrived at. The traditional concerns of philosophy have been submerged by sociological reason. Husserl's strategy has been reversed: it is

143

now the socially and culturally induced, supported and protected representations that are exempt from reduction and bracketing away, while the search for foundations is redirected from transcendental subjectivity to the immanent, this-worldly context of the practice of daily life. Arguably the most poignant prefiguration of the new relationship can be retrospectively gleaned from Wittgenstein's curt description of understanding as 'knowing how to go on'. A watershed separates this description from the pretence of legislative reason to the unique understanding that allows it and it alone to tell the goers how and where to go, and what for.

Freed from the blackmail of legislative reason, sociology may concentrate on the task for which – due to the nature of its inquiry – it has been always best prepared. It may 'come out' – openly become what it was destined to be all along: the informed, systematic commentary on the knowledge of daily life, a commentary that expands that knowledge while being fed into it and itself transformed in the process.

REFERENCES

1 A fuller discussion of the two categories can be found in my *Legislators and Interpreters: On Modernity, Postmodernity and the Intellectuals* (Cambridge: Polity Press, 1987).

2 All quotations from Kant in this section are from J.M.D. Meiklejohn's translation (*Critique of Pure Reason*, London: Dent, 1969). Quotations from Descartes come from Margaret D. Wilson's edition of *The Essential Descartes* (London: New English Library, 1969). Plato is quoted in W.H.D. Rouse's translation (*Great Dialogues of Plato*, London: New English Library, 1956). Spinoza's 'On the Correction of the Understanding' is quoted from Andrew Boyle's translation, included in Dent's 1986 edition of Spinoza's *Ethics*.

3 Philosophy can be foundational in respect to the rest of culture because culture is an assemblage of claims to knowledge, and philosophy adjudicates such claims. . . . We owe the notion of philosophy as the tribunal of pure reason, upholding or denying the claims of the rest of culture to the eighteenth century, and especially to Kant, but this Kantian notion presupposed general assent to Lockean notions of mental processes and Cartesian notions of mental substance.
(Richard Rorty, *Philosophy and the Mirror of Nature*, Oxford: Basil Blackwell, 1981, pp. 3–4)

Commenting on Kant's assertion that appearances must themselves have grounds which are not appearances, Hannah Arendt observed that 'the philosophers' "conceptual efforts" to find something beyond appearances have always ended with rather violent invectives against "mere appearance", (*The Life of the Mind*, Part One: 'Thinking', London: Secker & Warburg, 1978, p. 24). Philosophers sought to prove the 'theoretical supremacy of Being and Truth over mere appearance, that is, the supremacy of the *ground* that does not appear over the surface that does' (p. 25). Let us add that the postulated 'ground' was by definition out of the reach of ordinary, lay and commonsensical sensual impressions, and thus its supremacy reflected symbolically and legitimized the supremacy of the mental over the physical, and of the practitioners of 'theoretical practice' (Husserl) over those engaged merely in the menial, manual operations. The search for grounds and denigration of appearances was an integral part of the assault against non-philosophical, autonomous truth-claims. To quote Arendt again, 'the fact is, that there is hardly any instance on record of the many . . . declaring war on philosophers. As far as the few and the many are concerned, it has been rather the other way round' (ibid., p. 81).

4   Karl Marx and Friedrich Engels, *German Ideology* (Moscow: International Publishers, 1968), p. 413.

5   Alvin Gouldner, *For Sociology: Renewal and Critique in Sociology Today* (New York: Basic Books, 1973), p. 420.

6   Emile Durkheim, *Les règles de la méthode sociologique* (1895). Quoted in Anthony Giddens's translation from *Emile Durkheim: Selected Writings* (Cambridge: Cambridge University Press, 1972), pp. 59–60.

7   Quoted in *Max Weber: The Interpretation of Social Reality*, ed. by J.E.T. Eldridge (London: Nelson, 1972), p. 102. Note that from the Weberian perspective awareness and knowledge can be accredited to lay actors only if put in inverted commas; that is, only allegorically.

8   Quoted in translation by A.M. Henderson and Talcott Parsons in Max Weber, *The Theory of Social and Economic Organization* (New York: Free Press, 1947), pp. 88, 92–3, 97.

9   I have discussed this question at greater length in 'Legislators and interpreters: culture as ideology of intellectuals', in: *Social Structure and Culture*, ed. by Hans Haferkamp (Berlin: Walter de Gruyer, 1989).

10 Hans Georg Gadamer, *Truth and Method*, trans. by Garrett Burden and John Cumming (London: Sheed & Ward, 1975), pp. 263–5. Note the striking affinity between these formulations of Gadamer and the interpretive scepticism of Freud, ever more pronounced toward the end of his long life devoted to the 'hermeneutics of human self'. From 1936 on, Freud repeatedly asked the question 'is there such a thing as a natural end to an analysis or is it really possible to conduct it to such an end?' ('Analysis terminable and interminable'), 'what guarantee we have while we are working on these constructions'? ('Construction in analysis'), only to admit that 'it may seem that no general reply can in any event be given to this question', and, more seminally yet, that the practitioners of psychoanalysis may not 'pretend that an individual construction is anything more than a conjecture which awaits examination, confirmation or rejection' (comp. *Collected Papers Vol. V*, London: Hogarth Press, 1950, pp. 319, 363–5). Freud retained the vocabulary of 'confirmation' and 'rejection' while the thrust of his

argument suggested the absence of an operational procedure that could make such ideal types of legislative reason applicable in psychoanalytical practice.

11 Roland Barthes, *The Pleasure of the Text*, trans. by Richard Miller (New York: Hill & Wang, 1975), pp. 40, 64. In *The Visible and the Invisible* (Evanston, 1969, pp. 40–1) Maurice Merleau-Ponty brought into relief the new image of interpretation as a continuous and, in the end, monotonous process:

> For when an illusion dissipates, when an appearance suddenly breaks up, it is always for the profit of a new appearance which takes up again for its own account the ontological function of the first. . . . The dis-illusion is the loss of one evidence only because it is the acquisition of *another evidence*.

The break in quality the linear vision of legislative reason made us to expect is not forthcoming in the process.

12 Comp. Susan A. Handelman, *The Slayers of Moses: The Emergence of Rabbinical Interpretation in Modern Literary Theory* (Albany: State University of New York Press, 1982), particularly pp. 49–50, 91, 131. Handelman presents Derrida's philosophy of deconstruction as a reassertion of the Rabbinical tradition of interpretations that 'form part of the mesh and interweave with the text itself' as against the 'protestant literalism' – that 'hermeneutics of immanence and univocal meaning'.

13 Comp. Joseph H. Smith's and William Keniger's introduction to *Taking Chances: Derrida, Psychoanalysis and Literature*, the book they edited (Baltimore: Johns Hopkins University Press, pp. x–xi, 1984).

14 Comp. *Midrash and Literature*, ed. by Geoffrey H. Hartman and Sanford Budick (Yale University Press, 1986), p. xi.

15 *Philosophy and the Mirror of Nature*, p. 179. In 'Truth and Falsehood' (comp. *History and Truth*, trans. by Charles A. Kelbley (Northwestern University Press, 1979), Paul Ricoeur insists that

> science is never more than one 'praxis' among others, a 'theoretical praxis', as Husserl says, constituted by the decision to suspend all affective, utilitarian, political, aesthetic, and religious considerations and to hold as true only that which answers to the criteria of the scientific method in general, and the particular methodology of such and such a discipline.

In Ricoeur's view, it is the 'ambiguous nature of our will to unity' that is at one and the same time 'the goal of reason and violence', and a constant source of a temptation 'to unify the true by violence'. A temptation, Ricoeur says, that was surrendered to by the Church and the state, but which, one may add, always threatens to seduce the philosophy of legislative reason.

16 Comp. *Fin-de-siècle Socialism and Other Essays*, by Martin Jay (London: Routledge, 1988), pp. 34, 50, 60.

17 Hayden White, *Tropics of Discourse: Essays in Cultural Criticism* (Baltimore: Johns Hopkins University Press 1978), p. 3. White indicates that every '*applied* syllogism contains an enthymemic element, this element

consisting of nothing but the *decision* to move' from one plane to another, a decision which 'logic cannot preside over'.

And if this is true even of the classical syllogism, how much more true must it be of those pseudosyllogisms and chains of pseudosyllogisms which make up mimetic-analytic prose discourse, of the sort found in history, philosophy, literary criticism, and the human sciences in general?'

18 Agnes Heller, *Can Modernity Survive?* (Cambridge: Polity Press, 1990), pp. 25–6.
19 Manning Nash, *The Cauldron of Ethnicity in the Modern World* (University of Chicago Press, 1989), pp. 128–9.
20 Chantal Mouffe, 'Radical democracy: modern or postmodern?', in *Universal Abandon?; The Politics of Postmodernism* (Edinburgh University Press, 1988), p. 37.
21 As Peters and Rothenbuler wittily commented,

> just as the street criminal is too productive a worker in our society to be utterly stamped out (he sustains the law, prisons, police, burglar alarm installers, crime beat reporters, and prime-time TV writers), so the positivist, with his adoring attachment to a reality apart from everything human, has sustained a major part of the academic criticism for the past decade (supporting Marxist, hermeneutic, and deconstructive criticisms, for instance, since he takes the political as the neutral, the made as the given, and the exercise of will as apparent truth).

(John Durham Peters and Eric W. Rothenbuler, 'The reality of construction', in *Rhetoric in the Human Sciences*, ed. by Herbert W. Simons, London: Sage Publications, 1989, pp. 16–17)
22 Comp. Richard Bernstein, *Philosophical Profiles: Essays in a Pragmatic Mode* (Cambridge: Polity Press, 1985), pp. 53, 57.
23 Thirty-five years have passed since Dwight Macdonald offered the myth of 'community' as a cure for present-day atomization and loneliness, yet his lyric poetry (replicated in this country to great effect by F.R. Leavis) is still distinctly audible in the confident, no–doubts-allowed conviction that the 'community' will do what the discredited 'society' spectacularly fails to achieve. Community, in Macdonald's memorable rendition, is

> a group of individuals linked to each other by common interest, work, traditions, values, and sentiments; something like a family, each of whose members has a special place and function as an individual while at the same time sharing the group's interests (family budget), sentiments (family quarrels), and culture (family jokes). The scale is small enough so that it 'makes a difference' what the individual does, a first condition for human – as against mass [Macdonald would have probably written today 'contingent' – Z.B.] – existence.

(Dwight Macdonald (1953) 'A theory of mass culture', in *Diogenes* 3: 1–17)

24 Comp. Michel Maffesoli, 'Jeux de masques', in *Design Issues* IV (1988), nos.1 & 2, pp. 141ff. Maffesoli draws on earlier ideas of Gilbert Durand and Edgar Morin. Maffesoli's term, it seems, tries to capture the phenomenon similar to that discussed by Eric Hobsbawm under the heading of the *inventing of tradition*, and by Benedict Anderson under the heading of *imagined community*.

25 Jean-François Lyotard, *Peregrinations: Law, Form, Event* (Columbia University Press, 1988), p. 32.

26 Ibid., p. 38.

27 Comp. Richard H. Popkin, *The History of Scepticism from Erasmus to Spinoza* (University of California Press, 1979).

28 A comprehensive discussion of these arguments can be found in Léon Robin, *Pyrrhon et le Scepticisme Grec* (Paris: Presses Universitaires de France, 1944) part 3, chap. 1; or Adam Krokiewicz, *Sceptycyzm Grecki* (Warszawa: Pax, 1964) vol. 2.

6

THE WORLD ACCORDING TO JEAN BAUDRILLARD

In one of his essays George Orwell recalled the long extinct American journal *The Booster*, which used to advertise itself as '*non-political, non-ethical, non-literary, non-educational, non-progressive, non-consistent, and non-contemporary*'. I remember *The Booster* whenever I try to visualize the world as portrayed by Jean Baudrillard, professor of sociology at Nanterre and for the last decade or two one of the most talked about analysts of our times. Like that obscure journal, though with much more sound and fury, Baudrillard patches up the identity of his world out of absences alone. The world according to Baudrillard is like a party, noted mostly for the extraordinary number of people we knew and thought of highly, who have – alas – failed to turn up.

Baudrillard writes of what is not there, what went missing, what is no more, what lost its substance, ground or foundation. The major trait of our times, he insists, is disappearance. History has stopped. So has progress, if there ever was such a thing. Things we live with today are identifiable mostly as vestiges: once parts of a totality which gave them a place and function, but today just pieces condemned to seek a meaningful design in vain and destined for a game without end.

So far, I admit, nothing to shock a seasoned reader of the many biographies of these curious times of ours, to which most biographers give the name of *postmodernity*, which means hardly anything more than the end, absence or disappearance. After all, how can one write about change which is still happening and far from being complete? All change is about something which has been but is no more, or something else losing its old look or habits. . . . But the change Baudrillard writes about is not an ordinary change. It is, so to speak, a change to put paid to all changes. A change after which we cannot speak of change any more. Even the phrase 'no longer' loses its sense.

149

No longer is there 'no longer', as the base-line against which we measure what is and what is not, and how the first differs from the second, has also disappeared.

Speaking of change implies solidity. To alter identity, the changing object must first have one. Objects must possess clear boundaries and unmistakeable features of their own. They must differ, first of all, from their images and representations. That world in which we confidently spoke of change, renewal, trends or directions was a firm and trusty world where one could tell the difference between an idea and its referent, representation and what it represented, simulation and truth, image and reality. All these things are hopelessly mixed up now, says Baudrillard. Hence, it is not only that we are bound to speak of disappearance: it is the last time that we can do so. From now on, even the talk of 'no more' will be no more. Even disappearance disappears.

If all this boggles the mind too much for our liking, it is because our language is not well geared to discuss the 'post-change' era. Our language implies objects 'out there'. It invokes an image of things which can be touched and handled, examined and measured. Above all, the things it invokes stand apart from each other and occupy their own sites in space and in the flow of time. No wonder that once we use such a language (mind you, this is the only language we have) to describe Baudrillard's world, whatever we may say will sound clumsy, obsure and confused.

The reason is that in Baudrillard's world we have no right to speak of distinctions and differences, yet we do speak of them whenever we use our language – that is, whenever we speak. Take the most important of Baudrillard's concepts: this of *simulation* ('feigning to have what one hasn't'). Simulation, we are told, 'is no longer that of a territory, a referential being or a substance'. In simulation – this crucial, universal, perhaps exclusive, mode in which all things today are – the territory no longer precedes the map. It is rather the map that precedes the territory. The map 'engenders the territory'. Well, you would say, one can agree or disagree with this proposition, but at least one knows what the proposition is about and how to find out whether it is true or not. Alas, your satisfaction is, to say the least, premature. Simulation, you think, consists in *pretending* that something is not what it *really* is; you are not alarmed because you feel that you know how to tell pretence from reality. The simulation Baudrillard talks about is not like that, however. It effaces the very difference between true and false, real and imaginary. We no longer have the means of testing pretence against reality, or just know which is which. There is no exit from our quandary. To report the change, we must say that 'from now on' the 'relationship has been reversed' and the map precedes the territory. The fact is, however, that all this talking about map, territory, their relationship, reversal of relationship, etc. is illegitimate. With simulation rampant and in full swing, even the words we use 'feign to have what they havn't': meanings, referents. In fact we do not know the difference between map and territory, and would not know it even with our noses pressed against the very thing.

Together with the rest of our language, the ordinary concept of 'simulation' upholds the reality principle; Baudrillard's 'simulation' undermines it. All simulation is a deception, but the simulation Baudrillard speaks about is doubly so: 'It is no longer a question of a false representation of reality (ideology), but of concealing the fact that the real is no longer real' – at least no more real than the next thing, no firmer than the thing which feigns it. What we face here is, so to speak, a simulation of the second order, or – to use Baudrillard's favourite prefix – the *hyper*simulation.

Everything is 'hyper' in Baudrillard's world. Everything transcends and leaves behind the very opposition which it stood for and which used to lend it an identity of its own. This transcendence itself is 'hyper': the oppositions have been in fact *dissolved*, and so things have lost their identity. We live in *hyperreality*. Reality is 'more real than real', in that it no longer sets itself against something else, which unlike itself is phoney, illusionary or imaginary. Reality has devoured everything, and everything can claim reality with equal justice (or injustice, which amounts to the same). What is real politics, for instance? Smiling faces on the TV screen emitting headline-catching one-liners, or the profound visions and world-shattering deeds they simulate? Or what is the real product we inhale – the vicarious joy of riding through the windswept canyons of Marlboro country, or the pungent smoke of smouldering weed? Which one is more, which is less real? And – does it matter? In hyperreality, truth has not been destroyed. It has been made irrelevant.

In hyperreality, everything is in excess of itself (not 'too much'; how would one go about deciding what is too much, what too little, what just enough?). Piles of images, heaps of information, flocks of desires. So multiplied, the images represent nothing but themselves, information does not inform, desires turn into their own objectives. The world is no longer a *scene* (a place where the play is staged which, as we have the right to suspect, will be directed towards some concrete ending, even if we do not know in advance what it is); instead, it is *obscene*: a lot of noise and bustle without plot, scenario, director – and direction. It is a *contactual*, not a *contractual*, world. It has been patched together from hasty and perfunctory, skin-deep encounters, events with no past and no future, and above all no consequence. Mark Poster, Baudrillard would say, had no right to criticize him for poorly defining his major concepts, refraining from a sustained and systematic analysis and writing about particular experiences as if that could replace reliable synthesis. What under the dominion of the reality principle would be a crime against reason and scholarly decency, in hyperreality is the only responsible way of representing this fluidity which simulates something it is not. To follow Mark Poster's call, Baudrillard would say, would mean joining the conspiracy to hide the absence of a line dividing the real from the unreal . . . .

If *The Booster* is one thing which comes to mind when wading through Baudrillard's universe, François Rabelais is another. The world according to Jean Baudrillard is much like the world vividly painted by Rabelais; only Rabelais wrote a satire, while Baudrillard is dead serious.

Both worlds – the one inhabited by Gargantua and Pantagruel, and the one, as Baudrillard insists, populated by us – have been painted in fleshy colours. In both worlds men and women pass their time eating, drinking, fornicating and enjoying the desire to enjoy themselves. Both worlds are monstrously overgrown, run riot and go to the extremes. In Baudrillard's world, however, unlike in Rabelais's, the colours are drawn from decomposing flesh and diseased blood; eating, drinking and fornicating look strikingly similar to the jitters in the penultimate stage of delirium; while the world's exuberance is that of the cancer cell and the bacteria of putrefaction. What Rabelais celebrated, Baudrillard bemoans. From revisiting the domicile of Gargantua and Pantagruel, Baudrillard returns shattered and full of disgust – he has found there a social body which he could only describe as *mammaire, cellulaire, glandulaire*, in a state of advanced degeneracy, necrosis and decay. With all solid ground flushed away by the effluvia of decomposing reality, there is no Archimedes' point left, either accessible or at least imaginable, on which one could pivot the lever needed to force the derailed world back on its track.

Baudrillard brooks no hope, as the all-powerful simulation destroys all opposition to itself. Everything colludes to hide the fact that reality has been banished. The brave *Washington Post* journalists only added to the illusion that Watergate was a *scandal*, that away from Watergate there are some binding principles and some 'real', solid, reliable politics. Even Italian detonator-happy terrorists took part in the universal conspiracy, as they resuscitated the outdated belief in the difference between proper and improper, clean and unclean, simulated and real. Simulation hides the fact that everything is part of the same game; it offers the reality principle another lease of life – this time as a zombie. One cannot step outside simulation. Whatever one does to pierce through its veil, will only thicken the camouflage. Fighting simulation is itself a simulation. In the world of hyperreality, we are all like *hostages* – in the sense that we have been picked without relation to what we have done and that our fate will bear no relation to what we might yet do.

Mark Poster's brief yet comprehensive survey of Baudrillard's intellectual biography, together with the selection of fragments of his successive works,[1] provide an excellent opportunity to scan the long road which brought him to his present image of the world as a collage of absences and the palette of paints he uses today to paint it. Baudrillard embarked on that road twenty years ago (in *Le système des objets*, Gallimard, 1968, and *La société de consommation*, Gallimard, 1970) with an attempt to fix the frayed and tottery Marxist denture with new, sharp and high-tech teeth, better fit to bite critically into the brave new world of consumption. As the intoxication of the 1960s gave way to the *Katzenjammer* of the 1970s, Baudrillard's dental ambitions ran out of steam. Instead, a series of works were produced (most to the point, *L'échange symbolique et la mort*, Gallimard, 1976, and *De la séduction*, Galilée, 1979), remarkable mainly for the post-revolutionary gloom and despondency they exuded. Most recently, *Les stratégies fatales* (Bernard Grasset, 1983), and *La gauche divine* (Bernard Grasset, 1985), have introduced us into the fully-fledged Baudrillardian vision of the Gargantuan universe mark II – with its exuberant obscenity and wanton intemperance. They have also shown the author's latest mood: a curious quasi-Hegelian synthesis of early hopes and later resignation. We are now being told that the bovine immobility of the masses is the best form of activity we have, and that their doing nothing is the most excellent form of resistance.

In *America*, his most recently translated book, Baudrillard embarks on a search for *l'Amérique sidérale* – one which can only be found 'in the indifferent reflex of television, in the film of days and nights projected across the empty space, in the marvellously affectless succession of signs, images, faces, and ritual acts on the road'. Even when he watches the scene through the window of his fast-moving car, what he sees looks *like* TV film, can be understood only in terms set by such film, perhaps it is such film – but surely it would not matter much were it not. When Baudrillard's *flâneur* gets up and starts his car, it is not to explore the promenades of the city centre. He drives into the desert, looking for the most prominent mark of our times: the *disappearance*. The postmodern era is in its fullest of blossoms in the desert – '*for the desert is simply that: an ecstatic critique of culture, an ecstatic form of disappearance*'. For the same reason, one would guess, Baudrillard is fascinated with America: for the genius this country has shown 'in its irrepressible development of equality, banality, and indifference'.

America is a postmodern record of a postmodern world. The world recorded in the book and its record are postmodern because the first is not fully translatable, while the second is not a full translation. Much as the Third World would never make its own our capitalism and our democracy, so would Europe, burdened with its history and memory of class, never become as thoughtlessly equal and effortlessly indifferent as America. Among many things which have disappeared the hope of convergence and ensuing universality is perhaps the most salient. To replace the modern vision of an increasingly orderly garden of humanity, Baudrillard offers an image of a chaotic-looking site split into many minuscule allotments each with its own mini-order. To scan it all, one needs a fast car. Or a fast flow of pictures on the TV screen. Such scanning is entertainment. A fascinating variety of experience, at a breath-taking pace. An endless play of simulation. Freedom from responsibility. Freedom from the need to be serious. There is, it seems, another way in which the intellectual story of Jean Baudrillard may be told. The world he paints seems to be one likely to be seen by a person glued to the television screen; a person who replaced with TV screens the windows in the apartment he inhabits and in the car in which he travels to his university lectures; a person whose attention is at its sharpest during the commercial breaks in the constant flow of televised images he so avidly ingests. More than a century ago another Frenchman, the poet and critic Baudelaire, suggested that the right way to observe and make sense of the modern world is to stroll along the streets and past the shops of the urban metropolis. It is the *flâneur*, Baudelaire proposed, who has the best view of the true essence of modernity. Baudrillard tied the *flâneur* to the armchair in front of the TV set. The stroller does not stroll any more. It is the TV images, TV commercials, the goods and joys they advertise who now stroll, and run, and flow in front of the hypnotized viewer. Viewing is the only activity left to the former stroller. Baudelaire's stroller has turned into Baudrillard's watcher. The watcher knows well the immobility of the masses. From his own experience.

Personal experiences can be enclosed by the frame of the television screen. One doubts whether the world can. One suspects, *pace* Baudrillard, that there is life left after and beyond the television. To many people, much in their life is anything but simulation. To many, reality remains what it always used to be: tough, solid, resistant and harsh. They need to sink their teeth into some quite real bread before they abandon themselves to munching images.

It becomes a philosopher and an analyst of his time to go out and use his feet now and again. Strolling still has its uses.

NOTE

1 Jean Baudrillard, *Selected Writings*, edited and introduced by Mark Poster (Cambridge: Polity Press, 1988).

7

COMMUNISM:
A POSTMORTEM

The events of 1989 in the East-Central European belt of satellite communist regimes was a most fitting finale for the twentieth century, bound to be recorded in history as the age of revolutions. They changed the political map of the globe, affecting even parts ostensibly distant from the scene of the upheaval in ways which are still far from being fully grasped. They are also certain to be scrutinized for the updating they offer to our orthodox views of how revolutions come about and how are they conducted in a new sociocultural context.

Among *political* revolutions with which the modern era was fraught, genuinely *systemic* ones have been relatively rare. All political revolutions involved a change in the way in which the style of political rule affected the politically administered social system. Systemic revolutions, in addition, entailed a transformation of the system itself; a contrived, government-managed or at least government-initiated change of socio-economic structure, which took off at a moment when the political revolution has been completed. The two concepts are, of course, liminal; two opposite ends of a continuum along which the known revolutions – all or almost all of which have been 'mixed' cases – can be plotted.

Ideally-typically, revolution is 'merely political' (or, rather, non-systemic) in so far as it 'shakes off' a political regime dysfunctional in relation to a fully-fledged socio-economic system. Political revolution 'emancipates' the system from its political constraints. Recent revolutions in Portugal, Spain or Greece belong by and large to this category. They swept off oppressive dictatorial regimes, redundant from the point of view of fully developed bourgeois societies capable of self-sustained reproduction, already fully formed and capable of supporting a democratic order. Though it normally takes an organized, even conspiratorial minority, to overcome the coercive government of the day, such a minority may be justly seen in the traditional way: as an agent acting on behalf of certain well-established collective interests, an active and self-conscious vanguard of relatively integrated (economically and socially powerful, though politically disarmed) forces. One may say that the political revolutions of this kind simply remove an obstacle on the road already taken; or that they adjust the political dimension of the system to the other, economic and social, dimensions. This was, indeed, the original view of the revolution: having matured, like a butterfly inside the carapace of a pupa, society has to shatter the oppressive and gratuitous constraints that arrest its development. That imagery was a faithful reflection of the revolutions which accompanied the advance of the capitalist order: those revolutions were, so to speak, the instances of *bürgerliche Gesellschaften* shaking off the already obsolete frames of absolutist and despotic states within which they gestated.[1]

The recent anti-communist revolutions come close to the other pole of the continuum. In this respect, paradoxically, they are akin to the bolshevik revolution of 1917 rather than to classic capitalist revolutions that brought the unduly archaic body politic into agreement with the needs of the socio-economic traits of the system. Recent anti-communist revolutions have been *systemic* revolutions: they face the task of *dismantling* the extant system and *constructing* one to replace it. True, they toppled old dictatorial or despotic political regimes, like the other revolutions did; but here the similarity ends. A society capable of sustaining and reproducing itself without the perpetual and ubiquitous wardenship and command of political rulers (this is precisely the meaning of *bürgerliche Gesellschaft*) has yet to be constructed there; and the political stage of the revolution is only the act of site-clearing and condition-setting for the system-building job – a project that will have to be implemented under a close political supervision and through state initiative.

A corollary of this is a contradiction that has yet to reveal the full scale of its impact on further political history of post-communist Europe: the social forces which led to the downfall of the communist power (and so to the success of the political stage of the revolution) are not those that will eventually benefit from the construction of the new system. Forces whose interests will gain from the working of the new system will need to be brought into existence in the process of system-construction.

One of the reasons that even the most acute students of communist regimes were baffled and surprised by the sharply anti-communist direction of change prompted by the gathering social dissent, was the fact that before the series of revolutions started there were few, or no signs of organized social forces with interests pointing beyond the confines of the communist regime (as late as during the famous 'Round-Table Conference' in Poland there was no discussion of dismantling the planned economy or wholesale privatization of ownership; and none of the major participants indicated that they would put such matters on the political agenda, were the circumstances more favourable). Indeed, as the Polish sociologist Jadwiga Staniszkis observed, there were no 'transformative' interests among large classes of Polish society – none of the articulated groups raised the issue of private ownership or objected to the principle of the command economy.[2] In Aleksander Smolar's succinct summary of the situation barely a year before the end of the communist rule, 'the fundamental problem of a radical reform is the absence of any real social support'.[3] As I have indicated elsewhere, neither workers in the big industries who made up the core of the Solidarity movement, nor the state-protected individual farmers nor the few private entrepreneurs thriving on the inanities of clumsy central planning, wished a change that would go significantly beyond an essentially redistributive action.[4]

This was, let us emphasize, a *normal* picture for the state of social forces preceding any *systemic* revolution. Dissent the old system could not but generate tended to exceed the system's capacity for accommodation and thus pushed the crisis to breaking point; but this effect was precisely the result of couching demands in the language of the extant system (in the case of communist regimes – more planning, more centralized distribution, the reshuffling of resources within the order of administered justice, etc.) – and thus facing the system with output postulates it was unable to meet.[5] It is a constant and the constitutive attribute of systemic revolutions that the forces that destroy the *ancien regime* are not consciously interested in the kind of change which would eventually follow the destruction; before the old powers are removed, the design of a new system exists at the utmost as a vision held by a selected, narrow intellectual elite – not as a platform of any massive contest movement.[6]

To put this in a different way: the systemic revolution is not a result of the mass mobilization of support for the blueprint of an alternative system. The first stage of the systemic revolution – the overthrow of the old rulers who hold to the past order of society – bears all the marks of the 'systemic crisis' (i.e., of the system failing to generate the resources, physical and moral, needed for its reproduction), but does not, by itself, determine the alternative to the system that failed. The link between the failure of the old system and the required traits of the new one is construed in a political struggle between competing *theories* conceived and preached by intellectual schools. The nature of social forces that brought about the downfall of the old regime is not a decisive factor in the choice between such theories. Neither does the enmity manifested by the contestant forces towards the old regime guarantee their support for the new one that would be eventually chosen. The toppling of the old rulers does not conjure up the 'transformative interests' missing in the old regime.

Because of this double non sequitur, the survival of the revolutionary alliance is the main issue any systemic revolution is likely to confront 'the morning after' its political victory.[7] The original revolutionary alliance – one that overwhelms the resistance of the administrators of the *ancien regime* – is not normally a reflection of the unity of interests among forces of dissent. As a matter of fact, grievances which bring variegated groups into a political alliance united by its opposition to the government of the day, are highly differentiated as a rule – and more often than not mutually incompatible. It was – let us repeat – the persistent crisis of the old regime that condensed diffuse grievances into a united revolutionary force. Condensation (and unanimity in blaming the state for whatever the objected-to drawback or injustice may be) can follow the appearance of a large issue that seems to stand in the way of each and every demand (like the issue of continuing war in Russia of 1917). In a totalitarian system like the communist one, the tendency to condense the dispersed dissent into an integrated, frontal assault against the state is permanent. Aiming at the regulation of all aspects of social and economic activity, the state assumes willy-nilly explicit responsibility for each and every failing and suffering. All grievances are authoritatively interpreted as malfunctionings of the state and automatically politicized.[8] But would the unity of opposing forces survive the fall of the communist state? And would such forces be similarly energized by the uncertain attractions of the future regime? Would they not rather oppose a change likely to invalidate the form of action and political purposes they learned to pursue?

CHANCES OF DEMOCRACY IN SYSTEMIC REVOLUTIONS

Systemic revolutions must yet create the social forces in the name of which they embark on the thorough systemic transformation. In this, let us emphasize once more, lies their deepest paradox – and also the dangers to the democracy they intend to install. As Jerzy Szacki, a leading Polish sociologist, observed in April 1990,

> the basis for the victory of Western liberalism was the spontaneous development of economic relations. Today's Polish liberalism still remains a *doctrine* that is meant to provoke such a development in the first place – a doctrine the main inspiration for which has been the desire to exit from communism. In effect, today's Polish liberalism is strongly coloured by a 'constructivism' which the classical liberal thinkers most energetically fought against.[9]

Unlike the purely political revolutions, the systemic ones do not end with the chasing away of the old rulers. The post-revolutionary state faces the awesome tasks of large-scale social engineering; of prompting the formation of a new social structure which – whatever gains it may promise 'in the long run' for everybody's interests – will certainly play havoc with the extant distribution of relative privileges and deprivations. It is likely, therefore, to give rise to discontents of its own and regroup the inherited political alliances. It is unlikely, on the other hand, to secure from the start a majority in support of the intended change. As it remains, however, an 'active state' to a degree not drastically different from that of its predecessor, the post-revolutionary state cannot count on that parcelling out and self-dispersion of social dissent which is so easily attained in the established, market-based democracies. It can be, on the contrary, pretty sure to turn against itself the discontent its actions cannot but generate. For quite a considerable time yet, it will continue to act as a 'dissent-condensing' factor, and hence find it difficult to push forward the systemic transformation while being guided by democratically generated support for its actions.

The consequences for various post-communist regimes differ. What differentiates them is the moment at which a given country joined the series of anti-communist revolutions, and their political and social characteristics at the moment of joining. The collapse of communism in East-Central Europe was indeed a serial process, and the 'state of the game so far' significantly modified the conditions under which the next step was taken and its sociological significance.

Jean Baudrillard wrote recently of 'un pouvoir s'effondrant presque sans violence, comme convaincu de son inexistence par le simple miroir des foules et de la rue'.[10] This powerful picture of a power deemed invincible suddenly collapsing at the mere sight of the crowds refusing to leave the public square – 'as if persuaded of its own non-existence' – represents the endings of various communist states with varying precision. Certainly, for Czechoslovakia and Hungary and East Germany it is more correct than for Poland, which triggered off the series. For the few thousands in a carnival mood gathered at Vatzlavske Namesti or at the squares of Leipzig and Dresden to be so swiftly and so thoroughly successful (there was not even a need for the public squares of Budapest to be physically occupied), the 'non-existence' of the communist power had to be already convincingly demonstrated at the far end of the long and tortuous process of Polish permanent insurrection. People who filled the Vatzlavske Namesti, much as those who came with rifles to chase them away, knew already what the Poles had discovered by trial, error and a lot of suffering.

There were many factors that combined to make Poland first in the communism-dismantling process; it seems, however, that prominent among them was the protracted process of self-instruction in the self-management of society, culminating in the relatively early 'polonization' of the state–nation conflict in the aftermath of the military *coup d'état* of 1981. The process and the event meant to stop it put the relation between the state and the society, the role of the national state in the perpetuation of the oppressive regime as well as the extent of change attainable within the frame of the national state, in an entirely new perspective and triggered off ambitions that elsewhere looked more like idle utopias.

Gorbachev's decision to abandon the European satellites to their own resources and fate found Poland in a state sociologically very different from the countries which had not accumulated similar experience: most importantly, Poland had a fully developed, articulated and self-sustained alternative political force in the shape of a politically seasoned, powerful workers' union.

Thorstein Veblen wrote once of the 'penalty for being in the lead'; indeed, the well entrenched, confident and politically skilled contestant labour movement gave Poland the lead it enjoyed in the sapping and in the end dismantling of the communist rule in the east of Europe. And yet the very assets which secured that advantage may turn into handicap when it comes to the construction of a stable liberal-democratic regime (and this on top of the sorry state of Polish, and other East European economies, particularly when emerging from the shelter of COMECON barter and forced to measure themselves by the competitive criteria of the world market). Dissident intellectuals of Hungary and Czechoslovakia, with the help of students and unsettled urban youth, shook off their respective communist rulers without a nationwide political mobilization and with minimum application of massive political forces of their own, taking advantage of the blows delivered to the confidence and will to resistance of their local rulers 'by proxy' – by the revelations made in the course of the Polish battles. Once in power, they may now proceed to further, evidently less popular and less enthusing, stages of the revolution without the powerful and politically alert, defiantly independent mass movement breathing down their neck and closely watching their hands. They may, indeed, count on the apathy and lack of political skills of the population at large to help them round the first, most awkward corners of economic and political transformation, so that no violation of democracy would be needed to pave the road towards stable liberal democracy of the future.

This chance seems to be denied to Poland. After all, the workers of the largest industrial enterprises, those most obsolete dinosaurs of the failed communist industrialization, least capable of entering the dream of Europe and marked for extinction – were exactly the force that brought communism down (and became such a force through being moved then, as they still are now, by essentially the 'non-transformative' interests of better wages, better work and living conditions, and better ways of defending both of them in the future); but they are now bound to be the first to bear the most severe hardships of the economic transformation – intensification of labour, sharpening of work discipline, loss of job security, unemployment and all.

THE HOLD OF THE PATRONAGE STATE

The distinctive feature of the systemic revolutions now taking place in East-Central Europe is that the system they need to dismantle is one of state-administered patronage: that coercively imposed trade-off between freedom and security. Under the rule of the patronage state, freedom of individual choice in all its dimensions was to be permanently and severely curtailed, yet in exchange the less prepossessing aspects of freedom – like individual responsibility for personal survival, success and failure – were to be spared. To the strong, bold and determined, the patronage state feels like a most sinister rendition of the Weberian 'iron cage'; yet to many weak, shy and lacking in will it may also feel like a shelter. While the end of the oppressive supervision by the agencies of the state and the opening up of space for individual initiative is a change likely to be warmly greeted by all, the removal of the safety net and the burdening of the individual with responsibility previously claimed by the state may well arouse mixed feelings; it may also induce the past wards of state patronage to tune their antennae to populist promises of collective security, and make them into willing followers of any aspiring leader prepared to make such promises and lend his authority to popular suspicions about the dangers of unconstrained liberalism.

The tense period of the dismantling of the patronage state is ripe for complaints, Carlyle style, against the 'cash nexus' replacing much more fulsome, comradely, relations between masters and their men. The patronage the passing of which Carlyle bewailed was, however, unlike that of the communist state, diffuse and unpolitical; the patronage engraved in popular habits and thought by communist rule is state-centred and thoroughly political. It militates against the self-reliant individual and against the order of liberal democracy cut to the measure of such an individual. This is why the individuals ready for self-reliant life oppose patronage. In the west, they tended to buy themselves off the welfare state services (admittedly a considerably milder, and certainly only a one-sided version of state patronage in the comprehensive, communist style, individually, until the camp of the get-aways reached the critical mass enabling them to take a stand, collectively, against the burden which the continuing existence of the welfare institutions put on them all. In the post-communist east, with its middle classes mortally wounded and unlikely to recover vigour without the active patronage of the state, the prospects of a similar 'buy-out' are rather remote. Looking towards the state for guarantees of security (in private and business life alike) could be a habit which the post-communist reconstruction may reinforce rather than uproot.

Political formulae articulated by the anti-communist intellectuals in the east differ between themselves in the way they balance individual freedom against state-administered distributional justice. One can explain the division by reference to the controversial prospects of the state-patronage heritage. But another factor seems to interfere, rooted not so much in the communist past, as in the present of the 'professional society' which, according to many contemporary commentators from Daniel Bell on, the capitalist society becomes in its modern stage. From his thorough study of the mechanics of the contemporary western type of professional society Harold Perkin concludes that 'the struggle between the public and private sector professions is the master conflict of professional society', and that 'ostensibly class-based political parties' are 'in reality large coalitions of diverse professional interests'. Perkin suggests that the rivalry between two groups of professionals (two sections of the knowledge class) is grounded in the rift between genuinely incompatible interests. The rivalry is about resources, or rather about the principle of their distribution. Each one of the two sections obviously prefers principles better geared to the kind of skills it possesses. Thus the

> ideology of free market appeals to the professional managers of great corporations and their allies because it protects them from the accusation they most fear, that they themselves are the major threat to competition and the freedom of the citizens.

Presenting themselves as the gallant knights of freedom expressed in market competition, they conceal the fact that all competition drives out competitors and tends toward monopoly – and thus hope to pass in the public eye as the guarantors of freedom of choice and even political liberty. The professionals of the public sector, on the other hand, prefer to argue

> in terms of social justice for every citizen, rather than self-interest of each profession; [as this argument is accepted], once a service becomes professionalized under public auspices, the professionals discover further needs to be met and problems to be solved and a host of reasons for extending their activities. Hence the self-generating expansion of the State in all the advanced countries.[11]

From Perkin's vantage point, the communist system could be seen as the domination of 'public sector professionals' pushed to the radical extreme and secured with the help of the coercive resources of the state. The collapse of the communist system brings the post-communist societies closer to the conditions prevalent in the professional societies of the west. The process of the dismantling of the patronage state will need to be performed under those conditions. It will not be guided, therefore, by its own logic alone. The moves explicable by reference to the leftovers of state patronage (or by reference to the opposition they arouse) will intertwine with political developments that can only be understood in terms of modern competition for resources between the *public* and the *private* sector professionals.

The patronage state offered poor services, yet it did cut down on both gains and losses that might have resulted from individual decisions. The overall result was the diminution of risk (except for the area in which initiative was strictly off limits, that is in the space defined by the state as belonging to politics, its monopolistic domain) and the development of economic skills and attitudes that provide little support in situations of contingency, where probabilities are even and outcomes of decisions uncertain. Behaviour proper to unrestrained market conditions has not been learned even among private entrepreneurs and farmers as long as they acted under the conditions of a planned economy. The climate of market competition may feel too inclement for their liking. There is no necessary connection between private business and enthusiasm for a *laissez-faire* style of economic setting; an absence which the charges repeatedly raised by the Polish Peasant Party (and various political spokesmen vying for the votes of urban businessmen) against the government 'that lacks economic policy' profusely demonstrate.

THE COLLAPSE OF COMMUNISM AND THE ADVENT OF POSTMODERNITY

Communism was made to the measure of modern hopes and promises. Socialism's younger, hotheaded and impatient brother, it wholeheartedly shared in the family trust in the wonderful promises and prospects of modernity, and was awe-struck by the breathtaking vistas of society doing away with historical and natural necessity and by the idea of the ultimate subordination of nature to human needs and desires. But unlike the elder brother, it did not trust history to find the way to the millennium. Neither was it prepared to wait till history proved this mistrust wrong. Its war cry was: 'Kingdom of Reason – now!'

Like socialism (and all other staunch believers in the modern values of technological progress, the transformation of nature and a society of plenty), communism was thoroughly modern in its passionate conviction that a good society can only be a carefully designed, rationally managed and thoroughly industrialized society. It was in the name of those shared modern values that socialism charged the capitalist administrators of modern progress with mismanagement, inefficiency and wastefulness. Communism accused socialism of failing to draw conclusions from the charges: stopping at critique, denunciations, prodding – where an instant dismissal of inept and corrupt administrators was in order.

Lenin's redefining of the socialist revolution as a *substitution for*, instead of *continuation of*, the bourgeois revolution, was the founding act of communism. According to the new creed, capitalism was a cancerous growth on the healthy body of modern progress; no longer a necessary stage on the road to a society that will embody modern dreams. Capitalists could not be entrusted (as they once were by the founders of modern socialism, Marx and Engels) with even the preliminary job of site-clearing: 'melting the solids and profaning the sacred'. As a matter of fact, the site-clearing itself was neither a necessity, nor a job useful enough to justify the waste of time needed for its performance. As the principles of a rationally organized, good society (more factories, more machines, more control over nature) were well known and agreed upon, one could proceed directly to usher any society (and particularly a society without factories, without machines, without the capitalists eager to build them, without the workers oppressed and exploited in the process of building) into a state designed by those principles. There was no point in waiting till the good society arrived through the action of workers, fed up with the sufferings caused by capitalist mismanagement of progress. As one knew what the good society would be like, to delay or even slow down its construction was an unforgivable crime. The good society could be, had to be constructed right away, before the capitalists had a chance to mismanage and the workers to sample the outcomes of their mismanagement; or, rather, its designers should take over the management of society right away, without waiting for the consequences of mismanagement to show up. Capitalism was an unnecessary deflection from the path of Reason. Communism was a straight road to its Kingdom. Communism, Lenin would say, is Soviet power together with the 'electrification of the whole country': that is, modern technology and modern industry under a power conscious of its purpose in advance and leaving nothing to chance. Communism was modernity in its most determined mood and most decisive posture; modernity streamlined, purified of the last shred of the chaotic, the irrational, the spontaneous, the unpredictable.

To be fair to Lenin and other communist dreamers, we ought to recall that the good society of the nineteenth-century economists and politicians, disciples of Smith, Ricardo, James and John Stuart Mill, was not a society of *growth* (difficult as this is today to comprehend), but a society of *stability* and *equilibrium*; one of a steady, well-balanced economy, catering for all needs of the population – not an economy beefing up and pushing to new limits their consumptive needs and capacities. The goodness of society was to be measured by its productive performance, by the degree of gratification of needs (given, 'objective', finite), not by the growing richness and spectacularity of its consumptive display. Let us recall too that for the political theorists and practitioners of that century, disciples of Hegel, Comte or Bentham, the good society was one in which the individual conscience was well geared to the 'common interest', one in which the state acted as the supreme embodiment and the spokesman for the interests of all, while the members of the body politic were guided by awareness and loyalty to societal needs. The cravings and conscience of the individuals *mattered* to the state and to society as a whole. The well-being of society hung on the universal acceptance of its central values; to be effective, the body politic had to *legitimize* itself in terms of those shared values (which meant that the values shared had to be those defended and pursued by the leaders of society and organs of their leadership).

Let us also recall that long *after* the communist adventure started the memories of such a nineteenth-century vision found their most monumental codification in the theoretical system of Talcott Parsons, and that even at such a late date it was accepted at the time, on both sides of the capitalist/communist divide, as the crowning of modern sociology, the culmination of social-scientific wisdom, the long-awaited universal framework for analysis and comprehension of social, economic and political realities. That theoretical system viewed society from the vantage point of the managerial office (that is, posited society as first and foremost a managerial problem). It represented *equilibrium* as the supreme requisite and tendency of a social system, universal acceptance of *value-cluster* as the supreme means to that function's fulfilment, the *co-ordination* of individual and societal needs as the most conspicuous measure of a well-equilibrated society and the needs themselves (in tune with virtually all psychological teachings and the whole of the received humanistic wisdom) as unpleasant states of tension and anxiety which would cease to exist at the moment of needs–satisfaction.

Finally, let us recall that, well into the advanced stages of the communist experiment, the capitalist world watched its progress with bated breath, having little doubt that however wanting the emerging system might have been in other respects, it was a managerial and economic success. What counted for this overt or tacit admiration was that the productive capacity of that society quickly shortened the distance dividing it from the older and wealthier economies of the west. Giant steel mills (the more gigantic the better) and grandiose irrigation schemes (the vaster the better) were still accepted as a credible index of a well-managed society on the way to fulfilment of its mission: the satisfaction of the needs of its members. The communist state, in its own admittedly unprepossessing way, seemed to serve the same ideals of modern era which even its capitalist haters readily recognized as their own.

In these now uncannily distant times the audacious communist project seemed to make a lot of sense and was taken quite seriously by its friends and foes alike. Communism promised (or threatened, depending on the eye of the beholder) to do what everyone else was doing, only faster (remember the alluring charm of convergence theories?). The real doubts appeared when the others stopped doing it, while communism went on chasing now abandoned targets;

partly through inertia, but mostly because of the fact that – being communism in action – it could not do anything else.

In its practical implementation, communism was a system one-sidedly adapted to the task of mobilizing social and natural resources in the name of modernization: the nineteenth-century, steam and iron ideal of modern plenty. It could – at least in its own conviction – compete with capitalists, but solely with capitalists engaged in the same pursuits. What it could not do and did not brace itself to do was to match the performance of the capitalist, market-centred society once that society abandoned its steel mills and coal mines and moved into the postmodern age (once it passed over, in Jean Baudrillard's apt aphorism, from *metallurgy* to *semiurgy*; stuck at its metallurgical stage, Soviet communism, as if to cast out devils, spent its energy on fighting wide trousers, long hair, rock music and any other manifestations of semiurgical initiative).

Heller, Feher and Markus defined communist society as *dictatorship over needs*; and this it was, though only in that later, 'postmodern', stage did the dictating of needs become an abomination *per se*, regardless of the degree to which the needs experienced by its objects had been provided for. This happened because the society that throughout its modern development viewed itself as a social arrangement aimed at production capable of matching *established* needs, in its capitalist version turned consciously, explicitly and joyously to the production of *new* needs. Once seen as a state of suffering demanding reprieve, needs now became something to be celebrated and enjoyed. Human happiness had been redefined as the expansion of one's consuming capacity and the cultivation of new, more capacious and ever more refined needs.

For the social system, this meant that the balanced economy would no longer do and constant growth was needed instead. For the individual, this meant *choice* as the foremost criterion of good life and personal success: choice of the kind of person one would like to become (ever new personality-assembling kits are offered in the shops), choice of pleasures one would like to enjoy, choice of the very needs one would like to seek, adopt and gratify. Choice has turned into a value in its own right; the supreme value, to be sure. What mattered now was that choice be allowed and made, not the things or states that are chosen. And it is precisely *choice* that communism, this dictatorship over needs, could not and would not ever provide – even if it could provide for the needs it itself dictated (which more often than not it spectacularly failed to do anyway).

Well fed and clad, educated and cossetted young East German professionals stampeding to the west did not pretend to be running away from a disliked political philosophy; when pressed by the journalists, they admitted that what they were after (and what they could not get in the country they abandoned) was a wider assortment of goods in the shops and a wider selection of holidays. On my recent visit to Sweden I was told by quite a few even better fed, clad and otherwise provided for intellectuals that – supremely efficient as it prides itself on being – the bureaucracy of the social-democratic state becomes ever more difficult to live with; and this is due to the limits it puts on individual choice. I asked my conversationalists whether, given choice, they would abandon the doctor currently assigned by the National Health, or seek another school for their children. No, was the answer: the doctor is excellent, and so is the school our children attend; why on earth should we go elsewhere? But, they told me in the next sentence, I missed the point. Quite obviously, the point was not the quality of doctor or school, but the gratifying feeling of self-assertion, expressed in the act of consumer choice. This is what no bureaucratic provision, however lavish, could offer.

Even if communism could hope (erroneously, as it turned out in the end) to out-modernize the modernizers, it has become apparent that it cannot seriously contemplate facing the challenge of the postmodern world: the world in which consumer choice is simultaneously the essential systemic requisite, the main factor of social integration and the channel through which individual life-concerns are vented and problems resolved – while the state, grounding its expectation of discipline in the seduction of consumers rather than the indoctrination and oppression of subjects, could (and had to) wash its hands of all matters ideological and thus make conscience a private affair.

BUILDING A CAPITALIST SOCIETY IN A POSTMODERN WORLD

By common agreement, the passage from the state-administered to the market economy based on business initiative requires the accumulation of private capital as much as the presence of business motivations. What the latter are we know from Weber's unsurpassed analysis of the motives instrumental in the rise of the capitalist system. Greed and the pursuit of profit, Weber insisted,

170

have little to do with capitalism; unless restrained by rational calculation, they can hardly lead to the capitalist transformation – and they hardly ever led there, though they were ubiquitously present in all known societies and reached the height of ruthlessness and intensity well before the advent of modernity. On the other hand, the ideologically induced trait of *this-worldly asceticism* had everything to do with the emergence of the capitalist order. It was that trait which made capitalist accumulation and the passage to rationally calculated business both possible and in fact inevitable (the original accumulation of capital was, according to Weber, an *unanticipated consequence* of religiously induced self-denial coupled with the pursuit of workmanship as the mundane reflection of divine grace). This-worldly asceticism means first and foremost the *delay of gratification*; a suppression, rather than letting loose the natural predisposition to quick gain and fast enjoyment, to self-indulgence and ostentatious consumption.

There are few puritans left in the world at the time when the post-communist societies embark on the 'primary capitalist accumulation'. In fact, what enraged the rebels against communist command economy and what eventually brought communism down was not the envious comparison with the productive successes of capitalist neighbours, but the enticing and alluring spectacle of lavish consumption enjoyed under capitalist auspices. It was the postmodern, narcissistic culture of self-enhancement, self-enjoyment, instant gratification and life defined in terms of consumer styles that finally exposed the obsoleteness of the 'steel-per-head' philosophy stubbornly preached and practiced under communism. It was this culture that delivered the last blow to abortive communist hopes of competition with the capitalist rival. And it was the overwhelming desire to share (and to share immediately) in the delights of the postmodern world, not the wish to tread once more the tortuous nineteenth-century road of industrialization and modernization, that mobilized the massive dissent against communist oppression and inefficiency.

The postmodern challenge proved to be highly effective in speeding up the collapse of communism and assuring the triumph of anti-communist revolution in its supremely important, yet preliminary, political stage. This asset may however turn into a serious handicap at the stage of systemic transformation, on two accounts: first, the relative scarcity of puritan attitudes allegedly indispensable at the stage of primary capital accumulation; second, the possibility that the high hopes on which the anticipatory trust with which the post-communist governments have been credited has been based, will be frustrated – with adverse effects on the still barely rooted institutions of young democracy. Frustration may rebound in its usual sublimations, with scape-goating, witch-hunting and totalitarian intolerance most prominent and most vexing among them. The resulting socio-psychological climate may prove fertile for the growth of hybrid political formations with little resemblance to the liberal-democratic hopes of the intellectual leaders of the revolution.

East-Central European societies have victoriously accomplished their February revolution. The dangers of an October one are, as yet, far from being excluded. The revolutionary process has started, but its destination and the direction it will take in the foreseeable future is far from certain. One is reminded of Winston Churchill's view of the prospects of the war after the battle of El Alamein: 'This is not the end. This is not even the beginning of the end. This is only the end of the beginning.'

NOTES

1 Certain concepts, like certain wines, do not stand travel. The concept of *bürgerliche Gesellschaft* is one of them. In translation, it cannot but lose its unique semantic load: only in German the 'Bürger' stands *simultaneously* for the bourgeois *and* citizen, stating matter-of-factly the intimate bond between social and political characteristics. This bond is lost in the 'civil society' rendition of the term; it has been lost even more in recent faulty East European translations, which – having pared the concept down to the bare bones of political rights – induced a dangerous tendency to overlook the mutual dependency between political democracy and the presence of 'Bürgertum', and with that the difference between the tasks confronted by the anti-communist revolutions with those once faced by the capitalist ones.

2 Jadwiga Staniszkis, 'Stabilizacja bez uprawomocnienia', in *Legitimacja, Klasyczne Teorie i Polskie Doswiadczenia* , ed. by Andzej Rychard and Antoni Sulek (PTS Warszawa, 1988), p. 216.

3 Aleksander Smolar (1988) 'Perspektywy Europy Środkowo-Wschodniej' , *Aneks* 50: 22.

4 See Zygmunt Bauman (1988) 'Poland – on its own', *Telos* 77.

5 Lenin (helped as he was by his readings of Lavrov and Tkachev) was the first revolutionary to re-forge this contradiction into the major constitutive principle of his strategy: deliberately, he used the anger of the peasant mass, arising from 'non-transformative' interest in land and peace, as a battering ram to topple the old regime. Once in the saddle, Lenin proceeded to use the levers of government to impose systemic

change which the mass movement that destroyed the old rule neither planned for nor desired.

6 In the highly informative and perceptive volume *Studia nad ladem spolecznym* (ed. by Witold Nieciuński and Tomasz Zukowski, University of Warsaw, 1990), a number of authors – Edmund Wnuk-Lipiński, Ryszard Turski, Tomasz Zukowski and Winicjusz Narojek most prominent among them – point out in a variety of ways the mechanisms of incorporation of essentially anti-systemic interests and cravings (like the pursuit of personal gain, 'second economy', group and individual privileges, etc.) into the self-reproductive processes of the system; mechanisms which produced, on the one hand, the baffling lack of co-ordination between the radicalism of public attitudes and the conformism of private behaviour, and the equally puzzling 'insidedness' of actions arising from motives which could not be logically squared with the existing order.

The communist dictatorship over needs and monopoly over the means and procedures of needs-satisfaction makes the communist state an obvious target of individual disaffection; but it cannot but collectivize individual frustrations in the same way it collectivized the vehicles of gratification. Here, the state is the agency to which complaints are addressed as naturally and matter-of-factly as have been the expectations of better life. Unlike in the democratic/market/consumer world of privatized choices, the sources of diffuse unhappiness are not themselves diffuse and cannot be kept ex-directory; they are publicly announced, conspicuous and easy to locate. Admittedly, the communist regimes excelled in stifling the flow of information and pushed to elsewhere unknown heights the art of state secrecy; and yet they proved to be much less successful than market-oriented societies in dissipating and hiding the responsibility for socially produced ills, for irrational consequences of rational decisions and for overall mismanagement of social processes. They even failed to hide the fact of hiding information and thus stood accused, as of political crimes, of the kind of 'cover up' which market agencies of consumer society practice daily, effortlessly and without attracting attention (less still a public outcry).

7 With the sharpness of insight which has been his trademark, Claus Offe has sketched the more salient aspects of the 'morning after' awakening:

> In the European capitalist democracies, queues form in front of the job offices, while in the countries of 'really existing socialism' they do in front of butcher shops. In the first, there is a 'reserve army' of workers waiting to be employed (as well as a reserve army of commodities waiting for a customer), while in the second the managers wait for the workers and the workers wait for consumer goods.

These transmogrifications could have been expected; the others, which come in a package deal with the anticipated ones, less so: 'In the capitalist democracies one can say what one wants, but nobody listens. In the countries of 'really existing socialism' one *cannot* say what one wills, but this condition has in its own way sharpened human hearing (and not only the STASI ears!).' ('Ist der Sozialismus am Ende?', *Die Zeit*, 8 December 1989, p. 64). The last observation points to the particularly paradoxical 'morning after' feeling experienced by intellectuals, culture-makers and culture-brokers: freedom of expression sometimes feels like dispossession, and emancipation like a loss of social standing.

8 See note 6.

9 Jerzy Szacki, 'A revival of liberalism in Poland?', *Social Research* 57 (2) 491.

10 Jean Baudrillard, 'L'hystérésie du millenium', *Le Débat* 60 (mai-août 1990), p. 69.

11 See Harold Perkin, *The Rise of Professional Society, England since 1880* (London: Routledge, 1989), pp. 10–15. There are, according to Perkin, two possible renditions of the essentially identical 'professional ideal' arising from the place occupied by learned experts in the modern social figuration:

> The object of the professionals manning the system is to justify the highest status and rewards they can attain by the social necessity and efficiency they claim for the service they perform. That on occasion the service is neither essential nor efficient is no obstacle to principle. It only needs to be thought so by those providing and receiving it. Justification by service to the clients and society lies at the root of the professional ideal.
>
> (p. 360)

The battle of ideas between market and state service principles is a squabble inside the family, a sibling rivalry.

8

LIVING WITHOUT AN ALTERNATIVE

Communism has died. Some say, of senility. Some say, of shameful afflictions. All agree that it will stay dead for a long, long time.

The official opinion (whatever that means) of the affluent West greeted the news, arguably the least expected news of the century, with self-congratulating glee. The theme of the celebration is well known: 'our form of life' has once and for all proved both its viability and its superiority over any other real or imaginable form, our mixture of individual freedom and consumer market has emerged as the necessary and sufficient, truly universal principle of social organization, there will be no more traumatic turns of history, indeed no history to speak of. For 'our way of life' the world has become a safe place. The century remarkable for fighting its choices on the battlefield is over, ten years before the appointed time. From now on, there will be just more of the good things that are.

In the din of celebration, the few voices of doubt are barely audible. Some doubts do not dare to be voiced. Some inarticulate worries have not even congealed into doubts fit to be put into words. One can only guess what they are.

Those who deployed communism as a bugbear with which to frighten disobedient children ('look what would become of you if you do not do what I told you to') and bring them to their senses, feel slightly uneasy: where are they to find a substitute for the service the late communism rendered? How to keep people thankful for however little they have if one cannot get credit for defending them from having less still?

Some categories of people have more radical and immediate reasons to be worried. The huge warfare bureaucracy, for instance. It lived off the threat of the communist evil empire, and lived all the better the more it could make the threat look real and terrifying. That bureaucracy presided over, and derived its life juices from, the biggest arms industry that existed in any peacetime of history. That industry did not need actual warfare to thrive: the initial push of the communist threat sufficed to assure continuous, exponential development. After that, it has acquired its own momentum of self-perpetuation and growth. Producers of defensive weapons competed with the merchants of the offensive ones; navies with air forces, tanks with rocketry units. New weapons had to be developed one day because the weapons invented the day before made inadequate or downright obsolete the weapons deployed the day before that. Or new weapons had to be developed just because the laboratories, filled with high class brains and kept constantly at the highest pitch of tension by tempting commissions, prestigious ambitions and professional rivalry, could not stop spawning ever new ideas; and because there were spare or idle technological resources eager to absorb them. And yet this cosy arrangement needed the communist threat to secure the steady inflow of life juices. The weapons industry less than anyone else can survive without an enemy; its products have no value when no one is afraid and no one wants to frighten the others.

And there is another powerful industry that may bewail the passage of the communist enemy: thousands of university departments and research institutes, world-wide networks of congresses, conferences, publishing houses and journals all dedicated in full to 'Soviet and East European Studies' and now, like the warfare bureaucracy, facing the prospect of redundancy. Like all well-established and viable organizations (including the warfare bureaucracy), *sovietology* will certainly attempt to find a new topic to justify its continuing services, and this it can only do through construing new targets to match its impressive human and material resources. And yet one doubts whether the new targets, however defined, would attract as in the past the funds and the benevolence of the powers that be in quantities sufficient to keep the industry at its recent level of material wealth, academic prestige and self-congratulatory mood.

These and similar worries may be quite serious for the interests they affect directly, yet the globality of disaster to which they refer is, to say the least, a matter of contention. There are, however, other consequences of the demise of communism which may have truly global deleterious effects for the survival of the very same 'form of life' whose ultimate triumph they ostensibly augur.

It is widely assumed, particularly in the right-most regions of the political spectrum, that the bankruptcy of the communist system must have delivered a mortal blow not just to the preachers and outspoken devotees of the communist faith, but to any cause, however loosely related to the 'left' tradition of disaffection, critique and dissent, of value-questioning, of alternative visions. It is assumed that the practical discrediting of communism (construed as 'the Other' of *our form of life*, as the *negative* totality which injects meaning into *our positivity*), pre-empts by proxy and disqualifies in advance any doubts about the unchallengeable superiority of the *really existing* regime of freedom and the consumer market; that it discredits, moreover, any suggestion that this regime, even if technically more viable, may be still neither entirely flawless, nor the most just of conceivable orders; that it may be instead in urgent need of an overhaul and improvement. I will argue, however, that the assertion that the collapse of communism threatens the survival of the 'left alternative' and the left critique *alone* is invalid as a non sequitur; that such dangers as truly arise in the world that has abandoned the socialist alternative, ostensibly discredited once and for all by the now universally decried practices of its communist variant, apply to 'our form of life' (that is, to the *really existing* regime of free consumers and free markets) in the same (perhaps even greater) measure than they do to its left critique; and that this circumstance may only render the continuation of critique more imperative than it otherwise would have been.

THE HISTORICAL MEANING OF THE COLLAPSE OF COMMUNISM

What has been buried under the debris of the communist system? A number of totalitarian states, of course – specimens of a regime that left rule-unprotected individuals at the mercy of rule-free powers, and which insulated the self-reproduction of the political power-holders from all and any intervention by the powerless. The demise of the totalitarian state cannot, however, be said to be final or complete, as communism was just one of many political formulae of totalitarianism. Non-communist totalitarianism is neither logically incongruent as a notion nor technically inoperative as a practice. Even a cursory survey of the panoply of extant political regimes would show that to issue a death certificate to totalitarianism just because its communist version has disintegrated would be, to say the least, a premature and unwise decision. Even if every former communist state makes the parliamentary democratic procedure and the observance of individual rights stick (not by itself a foregone conclusion), this would not mean that 'the world has become safe for democracy' and that the struggle between liberal and totalitarian principles heretofore coexisting inside contemporary body politics has been settled. To suggest that the communist utopia was the only virus responsible for totalitarian afflictions would be to propagate a dangerous illusion, one that is both theoretically incapacitating and politically disarming – for the future chances of democracy a costly, perhaps even lethal mistake.

There are, however, other graves hidden under the rubble that are still waiting to be uncovered in full. The fall of communism was a resounding defeat for the project of a *total order* – an artificially designed, all-embracing arrangement of human actions and their setting, one that follows the rules of reason instead of emerging from diffuse and uncoordinated activities of human agents; it was also the downfall of the grandiose dream of *remaking* nature – forcing it to yield ever more of anything human satisfaction may require, while disregarding or neutralizing such among its unplanned tendencies as could not be assigned any sensible human benefit; it demonstrated as well the ultimate frustration of the ambitions of global management, of replacing spontaneity with planning, of a transparent, monitored, supervised and deliberately shaped order in which nothing is left to chance and everything derives its meaning and *raison d'être* from the vision of a harmonious totality. In short, the fall of communism signalled the final retreat from the dreams and ambitions of *modernity*.

One of the most conspicuous traits of modernity was an overwhelming urge to replace spontaneity, seen as meaningless and identified with chaos, by an order drawn by reason and constructed through legislative and controlling effort. That urge gestated (or was it gestated by?) what has become a specifically *modern* state: one that modelled its intentions and the prerogatives it claimed after the pattern of a gardener, a medical man, or an architect: a *gardening* state, a *therapeutic/surgical* state, a *space-managing* state. It was a gardening state, in so far as it usurped the right to set apart the 'useful' and the 'useless' plants, to select a final model of harmony that made some plants useful and others useless, and to propagate such plants as are useful while exterminating the useless ones. It was a therapeutic/surgical state, in so far as it set the standard of 'normality' and thus drew the borderline between the acceptable and the intolerable, between health and disease, fighting the second to support the first – and in so far as it cast its subjects in the role of the patients: the sites of ailments, yet not themselves agents able to defeat the malady without the instruction of a knowledgeable and resourceful tutor. It was a space-managing state, in so far as it was busy landscaping the wasteland (it was the landscaping intention that cast the operating territory as wasteland), subjecting all local features to one, unifying, homogenizing principle of harmony.

Communism and modernity

As it happened, communism took the precepts of modernity most seriously and set out to implement them in earnest. Indeed, its logic as a system had geared it to perform the gardening/therapeutic/architectural functions to the detriment of all, indeed any, prerequisites or demands unjustified by the reason of the enterprise.

Throughout its history, communism was modernity's most devout, vigorous and gallant champion – pious to the point of simplicity. It also claimed to be its only true champion. Indeed, it was under communist, not capitalist, auspices that the audacious dream of modernity, freed from obstacles by the merciless and seemingly omnipotent state, was pushed to its radical limits: grand designs, unlimited social engineering, huge and bulky technology, total transformation of nature. Deserts were irrigated (but they turned into salinated bogs); marshlands were dried (but they turned into deserts); massive gas-pipes criss-crossed the land to remedy nature's whims in distributing its resources (but they kept exploding with a force unequalled by the natural disasters of yore); millions were lifted from the 'idiocy of rural life' (but they got poisoned by the effluvia of rationally designed industry, if they did not perish first on the way). Raped and crippled, nature failed to deliver the riches one hoped it would; the total scale of design only made the devastation total. Worse still, all that raping and crippling proved to be in vain. Life did not seem to become more comfortable or happy, needs (even ones acknowledged by the state tutors) did not seem to be satisfied better than before, and the kingdom of reason and harmony seemed to be more distant than ever.

What the affluent west is in fact celebrating today is the official passing away of its own past; the last farewell to the modern dream and modern arrogance. If the joyous immersion in postmodern fluidity and the sensuous bliss of aimless drift were poisoned by the residues of modern conscience – the urge to do something about those who suffer and clamour for something to be done – they seem unpolluted now. With communism, the ghost of modernity has been exorcised. Social engineering, the principle of communal responsibility for individual fate, the duty to provide commonly for single survivals, the tendency to view personal tragedies as social problems, the commandment to strive collectively for shared justice – all such moral precepts as used to legitimize (some say motivate) modern practices have been compromised beyond repair by the spectacular collapse of the communist system. No more guilty conscience. No scruples. No supra-individual commitments contaminating individual enjoyment. The past has descended to its grave in disgrace.

THE POLITICAL SIGNIFICANCE OF THE COLLAPSE OF COMMUNISM

The demise of the communist system was also a defeat for the over-ambitious and over-protective state. Indeed it is because the last act of the protracted and tortuous process of demise was so final and dramatic that it is credible to describe ambitious and protective states as *over*-ambitious and *over*-protective. Such a state seemed to draw its last breath at the Vaclavske Namesti and the city square of Timisoara, though it survived, albeit temporarily, Tiananmen Square. What discredited that state more than anything else (*de facto*, if not in theoretical interpretations) is that it revealed an unbelievable inner weakness; it surrendered to an unarmed crowd while ostensibly threatened by nothing more than that crowd's resolute refusal to go home. Such a weakness seems to be a sole property of the communist state, and can be easily, and gladly, ascribed to everything it stood for. Can one imagine a similar effect of a public gathering at Trafalgar Square? Or the Champs Elysées? And can one imagine the gathering?

Because of the factors spelled out above, the subjects of the communist state could have more reasons to express disaffection than the population of most western countries. But – a point not stressed strongly enough, if at all – they also had a greater possibility of making their disaffection effective and of re-forging it into systemic change. The overbearing state had to pay a price for the formidable volume of its concerns and entitlements – and the price was *vulnerability*. To assert the state's right to command and control is to assume responsibility for the effects. The doorstep on which to lay the blame is publicly known and clearly marked, and for each and any grievance it is *the same* doorstep. The state cannot help but cumulate and condense social dissent; nor can it help turning the edge of dissent against itself. The state is the major, and sufficient, factor in forging the variety of often incompatible complaints and bids into a unified opposition – at least for long enough to produce a dramatic showdown. The state that assumes the right to structure society also induces a tendency to political polarization: the conflicts that otherwise would remain diffuse and cut the population in many directions tend to be subsumed under one overriding opposition between the state and society.

Thus it has not been proved that the illusory nature of state power and its incapacity to survive the mere refusal of obedience is solely the property of the communist state. What has been proved instead is that the communist regime created conditions most propitious to calling the bluff of state omnipotence. Most directly related to the nature of the regime was the possibility that refusal of obedience be synchronized, global and involving if not the total, then at least a sizeable part, of the population.

From the point of view of political sociology, the most important consequence of the present western tendency to de-étatization of the growing number of previously state-managed areas is the *privatization of dissent*. With both the global balance of social activities and the logic of the life-process split into finely-sliced and mutually autonomous functions, disaffections arising along separate task-oriented activities have no ground on which to meet and merge. Disaffection tends to generate one-issue campaigns, and dissent is functionally dispersed and either depoliticized or politically diluted. Seldom, if ever, is the grievance directed against the state, the frantic efforts of political parties notwithstanding. More often than not it stops short even of blending into social movements; instead, it rebounds in more disillusionment with collective solutions to individual troubles, and blames the sufferer for unfulfilled potential. The difference between the two systems

181

consists not so much in the size of the sum total of disaffection, as in the propensity of dissent in a communist system to cumulate to the point where the system is de-legitimated, and to condense into a system-subverting force.

It is for this reason that the sham of state omnipotence (sometimes represented in political theory as 'legitimacy'), even if it really were only a sham, would tend to remain invisible. Whether the communist and liberal-parliamentary states (one presiding over the command economy, the other letting loose the market game) do or do not share the inner weakness that only communist states have recently demonstrated, is bound to remain a moot question: it is unlikely to be put to a practical test. Hence the repeated assertions of the 'end of history', of the 'end of conflict', of 'from now on, more of the same' may boast immunity to empirical criticism. However wrong such assertions may *feel*, their detractors can find little in the political life of the apparently victorious system to make their doubts credible.

Indeed, what is often called *western civilization* seems to have found the philosopher's stone all other civilizations sought in vain, and with it the warranty of its own immortality: it has succeeded in re-forging its *discontents* into the factors of its own *reproduction*. What could be described in other systems as aspects of 'dysfunctionality', manifestations of crisis and imminent breakdown, seem to add to this system's strength and vigour. Deprivation breeds and further enhances the alluring power of market exchange, instead of gestating politically effective discontent: public risks and dangers spawned by 'single task' technologies and narrowly focused expertise supply further legitimation for problem-oriented action and generate demands for more technology and specialized expertise instead of questioning the wisdom of 'problem-limited' thinking and practice; impoverishment of the public sphere boosts the search for, and the seductive power of, private escapes from public squalor and further decimates the ranks of the potential defenders of the common weal. Above all, system-generated discontents are as subdivided as the agencies and actions that generate them. At most, such discontents lead to 'single-issue' campaigns that command intense commitment to the issue in focus while surrounding the narrow area of attention with a vast no-man's land of indifference and apathy. Party-political platforms do not reflect integrated group interests, real or postulated; instead, they are carefully patched together following a scrupulous calculation of the relative popularity (that is, vote-generating capacity) of each single issue in the public attention. Party-political mobilization of votes does not detract from the volume of voters' apathy; indeed, one may say that the success of mobilization through single issues is conditional on the voters' inattention to the topics left out of focus.

As a result of all this, the current western form of life, with its market-sponsored production of needs, privatization of grievances and single task actions, seems to be in a position strikingly different from that of the regionally localized civilizations of yore. It has neither effective enemies inside nor barbarians knocking at the gates, only adulators and imitators. It has practically (and apparently irrevocably) de-legitimized all alternatives to itself. Having done this, it has rendered it uncannily difficult, nay impossible, to conceive of a different way of life in a form that would resist assimilation and hamper, rather than boost, the logic of its reproduction. Its courtly bards may therefore credibly pronounce it universal and *sub specie aeternitatis*.

THE COSTS OF VICTORY

One aspect of the situation in which the western form of life has found itself after the collapse of the communist alternative is the unprecedented freedom this form of life will from now on enjoy in construing 'the other' of itself and, by the same token, in defining its own identity. We do not really know what effects such freedom may bring: we can learn little from history, since it knows of no similar situations. For most of historically formed civilization, 'the other' had the power of self-constitution. Alternatives appeared as real contenders and resourceful enemies; as threats to be reckoned with, adapted to and actively staved off. Alternatives were sources of at least temporary dynamism even if the capacity for change proved in the end too limited to prevent ultimate defeat. For the better part of the twentieth century, communism seemed successfully to play the role of such an alternative. Even before that, virtually from the beginning of capitalist modernity, such a role was played by socialist movements. Vivid display of a social organization that focused on the ends which capitalist modernity neglected made it necessary to broaden the systemic agenda, and enforced corrections which prevented the accumulation of potentially lethal dysfunctions. (The welfare state was the most conspicuous, but by no means the only, example.) This relative luxury of autonomous, self-constituted critique is now gone. The question is, where its functional substitute may be found, if at all.

The most immediate part of the answer is the radically enhanced role of intellectual, rational analysis and critique; the latter would now need to carry on its own shoulders a task shared in the past with the contenders in the political battle of systemic alternatives. What is at stake here is not merely an extension and intensification of the old role of intellectuals. Throughout the modern era, in which state have relied for their operative capacity mostly on ideological legitimation, intellectuals and their institutions – the universities most prominent among them – were first and foremost the suppliers of current or potential legitimating formulae, whether in their conformist or rebellious mode. These goods are not today much in demand, as the state by and large cedes the integrative task to the seductive attractions of the market. (This absence of demand stands behind the process dubbed the 'crisis of universities', the relentless erosion of the cultural role from which they derived their high status in the past.) This loss of state-assisted status, however alarming at the moment, may yet prove a blessing in disguise. Prised from automatically assumed or ascribed legitimizing or de-legitimizing function, intellectual work may share in a general freedom of cultural creation derived from the present irrelevance of culture for systemic reproduction. (I have discussed this process more extensively in the third chapter of *Freedom*.)[1] This gives intellectual work a chance of considerable autonomy; indeed, a radical shift of balance inside the modern power/knowledge syndrome becomes a distinct possibility.

On the other hand, the waning of the communist alternative lays bare the inner shortcomings of the market-centred version of freedom, previously either de-problematized or played down in confrontation with the less alluring aspects of the system of comparative reference. Less can now be forgiven, less is likely to be placidly endured. An immanent critique of the maladies of freedom reduced to consumer choice will be less easy to dimiss by the old expedient of imputed approval of a discredited alternative, and the inanities the critique discloses will be more difficult to exonerate as 'the lesser of two evils'. Market freedom would need to explain and defend itself in its own terms; and these are not particularly strong or cogent terms, especially when it comes to justifying its social and psychological costs.

The costs are, indeed, enormous. And they can no longer be made less appalling by showing that the attempts which have been made to rectify them elsewhere have increased the total volume of human suffering instead of diminishing it. Those attempts are no longer on the agenda, yet the costs show no sign of abating and call for action no less loudly than before; only the call is now more poignant than ever since inactivity cannot be apologized for by proxy. The continuing polarization of well-being and life chances cannot be made less repulsive by pointing to the general impoverishment which had resulted elsewhere from efforts to remedy it. The traumas of privatized identity-construction cannot be easily whitewashed by pointing to the stultifying effects of the totalitarian alternative. Indifference only thinly disguised by ostensible tolerance cannot be made more acceptable by the impotence of power-enforced coexistence. The reduction of citizenship to consumerism cannot be justified by reference to the even more gruesome effects of obligatory political mobilization. The ironical dismissal of forward dreaming loses much of its cogency once the now-discredited promotion of 'total order' and gardening utopias ceases to be its most conspicuous and tangible incarnation.

All this points to an opportunity. It does not necessarily guarantee success. (I have discussed above the astonishing ability of the postmodern habitat to absorb dissent and avant-garde-style criticism and to deploy them as the sources of its own renewed strength.) We, the residents of the postmodern habitat, live in a territory that admits of no clear options and no strategies that can even be *imagined* to be uncontroversially correct. We are better aware than ever before just how slippery are all the roads once pursued with single-minded determination. We know how easily the critique of 'market only' freedom may lead to the destruction of freedom as such. But we know as well – or we will learn soon, if we do not know it yet – that freedom confined to consumer choice is blatantly inadequate for the performance of the life-tasks that confront a privatized individuality (for instance, for the self-construction of identity); and that it therefore tends to be accompanied by the renascence of the selfsame irrationalities that grandiose projects of modernity wished to eradicate, while succeeding, at best, in their temporary suppression. Dangers lurk on both sides. The

9

A SOCIOLOGICAL THEORY OF POSTMODERNITY[1]

I propose that:

1. The term *postmodernity* renders accurately the defining traits of the social condition that emerged throughout the affluent countries of Europe and of European descent in the course of the twentieth century, and took its present shape in the second half of that century. The term is accurate as it draws attention to the continuity and discontinuity as two faces of the intricate relationship between the present social condition and the formation that preceded and gestated it. It brings into relief the intimate, genetic bond that ties the new, postmodern social condition to *modernity* – the social formation that emerged in the same part of the world in the course of the seventeenth century, and took its final shape, later to be sedimented in the sociological models of modern society (or models of society created by modern sociology), during the nineteenth century; while at the same time indicating the passing of certain crucial characteristics in whose absence one can no longer adequately describe the social condition as modern in the sense given to the concept by orthodox (modern) social theory.

2. Postmodernity may be interpreted as fully developed modernity taking a full measure of the anticipated consequences of its historical work; as modernity that acknowledged the effects it was producing throughout its history, yet producing inadvertently, rarely conscious of its own responsibility, by default rather than design, as by-products often perceived as waste. Postmodernity may be conceived of as modernity conscious of its true nature – *modernity for itself.* The most conspicuous features of the postmodern condition: institutionalized pluralism, variety, contingency and ambivalence – have been all turned out by modern society in ever increasing volumes; yet they were seen as signs of failure rather

than success, as evidence of the unsufficiency of efforts so far, at a time when the institutions of modernity, faithfully replicated by the modern mentality, struggled for *universality, homogeneity, monotony* and *clarity*. The postmodern condition can be therefore described, on the one hand, as modernity emancipated from false consciousness; on the other, as a new type of social condition marked by the overt institutionalization of the characteristics which modernity – in its designs and managerial practices – set about to eliminate and, failing that, tried to conceal.

3. The twin differences that set the postmodern condition apart from modern society are profound and seminal enough to justify (indeed, to call for) a separate sociological theory of postmodernity that would break decisively with the concepts and metaphors of the models of modernity and lift itself out of the mental frame in which they had been conceived. This need arises from the fact that (their notorious disagreements notwithstanding), the extant models of modernity articulated a shared vision of modern history as a *movement with a direction* – and differed solely in the selection of the ultimate destination or the organizing principle of the process, be it universalization, rationalization or systemization. None of those principles can be upheld (at least not in the radical form typical of the orthodox social theory) in the light of postmodern experience. Neither can the very master-metaphor that underlies them be sustained: that of the process with a pointer.

4. Postmodernity is not a transitory departure from the 'normal state' of modernity; neither is it a diseased state of modernity, an ailment likely to be rectified, a case of 'modernity in crisis'. It is, instead, a self-reproducing, pragmatically self-sustainable and logically self-contained social condition defined by *distinctive features of its own*. A theory of postmodernity therefore cannot be a modified theory of modernity, a theory of modernity with a set of negative markers. An adequate theory of postmodernity may be only constructed in a cognitive space organized by a different set of assumptions; it needs its own vocabulary. The degree of emancipation from the concepts and issues spawned by the discourse of modernity ought to serve as a measure of the adequacy of such a theory.

CONDITIONS OF THEORETICAL
EMANCIPATION

What the theory of postmodernity must discard in the first place is the assumption of an *'organismic'*, equilibrated social totality it purports to model in Parsons-like style: the vision of a 'principally co-ordinated' and enclosed totality (a) with a degree of cohesiveness, (b) equilibrated or marked by an overwhelming tendency to equilibration, (c) unified by an internally coherent value syndrome and a core authority able to promote and enforce it and (d) defining its elements in terms of the function they perform in that process of equilibration or the reproduction of the equilibrated state. The sought theory must assume instead that the social condition it intends to model is essentially and perpetually *unequilibrated*: composed of elements with a degree of autonomy large enough to justify the view of totality as a kaleidoscopic – momentary and contingent – outcome of interaction. The orderly, structured nature of totality cannot be taken for granted; nor can its pseudo-representational construction be seen as the purpose of theoretical activity. The randomness of the global outcome of uncoordinated activities cannot be treated as a departure from the pattern which the totality strives to maintain; any pattern that may temporarily emerge out of the random movements of autonomous agents is as haphazard and unmotivated as the one that could emerge in its place or the one bound to replace it, if also for a time only. All order that can be found is a local, emergent and transitory phenomenon; its nature can be best grasped by a metaphor of a whirlpool appearing in the flow of a river, retaining its shape only for a relatively brief period and only at the expense of incessant metabolism and constant renewal of content.

The theory of postmodernity must be free of the metaphor of progress that informed all competing theories of modern society. With the totality dissipated into a series of randomly emerging, shifting and evanescent islands of order, its temporal record cannot be linearly represented. Perpetual local transformations do not add up so as to prompt (much less to assure) in effect an increased homogeneity, rationality or organic systemness of the whole. The postmodern condition is a site of constant mobility and change, but no clear direction of development. The image of Brownian movement offers an apt metaphor for this aspect of postmodernity: each momentary state is neither a necessary effect of the preceding state nor the sufficient cause of the next one. The postmodern condition is both *undetermined* and *undetermining*. It 'unbinds' time; weakens the constraining impact of the past and effectively prevents colonization of the future.

Similarly, the theory of postmodernity would do well if it disposed of concepts like *system* in its orthodox, organismic sense (or, for that matter, *society*), suggestive of a sovereign totality logically prior to its parts, a totality bestowing meaning on its parts, a totality whose welfare or perpetuation all smaller (and, by definition, subordinate) units serve; in short, a totality assumed to define, and be practically capable of defining, the meanings of individual actions and agencies that compose it. A sociology geared to the conditions of postmodernity ought to replace the category of *society* with that of *sociality*; a category that tries to convey the processual modality of social reality, the dialectical play of randomness and pattern (or, from the agent's point of view, of freedom and dependence); and a category that refuses to take the structured character of the process for granted – which treats instead all found structures as emergent accomplishments.

With their field of vision organized around the focal point of system-like, resourceful and meaning-bestowing totality, socio-logical theories of modernity (which conceived of themselves as sociological theories *tout court*) concentrated on the vehicles of homogenization and conflict-resolution in a relentless search for a solution to the 'Hobbesian problem'. This cognitive perspective (shared with the one realistic referent of the concept of 'society' – the national state, the only totality in history able seriously to entertain the ambition of contrived, artificially sustained and managed monotony and homogeneity) a priori disqualified any 'uncertified' agency; unpatterned and unregulated spontaneity of the autonomous agent was pre-defined as a destabilizing and, indeed, anti-social factor marked for taming and extinction in the continuous struggle for societal survival. By the same token, prime importance was assigned to the mechanisms and weapons of order-promotion and pattern-maintenance: the state and the legitimation of its authority, power, socialization, culture, ideology, etc. – all selected for the role they played in the promotion of pattern, monotony, predictability and thus also manageability of conduct.

A sociological theory of postmodernity is bound to reverse the structure of the cognitive field. The focus must be now on agency; more correctly, on the *habitat* in which agency operates and which it produces in the course of operation. As it offers the agency the sum total of resources for all possible action as well as the field inside which the action-orienting and action-oriented relevancies may be plotted, the habitat is the territory inside which both freedom and dependency of the agency are constituted (and, indeed, perceived as such). Unlike the system-like totalities of modern social theory, habitat neither determines the conduct of the agents nor defines its meaning; it is no more (but no less either) than the setting in which both action and meaning-assignment are *possible*. Its own identity is as under-determined and motile, as emergent and transitory, as those of the actions and their meanings that form it.

There is one crucial area, though, in which the habitat performs a determining (systematizing, patterning) role: it sets the agenda for the 'business of life' through supplying the inventory of ends and the pool of means. The way in which the ends and means are supplied also determines the meaning of the 'business of life': the nature of the tasks all agencies confront and have to ʋᴗᴋe up in one form or another. In so far as the ends are offered as potentially alluring rather than obligatory, and rely for their choice on their own seductiveness rather than the supporting power of coercion, the 'business of life' splits into a series of choices. The series is not pre-structured, or is pre-structured only feebly and above all inconclusively. For this reason the choices through which the life of the agent is construed and sustained is best seen (as it tends to be seen by the agents themselves) as adding up to the process of *self-constitution*. To underline the graduated and ultimately inconclusive nature of the process, self-constitution is best viewed as *self-assembly*.

I propose that sociality, habitat, self-constitution and self-assembly should occupy in the sociological theory of postmodernity the central place that the orthodoxy of modern social theory had reserved for the categories of society, normative group (like class or community), socialization and control.

MAIN TENETS OF THE THEORY OF POSTMODERNITY

1. Under the postmodern condition, habitat is a *complex system*. According to contemporary mathematics, complex systems differ from mechanical systems (those assumed by the orthodox, modern theory of society) in two crucial respects. First, they are unpredictable; second, they are not controlled by statistically significant

factors (the circumstance demonstrated by the mathematical proof of the famous 'butterfly effect'). The consequences of these two distinctive features of complex systems are truly revolutionary in relation to the received wisdom of sociology. The 'systemness' of the postmodern habitat no longer lends itself to the organismic metaphor, which means that agencies active within the habitat cannot be assessed in terms of functionality or dysfunctionality. The successive states of the habitat appear to be unmotivated and free from constraints of deterministic logic. And the most formidable research strategy modern sociology had developed – statistical analysis – is of no use in exploring the dynamics of social phenomena and evaluating the probabilities of their future development. Significance and numbers have parted ways. Statistically insignificant phenomena may prove to be decisive, and their decisive role cannot be grasped in advance.

2. The postmodern habitat is a complex (non-mechanical) system for two closely related reasons. First, there is no 'goal setting' agency with overall managing and co-ordinating capacities or ambitions – one whose presence would provide a vantage point from which the aggregate of effective agents appears as a 'totality' with a determined structure of relevances; a totality which one can think as of an *organization*. Second, the habitat is populated by a great number of agencies, most of them single-purpose, some of them small, some big, but none large enough to subsume or otherwise determine the behaviour of the others. Focusing on a single purpose considerably enhances the effectiveness of each agency in the field of its own operation, but prevents each area of the habitat from being controlled from a single source, as the field of operation of any agency never exhausts the whole area the action is affecting. Operating in different fields yet zeroing in on shared areas, agencies are *partly* dependent on each other, but the lines of dependence cannot be fixed and thus their actions (and consequences) remain staunchly under-determined, that is autonomous.

3. Autonomy means that agents are only partly, if at all, constrained in their pursuit of whatever they have institutionalized as their purpose. To a large extent, they are free to pursue the purpose to the best of their mastery over resources and managerial capacity. They are free (and tend) to view the rest of the habitat shared with other agents as a collection of opportunities and 'problems' to be resolved or removed. Opportunity is what increases output in the pursuit of purpose, problems are what

threatens the decrease or a halt of production. In ideal circumstances (maximization of opportunities and minimization of problems) each agent would tend to go in the pursuit of their purpose as far as resources would allow; the availability of resources is the only reason for action they need and thus the sufficient guarantee of the action's reasonability. The possible impact on other agents' opportunities is not automatically re-forged into the limitation of the agent's own output. The many products of purpose-pursuing activities of numerous partly interdependent but relatively autonomous agents must yet find, *ex post facto*, their relevance, utility and demand-securing attractiveness. The products are bound to be created in volumes exceeding the pre-existing demand motivated by already articulated problems. They are still to seek their place and meaning as well as the problems that they may claim to be able to resolve.

4. For every agency, the habitat in which its action is inscribed appears therefore strikingly different from the confined space of its own autonomic, purpose-subordinated pursuits. It appears as a space of chaos and chronic *indeterminacy*, a territory subjected to rival and contradictory meaning-bestowing claims and hence perpetually *ambivalent*. All states the habitat may assume appear equally *contingent* (that is, they have no overwhelming reasons for being what they are, and they could be different if any of the participating agencies behaved differently). The heuristics of pragmatically useful 'next moves' displaces, therefore, the search for algorithmic, certain knowledge of deterministic chains. The succession of states assumed by the relevant areas of the habitat no agency can interpret without including its own actions in the explanation; agencies cannot meaningfully scan the situation 'objectively', that is in such ways as allow them to eliminate, or bracket away, their own activity.

5. The existential modality of the agents is therefore one of insufficient determination, inconclusiveness, motility and rootlessness. The identity of the agent is neither given nor authoritatively confirmed. It has to be construed, yet no design for the construction can be taken as prescribed or foolproof. The construction of identity consists of successive trials and errors. It lacks a benchmark against which its progress could be measured, and so it cannot be meaningfully described as 'progressing'. It is now the incessant (and non-linear) *activity* of self-constitution that makes the identity of the agent. In other words, the self-organization of the agents in

193

terms of a *life-project* (a concept that assumes a long-term stability; a lasting identity of the habitat, in its duration transcending, or at least commensurate with, the longevity of human life) is displaced by the *process of self-constitution*. Unlike the life-project self-constitution has no destination point in reference to which it could be evaluated and monitored. It has no visible end; not even a stable direction. It is conducted inside a shifting (and, as we have seen before, unpredictable) constellation of mutually autonomous points of reference, and thus purposes guiding the self-constitution at one stage may soon lose their current authoritatively confirmed validity. Hence the self-assembly of the agency is not a cumulative process; self-constitution entails disassembling alongside the assembling, adoption of new elements as much as shedding of others, learning together with forgetting. The identity of the agency, much as it remains in a state of permanent change, cannot be therefore described as 'developing'. In the self-constitution of agencies, the 'Brownian movement'-type spatial nature of the habitat is projected onto the time axis.

6. The only visible aspect of continuity and of the cumulative effects of self-constitutive efforts is offered by the human body – seen as the sole constant factor among the protean and fickle identities: the material, tangible substratum, container, carrier and executor of all past, present and future identities. The self-constitutive efforts focus on keeping alive (and preferably enhancing) the *capacity* of the body for absorbing the input of sensuous impressions and producing a constant supply of publicly legible self-definitions. Hence the centrality of *body-cultivation* among the self-assembly concerns, and the acute atention devoted to everything 'taken internally' (food, air, drugs, etc.) and to everything coming in touch with the skin – that interface between the agent and the rest of the habitat and the hotly contested frontier of the autonomously managed identity. In the postmodern habitat, DIY operations (jogging, dieting, slimming, etc.) replace and to a large extent displace the panoptical drill of modern factory, school or the barracks; unlike their predecessors, however, they are not perceived as externally imposed, cumbersome and resented necessities, but as manifestos of the agent's freedom. Their heteronomy, once blatant through coercion, now hides behind seduction.

7. As the process of self-constitution is not guided or monitored by a sovereign life-project designed in advance (such a life-project can only be imputed in retrospect, reconstructed out of a series of

emergent episodes), it generates an acute demand for a substitute: a constant supply of orientation points that may guide successive moves. It is the other agencies (real or imagined) of the habitat who serve as such orientation points. Their impact on the process of self-constitution differs from that exercised by normative groups in that they neither monitor nor knowingly administer the acts of allegiance and the actions that follow it. From the vantage point of self-constituting agents, other agents can be metaphorically visualized as a randomly scattered set of free-standing and unguarded totemic poles which one can approach or abandon without applying for permission to enter or leave. The self-proclaimed allegiance to the selected agent (the act of selection itself) is accomplished through the adoption of *symbolic tokens* of belonging, and freedom of choice is limited solely by the availability and accessibility of such tokens.

8. *Availability* of tokens for potential self-assembly depends on their *visibility*, much as it does on their material presence. Visibility in its turn depends on the perceived *utility* of symbolic tokens for the satisfactory outcome of self-construction; that is, on their ability to reassure the agent that the current results of self-assembly are indeed satisfactory. This reassurance is the substitute for the absent certainty, much as the orientation points with the attached symbolic tokens are collectively a substitute for pre-determined patterns for life-projects. The reassuring capacity of symbolic tokens rests on borrowed (ceded) authority; of *expertise*, or of *mass following*. Symbolic tokens are actively sought and adopted if their relevance is vouched for by the trusted authority of the expert, or by their previous or concurrent appropriation by a great number of other agents. These two variants of authority are in their turn fed by the insatiable thirst of the self-constituting agents for reassurance. Thus *freedom* of choice and *dependence* on external agents reinforce each other, and arise and grow together as products of the same process of self-assembly and of the constant demand for reliable orientation points which it cannot but generate.

9. *Accessibility* of tokens for self-assembly varies from agent to agent, depending mostly on the resources that a given agent commands. Increasingly, the most strategic role among the resources is played by knowledge; the growth of individually appropriated knowledge widens the range of assembly patterns which can be realistically chosen. Freedom of the agent, measured by the range of realistic choices, turns under the postmodern condition into the main dimension of inequality and thus becomes the main stake

of the *re-distributional* type of conflict that tends to arise from the dichotomy of privilege and deprivation; by the same token, access to knowledge – being the key to an extended freedom – turns into the major index of social standing. This circumstance increases the attractiveness of *information* among the symbolic tokens sought after for their reassuring potential. It also further enhances the authority of experts, trusted to be the repositories and sources of valid knowledge. Information becomes a major resource, and experts the crucial brokers of all self-assembly.

POSTMODERN POLITICS

Modern social theory could afford to separate theory from policy. Indeed, it made a virtue out of that historically circumscribed plausibility, and actively fought for the separation under the banner of value-free science. Keeping the separation watertight has turned into a most distinctive mark of modern theory of society. A theory of postmodernity cannot follow that pattern. Once the essential contingency and the absence of supra- or pre-agentic foundations of sociality and of the structured forms it sediments has been acknowledged, it becomes clear that the politics of agents lies at the core of the habitat's existence; indeed, it can be said to be its existential modality. All description of the postmodern habitat must include politics from the beginning. Politics cannot be kept outside the basic theoretical model as an epiphenomenon, a superstructural reflection or belatedly formed, intellectually processed derivative.

It could be argued (though the argument cannot be spelled out here) that the separation of theory and policy in modern *theory* could be sustained as long as there was, unchallenged or effectively immunized against challenge, a *practical* division between theoretical and political practice. The latter separation had its foundation in the activity of the modern national state, arguably the only social formation in history with pretensions to and ambitions of administering a global order, and of maintaining a total monopoly over rule-setting and rule-execution. Equally policy was to be the state's monopoly, and the procedure for its formulation had to be made separate and independent from the procedure legitimizing an acceptable theory and, more generally, intellectual work modelled after the latter procedure. The gradual, yet relentless erosion of the national state's monopoly (undermined simultaneously from above and from below, by transnational and subnational agencies, and weakened by the fissures in the historical marriage between nationalism and the state, none needing the other very strongly in their mature form) ended the plausibility of theoretical segregation.

With state resourcefulness and ambitions shrinking, responsibility (real or just claimed) for policy shifts away from the state or is actively shed on the state's own initiative. It is not taken over by another agent, though. It dissipates; it splits into a plethora of localized or partial policies pursued by localized or partial (mostly one issue) agencies. With that, vanishes the modern state's tendency to condensate and draw upon itself almost all social protest arising from unsatisfied redistributional demands and expectations – a quality that further enhanced the inclusive role of the state among societal agencies, at the same time rendering it vulnerable and exposed to frequent political crises (as conflicts fast turned into political protests). Under the postmodern condition grievances which in the past would cumulate into a collective political process and address themselves to the state, stay diffuse and translate into self-reflexivity of the agents, stimulating further dissipation of policies and autonomy of postmodern agencies (if they do cumulate for a time in the form of a one-issue pressure group, they bring together agents too heterogeneous in other respects to prevent the dissolution of the formation once the desired progress on the issue in question has been achieved; and even before that final outcome, the formation is unable to override the diversity of its supporters' interests and thus claim and secure their *total* allegiance and identification). One can speak, allegorically, of the 'functionality of dissatisfaction' in a postmodern habitat.

Not all politics in postmodernity is unambiguously postmodern. Throughout the modern era, politics of *inequality* and hence of *redistribution* was by far the most dominant type of political conflict and conflict-management. With the advent of postmodernity it has been displaced from its dominant role, but remains (and in all probability will remain) a constant feature of the postmodern habitat. Indeed, there are no signs that the postmodern condition promises to alleviate the inequalities (and hence the redistributional conflicts) proliferating in modern society. Even such an eminently modern type of politics acquires in many cases a postmodern tinge, though. Redistributional vindications of our time are focused more often than not on the winning of *human rights* (a code name for the agent's autonomy, for that freedom of choice that constitutes the agency in the postmodern habitat) by categories of population heretofore denied them (this is the case of the emancipatory movements of oppressed ethnic minorities, of the black movement, of one important aspect of the feminist movement, much as of the recent rebellion against the 'dictatorship over needs' practiced by the communist regimes), rather than at the express redistribution of wealth, income and other consumable values by society at large. The most conspicuous social division under postmodern conditions is one between *seduction* and *repression*: between the choice and the lack of choice, between the capacity for self-constitution and the denial of such capacity, between autonomously conceived self-definitions and imposed categorizations experienced as constraining and incapacitating. The redistributional aims (or, more precisely, consequences) of the resulting struggle are mediated by the resistance against repression of human agency. One may as well reverse the above statement and propose that in its postmodern rendition conflicts bared their true nature, that of the drive toward freeing of human agency, which in modern times tended to be hidden behind ostensibly redistributional battles.

Alongside the survivals of the modern form of politics, however, specifically postmodern forms appear and gradually colonize the centre-field of the postmodern political process. Some of them are new; some others owe their new, distinctly postmodern quality to their recent expansion and greatly increased impact. The following are the most prominent among them (the named forms are not necessarily mutually exclusive; and some act at cross-purposes):

1. *Tribal politics.* This is a generic name for practices aimed at collectivization (supra-agentic confirmation) of the agents' self-constructing efforts. Tribal politics entails the creation of tribes as *imagined communities.* Unlike the premodern communities the modern powers set about uprooting, postmodern tribes exist in no other form but the symbolically manifested commitment of their members. They can rely on neither executive powers able to coerce their constituency into submission to the tribal rules (seldom do they have clearly codified rules to which submission could be demanded), nor on the strength of neighbourly bonds or intensity of reciprocal exchange (most tribes are de-territorialized, and communication between their members is hardly at any time more intense than the intercourse between members and non-members of the tribe). Postmodern tribes, are, therefore, constantly in *statu nascendi* rather than *essendi*, brought over again into being by repetitive symbolic rituals of the members but persisting no longer than these rituals' power of attraction (in which sense they are akin to Kant's *aesthetic*

communities or Schmalenbach's *communions*). Allegiance is composed of the ritually manifested support for positive tribal tokens or equally symbolically demonstrated animosity to negative (anti-tribal) tokens. As the persistence of tribes relies solely on the deployment of the affective allegiance, one would expect an unprecedented condensation and intensity of emotive behaviour and a tendency to render the rituals as spectacular as possible – mainly through inflating their power to shock. Tribal rituals, as it were, compete for the scarce resource of public attention as the major (perhaps sole) resource of survival.

2. *Politics of desire.* This entails actions aimed at establishing the relevance of certain types of conduct (tribal tokens) for the self-constitution of the agents. If the relevance is established, the promoted conduct grows in attractiveness, its declared purposes acquire *seductive* power, and the probability of their choice and active pursuit increases: promoted purposes turn into agents' needs. In the field of the politics of desire, agencies vie with each other for the scarce resource of individual and collective dreams of the good life. The overall effect of the politics of desire is heteronomy of choice supported by, and in its turn sustaining, the autonomy of the choosing agents.

3. *Politics of fear.* This is, in a sense, a supplement (simultaneously a complement and a counterweight) of the politics of desire, aimed at drawing boundaries to heteronomy and staving off its potentially harmful effects. If the typical modern fears were related to the threat of totalitarianism perpetually ensconced in the project of rationalized and state-managed society (Orwell's 'boot eternally trampling a human face', Weber's 'cog in the machine' and 'iron cage', etc.), postmodern fears arise from uncertainty as to the soundness and reliability of advice offered through the politics of desire. More often than not, diffuse fears crystallize in the form of a suspicion that the agencies promoting desire are (for the sake of self-interest) oblivious or negligent of the damaging effects of their proposals. In view of the centrality of body-cultivation in the activity of self-constitution, the damage most feared is one that can result in poisoning or maiming the body through penetration or contact with the skin (the most massive panics have focused recently on incidents like mad cow disease, listeria in eggs, shrimps fed on poisonous algae, dumping of toxic waste – with the intensity of fear correlated to the importance of the body among the self-constituting concerns, rather than to the statistical significance of

the event and extent of the damage).

The politics of fear strengthens the position of experts in the processes of self-constitution, while ostensibly questioning their competence. Each successive instance of the suspension of trust articulates a new area of the habitat as problematic and thus leads to a call for more experts and more expertise.

4. *Politics of certainty*. This entails the vehement search for social confirmation of choice, in the face of the irredeemable pluralism of the patterns on offer and acute awareness that each formula of self-constitution, however carefully selected and tightly embraced, is ultimately one of the many, and always 'until further notice'. Production and distribution of certainty is the defining function and the source of power of the experts. As the pronouncements of the experts can be seldom put to the test by the recipients of their services, for most agents certainty about the soundness of their choices can be plausibly entertained only in the form of *trust*. The politics of certainty consists therefore mainly in the production and manipulation of trust; conversely, 'lying', 'letting down', 'going back on one's words', 'covering up' the unseemly deeds or just withholding information, betrayal of trust, abuse of privileged access to the facts of the case – all emerge as major threats to the already precarious and vulnerable self-identity of postmodern agents. Trustworthiness, credibility and perceived sincerity become major criteria by which merchants of certainty – experts, politicians, sellers of self-assembly identity kits – are judged, approved or rejected.

On all four stages on which the postmodern political game is played, the agent's initiative meets socially produced and sustained offers. Offers potentially available exceed as a rule the absorbing capacity of the agent. On the other hand, the reassuring potential of such offers as are in the end chosen rests almost fully on the perceived superiority of such offers over their competitors. This is, emphatically, a *perceived* superiority. Its attractiveness relies on a greater volume of allocated trust. What is perceived as superiority (in the case of marketed utilities, life-styles or political teams alike) is the visible amount of *public attention* the offer in question seems to enjoy. Postmodern politics is mostly about the reallocation of attention. Public attention is the most important – coveted and struggled for – among the scarce commodities in the focus of political struggle.

POSTMODERN ETHICS

Like politics, ethics is an indispensable part of a sociological theory of postmodernity pretending to any degree of completeness. The description of modern society could leave ethical problems aside or ascribe to them but a marginal place, in view of the fact that the moral regulation of conduct was to a large extent subsumed under the legislative and law-enforcing activity of global societal institutions, while whatever remained unregulated in such a way was 'privatized' or perceived (and treated) as residual and marked for extinction in the course of full modernization. This condition does not hold anymore; ethical discourse is not institutionally pre-empted and hence its conduct and resolution (or irresolution) must be an organic part of any theoretical model of postmodernity.

Again, not all ethical issues found in a postmodern habitat are new. Most importantly, the possibly extemporal issues of the orthodox ethics – the rules binding short-distance, face-to-face intercourse between moral agents under conditions of physical and moral proximity – remain presently as much alive and poignant as ever before. In no way are they postmodern; as a matter of fact, they are not modern either. (On the whole, modernity contributed little, if anything, to the enrichment of moral problematics. Its role boiled down to the substitution of legal for moral regulation and the exemption of a wide and growing sector of human actions from moral evaluation.)

The distinctly postmodern ethical problematic arises primarily from two crucial features of the postmodern condition: *pluralism* of authority, and the centrality of *choice* in the self-constitution of postmodern agents.

1. Pluralism of authority, or rather the absence of an authority with globalizing ambitions, has a twofold effect. First, it rules out the setting of binding norms each agency must (or could be reasonably expected to) obey. Agencies may be guided by their own purposes, paying in principle as little attention to other factors (also to the interests of other agencies) as they can afford, given their resources and degree of independence. 'Non-contractual bases of contract', devoid of institutional power support, are thereby considerably weakened. If unmotivated by the limits of the agency's own resources, any constraint upon the agency's action has to be negotiated afresh. Rules emerge mostly as reactions to strife and consequences of ensuing negotiations;

still, the already negotiated rules remain by and large precarious and under-determined, while the needs of new rules – to regulate previously unanticipated contentious issues – keep proliferating. This is why the *problem* of rules stays in the focus of public agenda and is unlikely to be conclusively resolved. In the absence of 'principal coordination' the negotiation of rules assumes a distinctly *ethical* character: at stake are the principles of non-utilitarian self-constraint of autonomous agencies – and both non-utility and autonomy define *moral* action as distinct from either self-interested or legally prescribed conduct. Second, pluralism of authorities is conducive to the resumption by the agents of moral responsibility that tended to be neutralized, rescinded or ceded away as long as the agencies remained subordinated to a unified, quasi-monopolistic legislating authority. On the one hand, the agents face now point-blank the consequences of their actions. On the other, they face the evident ambiguity and controversiality of the purposes which actions were to serve, and thus the need to justify argumentatively the values that inform their activity. Purposes can no longer be substantiated *monologically*; having become perforce subjects of a *dialogue*, they must now refer to principles wide enough to command authority of the sort that belongs solely to ethical values.

2. The enhanced autonomy of the agent has similarly a twofold ethical consequence. First – in as far as the centre of gravity shifts decisively from heteronomous control to self-determination, and autonomy turns into the defining trait of postmodern agents – self-monitoring, self-reflection and self-evaluation become principal activities of the agents, indeed the mechanisms synonymical with their self-constitution. In the absence of a universal model for self-improvement, or of a clear-cut hierarchy of models, the most excruciating choices agents face are between life-purposes and values, not between the means serving the already set, uncontroversial ends. Supra-individual criteria of propriety in the form of technical precepts of instrumental rationality do not suffice. This circumstance, again, is potentially propitious to the sharpening up of moral self-awareness: only ethical principles may offer such criteria of value-assessment and value-choice as are at the same time supra-individual (carry an authority admittedly superior to that of individual self-preservation), and fit to be used without surrendering the agent's autonomy. Hence the typically postmodern heightened interest in ethical debate and increased attractiveness of the agencies

claiming expertise in moral values (e.g., the revival of religious and quasi-religious movements). Second, with the autonomy of all and any agents accepted as a principle and institutionalized in the life-process composed of an unending series of choices, the limits of the agent whose autonomy is to be observed and preserved turn into a most closely guarded and hotly contested frontier. Along this borderline new issues arise which can be settled only through an ethical debate. Is the flow and the outcome of self-constitution to be tested before the agent's right to autonomy is confirmed? If so, what are the standards by which success or failure are to be judged (what about the autonomy of young and still younger children, of the indigent, of parents raising their children in unusual ways, of people choosing bizarre lifestyles, of people indulging in abnormal means of intoxication, people engaging in idiosyncratic sexual activities, individuals pronounced mentally handicapped)? And, how far are the autonomous powers of the agent to extend and at what point is their limit to be drawn (remember the notoriously inconclusive contest between 'life' and 'choice' principles of the abortion debate)?

All in all, in the postmodern context agents are constantly faced with moral issues and obliged to choose between equally well founded (or equally unfounded) ethical precepts. The choice always means the assumption of responsibility, and for this reason bears the character of a moral act. Under the postmodern condition, the agent is perforce not just an actor and decision-maker, but a *moral subject*. The performance of life-functions demands also that the agent be a morally *competent* subject.

SOCIOLOGY IN THE POSTMODERN CONTEXT

The strategies of any systematic study are bound to be resonant with the conception of its object. Orthodox sociology was resonant with the theoretical model of the modern society. It was for that reason that the proper accounting for the self-reflexive propensities of human actors proved to be so spectacularly difficult. Deliberately or against its declared wishes, sociology tended to marginalize or explain away self-reflexivity as rule-following, function-performing or at best sedimentation of institutionalized learning; in each case, as an epiphenomenon of social totality, understood ultimately as 'legitimate authority' capable of 'principally coordin-ating' social space. As long as the self-reflexivity of actors remained reduced to the subjective perception of obedience to impersonal rules, it did not need to be treated seriously; it rarely came under scrutiny as an independent variable, much less as a principal condition of all sociality and its institutionalized sedimentations.

Never flawless, this strategy becomes singularly inadequate under the postmodern condition. The postmodern habitat is indeed an incessant flow of reflexivity; the sociality responsible for all its structured yet fugitive forms, their interaction and their succession, is a discursive activity, an activity of interpretation and reinterpretation, of interpretation fed back into the interpreted condition only to trigger off further interpretive efforts. To be effectively and consequentially present in a postmodern habitat sociology must conceive of itself as a participant (perhaps better informed, more systematic, more rule-conscious, yet nevertheless a participant) of this never ending, self-reflexive process of reinterpretation and devise its strategy accordingly. In practice, this will mean in all probability, replacing the ambitions of the judge of 'common beliefs', healer of prejudices and umpire of truth with those of a clarifier of interpretative rules and facilitator of communication; this will amount to the replacement of the dream of the legislator with the practice of an interpreter.

NOTE

1 The ideas sketched in this essay have been inspired or stimulated by readings and debates far too numerous for all the intellectual debts to be listed. And yet some, the most generous (even when unknowing) creditors must be named. They are: Benedict Anderson, Mikhail Bakhtin, Pierre Bourdieu, Anthony Giddens, Erving Goffman, Agnes Heller, Michel Maffesoli, Stefan Morawski, Alan Touraine. And, of course, Georg Simmel, who started it all.

APPENDIX

Sociology, postmodernity and exile: an interview with Zygmunt Bauman

Richard Kilminster and Ian Varcoe

This is an edited version of an interview with Professor Bauman held on 15th and 16th August, 1990 as part of the preparation for a collection of essays to be published under the provisional title *Power, Culture and Modernity: Essays in Honour of Zygmunt Bauman*.

Q. Even though your publications and research interests have covered a wide range of sociological fields over the years, we do nonetheless see you as having a distinctive and continuing intellectual personality. We see you broadly as a humanistic Marxist, interested in culture, a kind of critical theorist; and there also seems to be a continuing theme of rejection of system in your work. Can you comment on these suggestions? Are we on the right track here?

A. Well, I'm not a good judge of these matters because what you are proposing has hardly any structure. Your proposal is to take a number of objective categories and to ask me to situate myself, in a sense, objectively and externally, as an outsider, in relation to myself, in these objective categories. Now this is not a performance in which the person in question is the best performer. It is something which is much better done precisely by people standing outside, and being capable of exercising objective judgement, and referring to objective categories, and so on. . . . I would rather look for subjective categories, subjective categories which provide the framework for my own research, but which do not necessarily overlap with these objective categories which you mention, like critical theory, humanistic Marxism, and so forth.

I can simply tell you that there were actually two things with which I was concerned throughout my writings, throughout my academic life. One was the working class, standing for the downtrodden or the underdog, for suffering in general. For a long time there was the sign of identity between the two: the working class as the embodiment of suffering. That was one topic, and the other was the topic of culture.

Now, when I try to generalize from here, and to say why I was interested in these two things, then what follows is that one presumable motive was that of irritation with what I would call the arrogance or conceit, of a sort. The phrase which infuriated me very early in my intellectual life, I remember, was Hegel's concept of the identity between the real and the rational. That was something which I was furious about, and which, I think, projected far more than my interest, because the interest was in exposing the underside, in debunking, in disassembling, precisely that conceit, the conviction that we live in the best possible world, which has not only reality, but some sort of supra-real foundation for it. And the somewhat derivative issue in relation to this first one, which was an interest not so much in – I would put it – architectural design, as in the building techniques – that was my major preoccupation in sociology. Not so much the structures as the structured process. To understand how the visibility, tangibility and power, of reality – and the conviction concerning, the belief in, reality – are being constructed: that was why I got interested in culture. I would say that it was Antonio Gramsci who actually made the connection between these two questions clear to me. That was the major influence of my life, when I read Gramsci's *Prison Notebooks*. What Gramsci in fact presented to me for the first time, was reality as something flexible and fluid, to be retranslated into the language of organization in action. . . . I think that this element was present from the very first book I produced. A book which I am still very proud of, to this very day, is *Between Class and Elite* [1972]. . . . Even before this book, which I brought from Poland, as you know, I wrote another one about British socialism [1956], so it was a long-standing interest which culminated in *Memories of Class* [1982], which was, in a sense, a farewell, not to the working class, but to the identity between the working class and the problem of injustice, and inequality. The problem of inequality survived. But it is not related to the working-class problem especially. Rather, it is reincarnated in the Hellenic vision of postmodernity. It is the question of tolerance as assimilation and tolerance as solidarity, two options which stand in front of the postmodern mentality.

Then there were the problematics of culture. I published the first full-scale investigation of culture in 1966. But several years before that, I published other studies related to it. The cultural problematics book of 1966 was called *Culture and Society*: Gramsci's idea of society as the sedimented, ossified, petrified product of cultural creativity, juxtaposed to the ongoing cultural production, as a dead body against the life activity. It's partly from Gramsci, but it may also be seen as inspired by Simmel's theory of culture, his retranslation of the alienation problematics from the economic sphere to that of spirituality: spiritual products which are alienated, and then confront the creator as an alien reality. That was the beginning of my interest in culture. Then, as you know, there was *Culture as Praxis* [1973], which developed this theme of culture as the ongoing creative process, and I think the two themes [outlined above] merge in what I call this trilogy of modernity. There is *Legislators and Interpreters* [1987], *Modernity and the Holocaust* [1989] and *Modernity and Ambivalence* [1991].

Q. That was extremely useful because it gives us elements of continuity.

A. I can't prove that there was continuity. It's not just that continuity is in the mind of the beholder. It was the continuity of, I would say, only, of what made me angry – the continuity of certain passions. The passions wander; for example, you mentioned that I looked for a number of current spiritual inspirations and I rejected them: structuralism, hermeneutics, for example. Well, that would be a prime example of *dis*continuity. In my view, it was an element of continuity. I was seeking for an answer to the same questions all along, and if I didn't find it, I moved elsewhere. But I took my questions with me.

Q. Can you describe the most important influences in your intellectual development, both individuals and traditions of thought?

A. In my inaugural lecture at Leeds University I spoke about my two teachers, Hochfeld and Ossowski; so it is recorded there [1972]. Ossowski is known in the west, but Hochfeld is not. Again, there are two elements in intellectual motives, and there were two different teachers at the same time. I think there is some sort of symmetry between these two dualities in my life. In fact, the two teachers have something in common: they were very unlike most academic sociologists. They were convinced of the tremendous sociopolitical importance of their purely academic work. Theirs' was never detached work, for its own sake. But, on the other hand, if they were asked about their primary allegiances and loyalties, they would probably answer differently. Hochfeld would say he was dedicated to moral principles, and it was of secondary importance whether these are pursued through politics or academic work. And Ossowski would say that his prime allegiance was to truth, and he would reject any kind of activity which would require him to compromise these principles and enter some sort of negotiation – the art of the possible or some such thing. And so, in this sense, they were very different; and it was not very easy to square the influences, not to become schizophrenic, having two such teachers at the same time.

Personally, I feel quite a lot of their influence in what I am doing. For example, the late return to the problematics of morality, I think, is some sort of posthumous tribute to Hochfeld. It is the kind of work he was trying to do. . . . I have already mentioned Gramsci, who was probably the turning point in my intellectual life.

Q. How were Marxism and sociology combined in the influences on your development? Were they separate, or distinct? If they were not, how did the Polish intellectual tradition combine them?

A. There is some sort of inner ambiguity about Marxism, even if it is absorbed and accepted as the official ideology of a country. It is singularly unfit for this role, unless it is simply translated, as it was in Soviet Marxism, as the will of the Party – or, rather, the latest official document of the Party. It remains extremely ambiguous, because it legitimizes reality instrumentally. That is, it legitimizes reality as tending towards something which it is not, something different from itself. And, therefore, in a sense, organically, it supplies criteria for criticism of reality. Therefore, any attempt at using Marxism as the justification of a particular kind of reality is shot through with this element of criticism. Reality is short of perfect. It is not yet there. It is 'not yet': reality is always 'not yet', always not reached, not accomplished. And therefore the intellectuals who joined their lot with the communist movement were, at the same time, time-bombs: they were always potentially dissident. I wonder whether you ever noticed that, for example, in Nazi Germany, there was never the phenomenon of intellectual dissidence; but the history of Soviet Russia and Eastern European countries is fraught with waves of intellectual dissidence. Now why? It was not an accidental phenomenon because Nazi ideology was received 'all on a plate'. It was extremely honest, in a sense, extremely straightforward, everything that was said was meant. And those who joined it knew exactly what was involved. Intellectuals were lured to communism by the assurance that the future will be different from the present, that the latter is imperfect. This is something that intellectuals are inclined to think anyway: the present is not exactly as Reason would like it to be. Therefore, sooner or later, when they were asked to say that what they were hoping for had already been accomplished, the phenomenon of dissidence arose. . . . Marxism, as a legitimation of communist society, was a failure, I think. It was actually not fit for this role at all.

Q. Marxism *and* sociology: You seem to be suggesting that they were not separate categories, that Marxism was taught *as* sociology.

A. Yes, I would agree with that. I think that there is a parallelism between these inner qualities of Marxism and sociology in general. I think sociology is a schizophrenic discipline, organically dual, at war with itself. And that is why, in most countries, sociology is always an object of intense, and slightly morbid, fascination. Whether it is praised or castigated and condemned, it is always considered very much like, in simpler societies, blacksmiths were: people who were sort of alchemists, who sit astride the normal barricades which ought to be used to keep things apart. Now why is sociology so internally ambiguous and inherently schizophrenic? It is because, on the one hand, it cannot start from anywhere other than society as it is, that is, society which has already accomplished its work, which is already framed and trimmed and organized; and from individuals who are already manipulated, in whatever way they were: the natural human impulses, tendencies, lives, trends, and so on. So, reality as it is – this is the starting point. You cannot make a sociological statement without already assuming society 'in place'. It is already 'there'. . . . On the other hand, sociology does present society – any kind of society, any state of society, any form of society – as an accomplishment. Therefore, it relativizes it. Therefore it puts it in question. Therefore it is inherently against this arrogance which says that it is not just the reality, but the only reality there is; and that it has its own inner laws and rules that cannot be violated unless to the detriment of those who do the violation. So, on the one hand, there is this conservative potential in sociology. On the other hand, there is this reformatory, revolutionary, critical potential. And they can't be separated. This is the whole point. You can't be a fully, one hundred per cent, conservative, legitimating kind of sociologist without giving your legitimation such a form that it is potentially disruptive. And you cannot be subversive and disruptive sociologists without, at the same time, appealing to the power of realities, of dominance, of structures, and so on. This duality is also present in Marxism – I think that the way they function in their respective contexts, whether it is Marxist sociology or non-Marxist sociology, is, in fact, very similar.

Q. Like you, many other writers sympathetic to the western Marxist tradition came to see culture as of crucial importance, since it was from this realm, broadly conceived, that people drew the meanings they needed to make sense of their lives; and it was also the potent source of visions of a different society. But how autonomous, in your view, is culture?

A. In my discourse, the normal, global view of culture as an epiphenomenon, something like the icing on the cake, something extra to the 'real', hard stuff of social life, which is 'structure' – all these things are difficult to express in my language, let alone to make central. I already mentioned before my primary views on this matter: 'structure' is culture sedimented, the petrification of the cultural products of cultural activity. . . . Cultural activity never starts in any generation, in any particular place, from scratch. It always has to reckon with what has already been accomplished by previous generations. And, on the other hand, it is not entirely free activity, because the stuff on which it operates is given. The stuff is human beings with their natural propensities, and it is the resources which are made available for cultural activity by previous development. So it is always the manipulation of something. Culture is never conjuring these things up from nowhere – it's always operating on things which exist. But what is specific about the sociological way of looking at the actual reality is to see it as an accomplishment, a product of activity. So that is why I find it difficult to answer the question 'how far is culture autonomous ?'– autonomous in relation to what? It is a form of activity. You may ask how much everything else in human life is autonomous; but not culture.

Q. You wrote a great deal in the early 1970s on structuralism. Did this interest in structuralism logically follow from your interest in culture? It is noticeable, however, that your interest in this field seems to have waned subsequently. This is true of many other sociologists, who came to doubt structuralism on the grounds, amongst others, that it was ahistorical and inapplicable to advanced societies; and that the analogy between society and language was untenable. Did your thinking follow this path?

A. I am inherently, and probably incurably eclectic; that is, I am not very much interested in loyalty to any particular school or style. I am looking everywhere for things which seem to be relevant to what I am working on. And, once I have found them I am not very much bothered with the question of whether I transgressed some sacred boundary, or went into the area which I shouldn't, because I belong to a different school. . . that is one thing. During my intellectual career – if you want to put it this way – I flirted in this manner with a number of new fads which I thought might contain something relevant. Some I rejected out of hand as completely irrelevant to my interests. . . . Now, why I was enchanted and enthralled by Lévi-Strauss was not because of what some people ascribe to him, his alleged promise of providing some sort of a final answer to the structure of everything, the tough, ultimate foundations of reality, as quite a few people have interpreted him. . . . What I was fascinated by in the structuralism of Lévi-Strauss was precisely his insistence that there is no such thing as *the* structure, as the structure of society, for example. What is there, is only the constant urge – which is universal, according to him – to structure everything. . . . We are structuring music. We are structuring mythological thinking. We are structuring cooking. We are giving structures to every area of our lives. But what is universal here is this propensity, this inner push, to structure – and not any emergent structure. He rejected emphatically the idea of *the* social structure. Every aspect of social life is structured. But it doesn't mean that there is some final, ultimate, underlying structure of everything. So I really saw an opportunity in Lévi-Strauss, understood thus. I saw an idea very much resonant with my primary interest in these building techniques. *Modernity and Ambivalence*, for example, the work I have written very recently, is all about this modern compulsion to structure, to eliminate ambivalence and to drive out ambiguity, to classify, to design, to name, to separate and to segregate. I was interested in structuralism in this sense, and I don't regret this period of intense study of [structuralist writers] simply because what I learned from it is very much an organic part of my thinking.

Q. You're saying that you were interested in it for your own reasons, as it were, from the very beginning. . . . You were interested in some of the insights, perhaps, and how these could be extended and developed, applied, etc. to the study of culture.

A. I found very useful insights in this field, in particular – precisely in the writings of structuralists: language as a system in the sense that there is an arrangement of constant permutations, so the continuity, the reality, of existence is achieved only through continuous creativity and change; language existing in no other form but in the infinite collection of utterances. This frame of thinking, this mental attitude, I found so conducive and akin to my own interests.

Q. From various statements you have made over the years one gets a strong impression that you see an important function of sociology as being its role as a maverick discipline, spinning off ideas, relativizing hallowed absolutes, debunking established ways of thinking and acting, and exploring different social worlds. Two questions then: this model of sociology fitted very well into the nature of state socialist societies, where the communist state was fundamentally more affected by expressions of intellectual dissent which challenged its legitimacy. How well did this model transfer to a western setting? What is your opinion of another strategy for developing sociology which suggests that it is more important, at least in the west, to establish the institutional and professional credibility of the discipline as a science, through the generation of reliable knowledge of society?

A. I see sociology as inevitably and incurably two-faced: one face is potentially conservative and the other is potentially subversive; and, as two faces of the coin, they cannot be separated, they are always there – so you cannot have one without the danger of the other. That is the constant view of sociology, which hasn't changed in my mind. What has changed quite considerably, is the way in which I exemplify this basic duality, and how I explain it to myself.

For quite a long time, I thought about this dichotomy in terms of sociology always influencing, in a way, social reality, but capable of doing so in one of two different ways: through rationalization or manipulation. Now manipulation means simply, in a sense, informing the structure of society, its organization, and the legislation about it; informing the setting in which human activity takes place. Therefore, in a way, forcing people – by arranging the setting very skilfully – to do what those in charge require them to do. This sort of sociology serves the rulers, the factory managers and the bosses. This is influence through manipulation. Influence by rationalization would be of a very different kind, exercised by supplying the individual with more information about the setting, various parameters of life, the environment in which he or she must perform their life activity, and so forth. And by the same token, this second influence undermines the first. That is, if the first confines the freedom of the individual, of choice, the second enhances the freedom of choice, and therefore underlines individuals' part in the structuring of society. So, one hand in fact fights against the other. What sociology does on the one hand undermines the things which were done on the other. That was how I thought about it, for a long time. I thought in terms of sociology actually imposing solutions through the individual's choice, or through the legislative activity of the state – or whatever the head organization is – but always imposing itself upon reality and changing it.

Now I don't assume that sociology is a body of knowledge capable of performing such roles on its own. . . . I thought a lot about how Foucault's power–knowledge syndrome applied to sociology, and I came to the conclusion that it doesn't apply to it at all. I came to the conclusion that sociology is not a discursive formation. If it is a discursive formation, it is one which is made of holes only – of apertures – so there is a constant input of material from outside, as well as output. I am rather inclined to see sociology today as an eddy on a fast-moving river, an eddy which retains its shape but which changes its content all the time, an eddy which can retain its shape only in as far as there is a constant through-flow of water. That's metaphorically. Now more practically, more literally: what I would say is that sociology is a constant interpretation of, or commentary on, experience. It is not the experience of sociologists, but experience shared by sociologists with the wider society. And this commentary is sent back into the society itself. . . . To draw the boundary where sociology stops and the 'real' begins, to establish the property in the same sense as you put fences on land – 'that's my plot', 'that's their plot' – is, practically, out of the question: you can't do it. Rather, it is a constant involvement with reality, but in such a way that . . . again, to use a metaphor, I would recall the beautiful statement of Blaise Pascal about history: 'History is a book which we write and in which we are written.' Well, I would put the relationship between sociology and the social reality which it tries to grasp in the same way.

Now, how does the old dilemma present itself to me? It is between sociology as a legislating authority, sociology motivated by legislative reason, reason which asserts – claims – the right for the ultimate say, for the last word; and a second type of sociology that sets itself a different goal: that is, by its very presence, by its very impulsive and compulsive interpretive urge, to relativize the existing interpretations of reality. . . . The one right it claims to itself is the right to expose the conceit and arrogance, the unwarranted claims to exclusivity of others' interpretations, but without substituting itself in their place: 'Look, what you are convinced is the truth is not necessarily so, because here is another possibility of looking at the thing.' And you have at least realized that, ultimately, it is a matter of your responsibility to make the choice. The good choice is not given, it is not there already waiting to be learned and absorbed. The choice is something you have to work for.

Q. You are now saying that this view you used to have about the function of sociology as being rationalization or manipulation, is a 'modern' view of sociology. You now say we must look at this in a different way.

A. For most of my life, the *raison d'être* of, the reason for existence for, sociology was: to be a sort of missionary vision, conversion to truth. Very much like Spinoza said about the moral duty of the holder of truth: 'If I am right and you are wrong it is my moral duty to convert you to my point of view. It would be cruel of me if I did not do it.' In Plato you have the same thing, that when the philosophers actually went to this world where they contemplated pure ideas at close quarters, and their duty was to return to earth and to bring this wisdom to others – if they neglect this duty they are really immoral people. The idea of sociology as a converting, proselytizing, missionary activity always ended up in constructing new structures of domination, whatever the intentions were. Whether they were left or right, progressive or regressive, conservative or liberal, it always led in the same direction. I think it was all part of the modern project.

Q. Putting the interests of the profession, where do we fit into the structure of knowledge? Where do we fit in institutionally, into universities and research institutions, if this is our view of our discipline?

A. I feel no compunction about justifying the social significance of the discipline, of which I feel a part, by pointing out the role it plays in self-reflection, in the organically self-reflective life, in which we all live. And I think very few other areas of intellectual activity can actually claim the same possibility of this particular function – of playing it, as sociology does; that is, of serving this extremely crucial activity of self-reflection – and simply by supplying the resources for it, and also the patterns for it, without prejudicing, without pre-empting, the results of this self-reflection for the choices which eventually will follow. I am fully aware of the self-contained and self-sustained, institutionalized tradition of academic sociology, particularly, in part, American sociology, and I am quite aware, being a sociologist, that, once an institution has been established, it has the quality of self-perpetuation; and the major thing which a successful institution does is to erect impenetrable walls, which, in a way, make it immune to external influences, and keep it on course. I'm quite sure that the self-justification for the continuing existence of philosophy is the presence of thousands of philosophical texts, a continuous discourse which has been brought into being a very long time ago in Ancient Greece, and which goes on through the ages.

Q. What, though, on your more recent view of the nature of sociological knowledge distinguishes sociology from journalism, cultural critique, social philosophizing, and many other things? Is there any difference?

A. Well, what is distinctive is the certain tradition of which we are the guardians. We have our books, to which we go. We have our continuous discourse, of which we are the participants. And that is exactly what we bring as our dowry when we enter this self-reflective activity, which goes on anyway, everywhere. And we have something to bring. . . . According to Kant's *Critique of*

Judgment the aesthetic community will never reach reality, other than through the continuous participation of people, who, in fact, make the group a community. But, nevertheless, the *telos*, the purpose, of making this community a reality is a necessary requirement of this continuing activity of community-making, of this participation, of this commitment which is, in effect, the only flesh of the aesthetic community. There is no objective solution to the question, according to Kant, for example, of what is beauty, what is ugliness?; there is no 'objective', 'outside', 'objectively given', outside this continuing creation and disassembling of the aesthetic community, as process. . . . So that's how sociology acts, I think. And I know it's not good news for anybody who really wishes to have the assurance, the guarantee, of success, before the work has started. Most people probably would like this luxury very much: it truly comes in all sorts of forms, this guarantee. One of the forms specific to sciences is the guarantee given by scientific method. If you follow the method then you may reach something interesting, or utterly banal and unimportant. But it doesn't matter – what does, is that the method guaranteed it to be a valid finding. Now you would like to have this sort of guarantee, given in advance. But I don't believe that there is such a guarantee.

Q. Do you see any parallel between this view and what you were saying earlier about culture as making, and constantly building? What matters is not the structure but the building, the operations.

A. I think that sociology is a cultural activity *par excellence*. It is the exercise of human spirituality, the constant reinterpreting of human activity in the course of activity itself. So it is a very important element of the self-reflective, self-monitoring quality of human action.

Q. How can we be sure that this view of sociology isn't a transient one, reflecting how sociologists see themselves during the particular phase of development, on a national and global level, that we are living through at the moment?

A. We can't be sure because, simply, sociology *is* a transient activity, confined to its time and place. It is part and parcel of the stage in the development of culture and it is no worse for this reason. I think that is precisely where it derives its value from. It is always engaged with current, topical issues which are relevant to the particular stage in political, economic, social and cultural development. I see nothing wrong with that. Now, pretending that it speaks to the current moment from the point of view of some supratemporal, extra-territorial point of view – that would mean making false pretences. Of course, it is a good strategem in the fight for authority, but I don't think it has anything to do with scholarly honesty, which is the only ground to which I would point when claiming the right to be listened to.

Q. Your view of the main importance and function of sociology resembles that of the critical theory of the Frankfurt School – a sociological version of 'negative dialectics', if you like. At one stage in your career you were a convinced advocate of the work of Jürgen Habermas, as a writer who attempted to combine the positivists' insistence on reliable knowledge with acknowledgement of the hermeneutic dimension of social life in a science with 'emancipatory' intent, in the Marxist tradition. Would you still regard yourself as a 'critical sociologist'?

A. Yes, I do. I don't like Habermas, however.

Q. Not any more!

A. Not any more – yes. I think what attracted me to Habermas, really, was his ideal of a society shaped after the pattern of a sociology seminar; that is, that there are only participants and the one thing which matters is the power of argument. Therefore, the function of sociology is to debunk these other factors, which hide behind allegedly, ostensibly free discussion, and eliminate their influence. And, once that is achieved, then the problem of truth merges with the problem of consensus, of agreement, and so forth. So, I liked this as a utopian *focus imaginarius*, somewhat like the idea of the ideal experiment, which of course is never achieved, but unless you have it, you can't experiment at all. Now, I liked this horizon, this prospect, as the organizing, directing factor in our efforts – where we should aim at. But, once Habermas turned from there to a straightforward positivistic re-hashing of Parsons, then I lost any spiritual affinity with his project.

Q. We have been talking so far very much in terms of social philosophy. The sort of categories that we mainly employed were to do with social justice, culture, limits, possibilities, etc. But we also thought we discerned in your work over the years something closer to sociological theory in the narrower sense. That is, some sort of intellectual synthesis of the linkages between the contradictions of capitalism and cultural crisis. Are we right in discerning that sort of continuing level of interest in the way that advanced societies are tending?

A. I have been continuously interested in these issues – with one proviso, however: that the way in which I formulate them has changed. . . . I am against the consideration of the present world situation in terms of crisis or deformation of something else. So what I am after – what I am very keen to find out – is the possibility of treating this sort of reality in its own terms, as a system in its own right, a reality which is not an inferior or changed form of anything else, but just itself; and to find out how it functions. I think that the fact that we remain in the grip of old concepts: capitalism; industrial society; homogenizing culture; legitimation by unified, homogeneous ideology; and similar ideas – because we remain in the grip of these concepts, I think we overlook a number of things which are important in contemporary society. . . . The postmodernity idea was introduced as a pure collection of absences. It was formulated, articulated, in terms of: 'There is no'; 'this is absent'; 'these things have disappeared', and so on. Now, the sooner we get rid of this grip of historical memory, as I call it, the better.

Q. It is only in recent years – perhaps in response to the higher profile and legitimacy achieved by economic liberalism in the west in the era of the New Right – that you have systematically addressed the question of 'freedom', in your recent book [1988] with this title. Would you agree that, like many socialists, you have until now been preoccupied more with inequality than with freedom, of which, coming from a Marxist tradition, you were naturally sceptical?

A. In fact, I started from the classical writings of liberalism. My first book, on British socialism, was based on a study of Bentham, J.S. Mill and Herbert Spencer. I was actually struck by the fact that J.S. Mill, starting from some very straightforward liberal, individualistic assumptions . . . ended up, following the logic of utilitarianism, with becoming in fact a socialist. He actually deduced the necessity of the social manipulation of justice, the social arrangements of justice, from his dedication to individual freedom, as a necessary complement, as a supplement. One thing that liberalism cannot cater for is precisely the matter of justice, social justice. Whoever is concerned with the value of justice cannot simply stop by saying: 'Well, the only function of the state is to wither away, to disappear, and leave well alone.' That's one thing, and the other is that . . . the state of total freedom is, practically, unimaginable. It is a non-social state, and freedom in society means always the liberty of x to impose his or her will on y: in a sense, freedom is privilege. I come more and more to the conclusion that freedom is a tremendously important stratifying factor in society. That it is the substance of social stratification. What does it mean that you are higher? It means that you have more options open to you. The lower down you are, the more determined you are, the less free you are. The discussion – the notorious discussion – in sociology about the voluntaristic side of the social actor as such, is hopelessly abstract because the voluntariness, or voluntarism, of human action is a matter of social position, or the place in the social structure. You may be more voluntaristic or less so, depending on the situation which you are in. So I think that the divorce between the discourse of inequality and the discourse of freedom is detrimental to both of them. The only way of discussing either of the two issues is to bring them together. What is inequality about? In the end about unequal freedom. And what is freedom about? About advancing in the social ability to do things. . . . So I think that the two problematics can be understood only if they are conjointly treated. That's my answer to it.

Q. Now, you are somebody who, in your own lifetime, moved from a social system that was geared to the maximizing of equality, at least in its ideological pronouncements about itself, to another society which was the classic home of individualism, or economic liberalism, where the emphasis, in reality, would have been towards the freedom pole. As somebody who has experienced this transition, lived in these two societies, how has this fed into your process of reflection?

A. This is an extremely complicated question. The idea of welfare-state provision really was to engage the state in order to create for the ordinary people, who didn't have freedom, the conditions for it. It was very much like Aneurin Bevan's view of the National Health Service, that it was a 'one-off' expenditure. You introduce it, then everybody would become healthy; and then there would be no expenditure on national health any more – at least, it would be going down and down, year by year. That was the idea. And it was the same with the welfare state. The welfare state was thought of as an enabling institution, as a temporary measure to provide a sort of safety cushion for people, so that they know they can dare, they can take risks, they can exert themselves, because there is always this safety provision if they fail. . . . And the same thinking was behind the communist experiment, and that's why many people were so seduced, actually. A great part of the Polish intelligentsia was attracted to it. Poland was in a different state than England, anyway. In 1939, when the independent existence of Poland ended, there were eight million unemployed in the country. Around one-third of the population was without work. Poverty was unimaginable by British standards: there was no provision for the unemployed, and people would just sit on the street idly, without hope, without having any energy to do something, look for anything. So, to speak about freedom as the one thing that was missing there would immediately have aroused an ironical smile. . . . What most people were worrying about was the daily bread, and the security of work, the certainty that their children would get jobs – these sort of things. And so, freedom will come later when they actually . . . it's very much like Marx said, you remember: freedom begins when the necessities are satisfied, the basic necessities – when you are fed and sheltered. . . . Freedom was not exactly at the top of the agenda; what was on top of the agenda was providing people with these conditions of life. The effect of this specific situation of Eastern Europe at that time was that it made thinking persons more sensitive to people being in any condition of incapacitation. Poverty meant mostly this incapacity to be truly free. Therefore, the reception of liberalism and western freedom was tainted by this recognition that people who succeeded, people who actually made it, and who don't need any collective provisions to sustain their well-being, deny these provisions to others who really do need them. The balance between the two is not easy to find – taxpayers 'need' more freedom, the person who gets benefits 'needs' more constraint. I think I've remained sensitive to these dialectics of freedom, dependence and justice.

As far as academic freedom is concerned, freedom of speaking and writing, in Poland it was not like in Soviet Russia. It was not a Stalinist country at any time – perhaps for a very brief period of one or two years, too brief to leave any profound trace. . . .

Q. We have witnessed the dramatic demise of communism in Eastern Europe in recent years, as a failed historical experiment in state collectivism. It is obvious that you took seriously – as more than something simply to criticize as an ideological illusion – the classical liberal statements about freedom, the market, individualism and the dangers of statism. Would you say that Popper has been historically vindicated?

A. One thing Popper has said is, I think, extremely topical and invaluable, and that is something which emerges from these recent events very clearly – and only recent events in the east. It is this 'piecemeal social engineering', which he juxtaposes to the global order. I think that is the major issue; the major change; the major shift. The fall of the communists spectacularly dramatized this shift, but only because, in my view, the communist system was the extremely spectacular dramatization of the Enlightenment message. This was the common message, taken up by the west and the east – only its implementation was never attempted in so condensed a form anywhere else than in the east. I tried to explain the reasons in some of my articles, particularly in the article on the East European intelligentsia [1987], torn between the modernity already existing 'out there' and the hopelessly premodern world, which, because of that, felt the same way as America felt to Christopher Columbus, or even better, to Amerigo Vespucci, namely: 'it's just an empty land, uninhabited, a land of infinite possibilities, "anything goes"'. So, for this reason, it was a much more condensed, much more intense, practical exercise in the Enlightenment ideal of the global order than anywhere else. The collapse of this, was not only the collapse of communism – of course, it was the collapse of communism, to be sure – but it was also more than that: it was the collapse of a certain modern idea of a 'designed society'. Popper has been vindicated, not only for moral reasons, but also for the sheer impossibility of doing it, for the technical inaccessibility of achieving it.

Q. If your *Socialism: The Active Utopia* [1976] came out now in a second edition, what would you say in a new Preface? Is it possible any more to see socialism as the 'counter-culture' of capitalism?

A. Well, I'm much more concerned now with the counter-culture of modernity, having put traditional nineteenth-century capitalism and socialism in the same category. They were a family quarrel inside modernity. In the nineteenth-century, the reality and the inescapability of modernity was never under question – including Marxism. There was the Romantic movement, and there was Nietzsche, in the end, but basically the central discourse assumed this kind of 'reality as given once-and-for-all'; Progress; the Whig conception of history; 'we are fighting prejudice, ignorance and superstition'; and so on. And against this background, 'capitalism and socialism' was the quarrel of how best to implement it, this progress, which everybody agreed about. I think that now we are past this moment, and it is the very value of this vision of the world which is in question. Therefore, assuming that the world, to be sane and to be able to self-correct, to be able to monitor itself, needs a counter-culture, the question is: is it the counter-culture of capitalism, or is it the counter-culture of modernity? Which is really the call of the day, in a sense? Waiting for some sort of a new Marx who will formulate this counter-culture, not of capitalism this time, but of modernity. I'm not sure that I am quite aware, not so much of the answer to this query, but even of where to seek the answer to this question. But what I am convinced of is that the very problem of the counter-culture of capitalism is out-of-date. We seem to be at the crossroads now, with one road which contains both capitalism and socialism together, married for ever in their attachment to modernity, and another road which is still hard to describe.

Q. You would not accept the view that state socialism has failed and liberal capitalism triumphed?

A. I think that people who celebrate the collapse of communism, as I do, celebrate more than that without always knowing it. They celebrate the end of modernity actually, because what collapsed was the most decisive attempt to make modernity work; and it failed. It failed as blatantly as the attempt was blatant.

Q. Moving on to your interest in consumerism: why does the experience of relative affluence in western societies in the post-war period manifestly form such a large part of your recent thinking and writing?

A. It is connected to the question which you asked before. I am really looking for a theoretical model of contemporary society which is emancipated from the old concepts and which represents this society as an entity in its own right. And here I find consumerism a very central category. What I propose, you remember, tentatively, at the end of this little book on freedom [*Freedom*, 1988] is that the same central role which was played by work, by job, occupation, profession, in modern society, is now performed in contemporary society, by consumer choice. . . . The former was the lynch-pin which connected life-experience – the self-identity problem, life-work, life-business – on the one level; social integration on the second level; and systemic reproduction on the third level. . . . Consumerism stands for production, distribution, desiring, obtaining and using, of symbolic goods. *Symbolic goods*: that is very important. Consumption is not just a matter of satisfying material greed, of filling your stomach. It is a question of manipulating symbols for all sorts of purposes. On the level of the life-world, it is for the purpose of constructing identity, constructing the self, and constructing relations with others. On the level of society, it is in order to sustain the continuing existence of institutions, of groups, structures and things like that. And on the systemic level, it is in order to ensure the reproduction of the conditions in which all this is possible. . . . I think that sooner or later, we will rewrite the history of the nineteenth and twentieth centuries, because we understood nineteenth-century history only as the production of industrialism. What about the production of consumerism? It must have happened then, at some point. But we overlooked it. We were so fascinated with work, employment and production technology that we hardly ever looked at the other thing. There are some new books, for example Rosalind Williams's *Dreamworlds* [1989], which I think signal the beginning of such rewriting.

Q. Of course, that part of the productive process – work and industry – shifted globally, didn't it?

A. I wonder whether it is a question of shifting or whether it is the question of us being made sensitive to aspects which were always there, but which we were not inclined to see because we were dominated by the models which we, so to speak, created, like this job-centred model. We were subdued by the dominant ideology of the system, bent on producing more, and greater, profit.

Q. Other East Europeans have reported the shock they experienced when first confronting western consumerism, abundance and greater wastage. Was this your experience?

A. I don't remember that kind of shock. I came to the west many times before I actually settled here. I started travelling west in 1956. . . . It was a smooth introduction. . . . On a research scholarship my first insight was not into the life of the affluent but into that of the poor.

Q. So, in other words, your interest in consumerism is not prompted by a kind of moral response. It is much more to do with an analysis of the way that societies work.

A. Yes, it is intellectually fascinating to me, not only because it is such a useful category in creating these theoretical models, but also because, once it is accepted as the central category, it leads towards another look, another assessment, of very basic assumptions about human motives; about human attitudes; about the relationship between the individual and society; and about the whole logic of human existence. These were somewhat garbled and made one-sided by this perspective of the work-centred society. . . . I don't think moral evaluation is straightforward. I am far from castigating it for letting loose human materialism, greed and things like that. Consumer society is a different instrumentality, but in itself it is neither moral nor immoral, like any other.

Q. Your analogy in *Freedom* between consumer society and Rabelais's Abbey of Thélème is a pointed and revealing one. Do you, at some level, disapprove of consumerism? Are we correct in detecting in this work, particularly in the last two chapters, both an admiration of consumerism as a solution to the freedom–security paradox and a critical tone, because it does not advance us very far down the road towards the older socialist ideal of communal self-rule?

A. I am there accusing consumerism, or rather the Hayek-oriented view of it, of duplicity on two counts. One count is that, by comparison with consumerism, industrial capitalism was much more honest, because it was straightforward. It said: 'Here are the bosses; here are the labour-givers and the labour-takers; people are divided; they will stay divided; the only thing we can offer you is the chance that, if you really stretch yourself to the utmost, you will join your betters; but there will be winners and losers', and so on. Consumerism doesn't have this straightforwardness: consumerism promises something which it can't deliver. It actually promises universality of happiness. Everybody is free to choose, and, if everybody is let into the shop, then everybody is equally happy. That is one duplicity. Another duplicity is the limitation of its pretence that you resolve the issue of freedom completely once you offer a consumer freedom. So it is a reduction of freedom to consumerism. That is the other duplicity. People are led into forgetting that there could also be other ways of self-assertion than simply buying a better outfit.

Q. In saying that there are these duplicities in consumerism, you are implicitly criticizing this, from some point of view. What we read into it was: here is a socialist, still; here is someone who is talking about communal self-government or self-rule, workers' control, being in control of your life, and so on.

A. I have stated the *foci imaginarii*. The first of these duplicities is on account of flouting the justice principle; the second duplicity is on account of flouting the self-assertion principle. These principles stay with me all the time – if you call them socialist, fine; but I don't think they are particularly socialist, anyway. They are much wider than that. I really believe that communism was just the stupidly condensed and concentrated, naive effort to push it through; but the values were never invented by the communists. The values were there, much wider; they were western, Enlightenment values. I can't imagine a society which would dispose completely of these two values, ever. . . . Once the ideas of justice and self-assertion were invented, it is impossible to forget them. They will haunt and pester us to the end of the world.

Q. Finally, can we draw you a little on the subject of Jewish identity and its possible consequences for your outlook and sociological concerns. Your exile from Poland owed as much to anti-semitism as to political expediency. And we would not be the first to point out the advantages of marginality in the formation of the sociological outlook. Recently you have written on the Holocaust, strangers, outsiders and exiles, and seen the Jews as archetypical in these latter respects, as the only 'non-national nation', and been preoccupied with the meaning of 'assimilation' in this connection. Why do you think you have become more conscious of this dimension of your life in recent years?

A. Well, there were three stages in which Jewishness played some role in my life. On the whole, for most of my life and the greater part of it, Jewishness played a very small role, if at all. The first time it was brought to my awareness, was in 1968 – this eruption of anti-semitism. . . .

The second stage was Janina's [Bauman] Holocaust book [1986]. It may seem really bizarre, but I did understand for the first time what the Holocaust meant when I read her book. I knew that there was a Holocaust – everybody knew that there was a Holocaust – but it was an event 'over there', somewhere else. As I said in the Preface to my Holocaust book, I saw the Holocaust as a picture on the wall, and then, suddenly, I saw it as a window, through which you can see other things. So I became fascinated, intellectually fascinated, with this issue, and, step by step, while starting reading the literature and trying to recover this experience from other people's reports, I came to the third stage. . . . I discovered that peculiar condition in which Jews were cast first during the period of rapid modernization and assimilation in the second half of the nineteenth century. If one goes through the ideas of people like Marx, Freud, Georg Simmel, Kafka, all these people who actually created what we call modern culture and beyond that, to people like Lévi-Strauss, Levinas, Derrida, or lesser figures, lesser known, like Jabès or Shestov, but also quite influential in shaping the essential categories of modern culture – one can find some sort of (I will use the Weberian term) elective affinity between the enforced condition of social suspension in the process of assimilation, and the kind of penetrating, perceptive, insightful modern culture which saw through the modernity deception. So, in this sense, the Jewish experience could be helpful in the understanding of some general issues, through the conditions in which the essential categories of modern culture were conceived of.

I must say that all this is rather intellectual and unemotional. And so I am – in this sense, I was, and remain – a stranger. I like very much what three people said about the Jews. One is the playwright Frederic Raphael; he is extremely conscious of being a Jew, as you know, and quite active in spelling out what it means. But he said that 'the meaning of my being a Jew is that I am everywhere out of place'. That's one statement. The second statement is by George Steiner, who said that 'my homeland is my typewriter'. And the third statement, made by Wittgenstein, was that 'the only place where real philosophical problems could be tackled and resolved is the railway station'. These three statements point in the same direction. And I think this 'nowhere', as these people said, is an intellectually fertile situation. You are somewhat less constrained by the rules, and see beyond.

Q. So you are saying that the experience of this group, through, firstly, the Holocaust, and secondly, just their structural position in general, is a rich source of sociological insight.

A. The first is the lot of the Jewish people, as such. The second is not the Jewish problem generally, but is the problem of assimilating the Jewish intelligentsia: people who were the most avid and dedicated prophets of this great chance of modernity. As they sought to assimilate themselves to this new modern life, however, in fact they assimilated themselves to their own assimilation, since this was the only place where they could go. Kafka caught it very well, using the metaphor of a four-legged animal: its hind legs have already left the ground but the fore-legs cannot find a place on which to rest. That's the sort of a suspended situation which now becomes more or less universal – we all live in a situation of contingency and choice: nothing is given; everything must be made. And the Jews – this sort of intellectual Jew – simply happened to find themselves in this situation first.

Q. We like the phrase 'non-national nation', because you have Jewish people, who are, in western societies anyway, virtually invisible. They are not like Black or Asian people – they are invisible – but, at the same time, Jewish people have non-Christian beliefs, celebrate a different calendar of religious festivals and operate in small, fairly close-knit communities, with a good deal of intermarrying; and yet, at the same time, this group is part and parcel of the country in which they have settled, so that – the phrase is apt – they are both outsiders and insiders.

A. Yes, but this is very much less so than it used to be. The point I am making in *Modernity and Ambivalence* is that it was simply a 'one-off' historical chance. The life of assimilated Jews, whom you describe and whom you know, the only people you actually encountered, is dull, uninspiring and not peculiarly fertile. There is nothing to boost special intellectual currents, to give particularly wide vistas and to break horizons. It was just the one period in history when Jews were emerging from the straitjacket of the ghetto and entering the big society. That was the second half of the nineteenth century and the first part of the twentieth, and particularly the territories of intense, shortened modernization: Austria-Hungary, Germany, Central and Eastern Europe, where this chance was created of some sort of a prophetic vision, of opening eyes to things which other people did not yet see. . . . It is not a specifically Jewish phenomenon, this elective affinity. It is rather the phenomenon of a peculiar social situation in which part of the Jewish population happened to find itself in such circumstances. To emphasize: I am not ascribing a special mission to Jewishness – I am simply saying that, by accident of history, it so happened that the Jewish experience had a special significance for understanding the logic of modern culture.

REFERENCES

Bauman, Janina (1986) *Winter in the Morning: A Young Girl's Life in the Warsaw Ghetto and Beyond, 1939–1945*, London, Virago Press.

Bauman, Zygmunt (1956) *Socjalizm Brytyjski*, Warsaw, PWN.

Bauman, Zygmunt (1972) 'Culture, values and science of society', *University of Leeds Review*, 15(2) (October).

Bauman, Zygmunt (1987) 'Intellectuals in East-Central Europe: continuity and change', *Eastern European Politics and Societies*, 1(2) (Spring).

INDEX

Printed in the United Kingdom
by Lightning Source UK Ltd.
118360UK00001B/16